POMEGRANATE
YEARS

Pomegranate Years, an intimate account of three years lived on the island of Crete, documents a turbulent, stressful time of economic and political crisis in Greece. It is also deeply concerned with illness and death, as the author's husband Fotis Kafatos, a distinguished scientist, is increasingly affected by Alzheimer's disease.

Fotis remains a full human being, authentic and resilient despite his impairments. Sarah, in her journal, reflects on his situation as well as on current events, the vicissitudes of daily life, and the practice of art. Long walks in the mountains reveal hidden aspects of the island, and her understanding, and belonging, are enriched through historical awareness and conversations with friends.

As an account of a solitude, a couple, a family, and a culture, *Pomegranate Years* is concerned with the question of how to live well at any age, but especially as one grows older and a beloved life draws almost imperceptibly nearer to its end.

"When news that the exceptional scientist Fotis Kafatos had been diagnosed with Alzheimer's disease reached his many friends and colleagues, the only consolation was the devoted presence of his talented wife Sarah. In this diary, she recounts how she maintained his dignity and her own, as he set forth, an Odysseus destined not to return to his Penelope. It is a moving story, honestly told."—Harold Varmus, author of *The Art and Politics of Science*, Nobel Prize-winning scientist, former Director of the National Institutes of Health and the National Cancer Institute

"Six weeks before the celebrated scientist Fotis Kafatos died of Alzheimer's disease, his wife Sarah noted that the pomegranates in her Cretan garden 'are ripe, and Persephone will be eating her handful of seeds.' Whoever eats even a single pomegranate seed will overcome distress. Accordingly, Sarah Kafatou's journal focuses less on loss than on coping. Recorded so well here, these three pomegranate years reveal their Persephone emulating Milton's Eve who, hand in hand with Adam when expelled from Eden, wiped away her tears."—Peter Bien, Emeritus Professor of English and Comparative Literature, Dartmouth College, and past President of the Modern Greek Studies Association

POMEGRANATE YEARS

A Journal of Aging, Art, Love, and Loss on a Greek Island

SARAH KAFATOU

PAUL DRY BOOKS, INC.
Philadelphia, Pennsylvania

First Paul Dry Books Edition, 2019

Paul Dry Books, Inc.
Philadelphia, Pennsylvania
www.pauldrybooks.com

Printed in the United States of America

Library of Congress Control Number: 2019947653

ISBN: 978-158988-140-2

INTRODUCTION

I started this journal when my husband, Fotis Kafatos, became unable to continue his life in science and we began living year-round in the village of Fortetsa, at the edge of the city of Heraklion on the island of Crete. In it I recorded my impressions of daily life, the world around us, and Fotis in his illness. Much happiness, and some sadness, was intrinsic to what I wrote.

My original family was American, of English, French, and German descent, and I grew up in cities on the east and west coasts of the United States. Fotis was Greek, from Crete. When I was nineteen and he was twenty-two we met by chance at a social event. We talked, we met again, and soon we both felt that we should spend the rest of our lives together. At that time I felt very strongly about a few things and was very naive about much else. I loved reading and writing and knew they would be central to my life, and after meeting Fotis I knew I wanted to stay with him. I assumed that everything else, being of less importance, would fall into place.

I graduated from college in 1965 and went on to graduate school in English and American literature, but never completed my PhD. Fotis received his doctorate in the same year, was hired as an instructor and rapidly promoted, and in 1969 became a tenured professor at Harvard. At twenty-nine, he was the youngest full professor in the history of the university up to that time. This was the more remarkable because, before winning a Fulbright scholarship to attend college in the US, he had lived his entire life in Crete.

Fotis wanted to return to Greece and contribute to science there. When he was offered the Chairmanship of Biology at the University of Athens he took that on in addition to his role at Harvard. We divided our time between Cambridge, Massachusetts and Athens until 1982, when he left the University of Athens to help create a new university and research center in Crete. In 1994 he left both Harvard and the University of Crete to become Director General of the European Laboratory for Molecular Biology in Heidelberg, Germany. Twelve years later we moved from Heidelberg to London, where he was appointed to a Professorship at Imperial College. Shortly after that, he became the founding President of the European Research Council, the preeminent source of academic research funding in Europe. Several years passed before we noticed that, in small ways, he was becoming less able to orient himself in space and time.

During the early years of our life in Athens, Greece was under military dictatorship. Fotis affiliated himself with the democratic student resistance movement and helped it in small ways, but I needed to find some other way to express my opposition to the regime. I began writing a book, in Greek, about politics and economic development in Latin America. This was my roundabout way of responding to the situation of Greece as a relatively poor and troubled country on the outskirts of Europe.

After publishing my book, I did a variety of things that I hadn't anticipated doing. I volunteered in a homeless shelter, led a monthly academic seminar on modern Greece, joined the editorial board of a political journal, took piano lessons, and made a very gradual breakthrough in my longstanding, long frustrated, effort to write poems. I also began for the first time to draw and paint. My mother had been a fine professional artist, and, though I'd believed since childhood that I could never do anything of the kind, I happily discovered that I could. I studied painting for two stimulating years, then left art school to earn a Master of Fine Arts in poetry.

While we were living in Germany I played chamber music, painted and exhibited my work, taught poetry for a time, tried my hand at literary translation, published essays on European literature, and began writing a novel that would take me ten years to complete. After we moved to England, I continued with my essays, poems, and translations, finished the novel, and made my first foray into composing music. I also earned a diploma in life coaching, though I didn't go on to create a practice. All of that, not to mention my life with our family and friends, has been marvelously challenging, rewarding, and fun. None of it would have been possible without the loving support of my husband Fotis, to whom my life and this journal are dedicated.

2 0 1 4

Saturday, August 16, 2014

A new chapter in life has opened as we—our daughter Helen and I, with the agreement of all our family—have decided that Fotis should go to the Hjem, a residence for assisted living in the village of Gouves. It is a hundred percent Greek except for the director, who is Danish. We like its professionalism, the friendly, low-key atmosphere, and the Scandinavian philosophy and style. Our moving date is 7 September, and our preparations have already begun. The Hjem is only twenty minutes away by car, so I can easily go there, support Fotis, and monitor the environment for him. Our alternative options as to the best framework for him are still open, and, although none is perfect, all are acceptable.

One feels empowered when the alternatives before one seem good, and disempowered when they are mostly or all undesirable. One feels empowered, too, by the sense that one can freely choose to do one or another thing and then live with one's choice. I should remember that this is not only true for me, but it's very true for Fotis. He can't actually manage his life by himself anymore. But it's very important to him to feel that he decides, that he's in charge of everything that happens with him, and that other people are not taking his power of self-determination away.

I need to couch this move with that in mind. He often says that he doesn't like people to "grab" things from him and doesn't want them to "push" him. It's not that he does or doesn't want to do or have a certain thing, necessarily; instead it's important that he do whatever it is according to his own sense of time, that is, slowly and gently, carefully and attentively, and feeling that he's in charge. You can't rush him, and irritated impatience toward him will get you nowhere.

Established routines—for example, his lifting one foot and then the other so that I can put on or take off his shoes for him—work well. Explanations as to why we are doing a thing are a waste of time. Showing him gently and attentively that "this is the way we do it" when we're doing something unfamiliar is the best way to get it done.

Explaining that the Hjem is a good place for him won't work. I did show him the brochure and introduce him to the idea, but he still thinks of himself as a research scientist and objected because, he said, if he goes there he won't be a scientist anymore. I've decided to present the move by saying that we're going on a holiday. He will probably agree to this. Once settled in, he will hopefully accept his new room and environment as normal. He isn't very attached to our house here, though it is beautiful. He doesn't recognize it very well. I think that the Hjem, if comfortable, will be acceptable to him. The main thing is that he should accept it and be happy there, as he is here.

In fact he is happy, except when he's irritated and angry about being interfered with in some way or is overtired (for instance, when we walked on the beach for fifteen minutes yesterday. Ten would have been better). He's reported recently that he feels happier now than he did in the past.

I too am happy and content. I would prefer to continue looking after him as before, were it not that I can never get away, and even doing small errands has become difficult now that it tires him so much to go with me. It's also true that I can't handle him securely anymore, since I don't have the strength to lift or move him, and this will quickly become more important as he is able to do less and less. And what if I were to, let's say, trip and fall down the stairs? We don't have adequate backup support in the event that I couldn't care for him.

One last reflection: I don't miss the old Fotis. I like the Fotis there is now. This is quite the way it is with one's children: we adore them as babies, and toddlers, and as they get older we forget more or less how they were before and love them as they are now.

In *Still Alice*, the very good book by Lisa Genova about the disease, Alice and her husband are both high-powered professors in Cambridge when she gets early-onset Alzheimer's. Her husband complains to her at one point, "I miss the old Alice"; and not too long afterward he abandons her to their adult children and moves to an even more high-powered academic position in New York. He does this so that he won't have to change from the way he was when he was married to the old Alice, and one can understand this and see that the price of change for him would be very high.

I've always, throughout our life together, adapted to Fotis' initiatives and his pattern of life, and this has worked out very well for me. All the changes and challenges involved have enabled me to live probably the richest life I could have had. Thankfully, the price of the sort of change we are experiencing now is not high for me. It even offers me an opportunity to benefit and further enrich my own life. More about that later.

Sunday, August 17, 2014

Last night we had such a lovely dinner together on our kitchen patio. Fotis is just as good company as ever, and maybe even better. He's entirely there, himself. I have to remind him to feed himself, and even prepare his fork for him, but that's not tedious when we do it casually in the course of sitting together and reviewing our day. I do the talking, but Fotis responds in a really understanding way, wanting to say that his former postdoc Mike, who talked with him on Skype in the afternoon, is a good person, and wanting to tell me that he loves me.

It will be lonely at home without him, and there won't be much social life here unless I create it. I will visit Fotis daily at the Hjem, and will see other people there, too, and learn from them. There are very good neighbors here in Fortetsa whom I can see by walking around the corner. I'll have to take initiative and make time to socialize with our friends in town. Most importantly, our daughter Zoe will visit soon, Helen will visit later, and a few other friends have also made tentative plans to visit.

Our house provides a fine base for exploring Crete, and a perfect retreat for people wanting to settle in for a while to do creative or intellectual work. I might try to develop this side of it, inviting friends here to write, as my novelist friend Annabel did last year.

Monday, August 18, 2014

A north wind is blowing and there's fog on the mountains.

This journal is about me as well as Fotis, and one of its purposes is to help me understand how to be in my personal life, not only with him. In a month or so I will have completed my translation of Pushkin's novel *Eugene Onegin* from Russian into English verse. It will have taken me two years, filling in almost exactly the time between our leaving London and Fotis' move to the Hjem. I didn't expect or plan to do it—I just, over many years, accumulated the necessary background, then one day happened to start, and then continued until the end. I never had to tell myself to do it, never had to stick to a work schedule. As soon as I'd done the first stanza I knew I could do it all, and I enjoyed doing it, and so I did.

This is surely the best way to do a thing. I'm lucky that so many of my activities—bringing up children, hiking, music, painting, poetry and short story writing—have been like that. Writing my one novel involved more heavy lifting and was more of a grind. (I'm very glad I did it, though.)

I wonder what I will do next. It seems that this year I will be home with enough opportunity to do what I want, and there will have to be something.

It is good to have a plan, but the best way is not to tell myself what to do. The best way is to watch myself intuitively find something to do, and then to be "the guide who walks beside."

Intention isn't the only factor, or even the most important one, in choosing hour by hour what to do. Habit, once formed, and environment are both very important. I do have art materials here, and a studio. I'm out of practice after five years of not painting, but it should only take a little push to set me off. I also have a piano, and since going to music camp at Dartington five years ago I've been learning to compose.

Since I have a diploma in life coaching, it's imaginable that I could do that. Should I try? If so, how shall I recruit clients? The best clients for me will be those with artistic aspirations or writing projects that are unfulfilled.

Friday, August 22, 2014

Right now I'm seated at the desk in our living room with Fotis opposite me on the couch. It's hard to concentrate with him there. Once again I'm grateful to have my *Onegin* translation, because I don't need to be entirely free of distraction in order to do it. Translation is like editing. It doesn't involve imagining something out of the blue, which for me demands full quietness.

Saturday, August 23, 2014

Fotis' morale has been excellent. Depression is a common hazard for people with Alzheimer's, but he hasn't been depressed at all. However, he is growing more easily upset and fearful, and he's especially afraid of falling. Usually when he's unwilling to get up or walk across the room, it's because he's afraid of falling.

He's also very focused on me, and has been for the past few years. He remembers and recognizes people very well, and only occasionally seems slightly confused (speaking to me of me in the third person, for example). He misses me when I'm not present. I'm the primary constant in his life.

It would be a lot easier to take him to the Hjem if this were not true. I plan to provide all the continuity I can, and will get up very early so as to be there when he wakes up in the morning, but I'm not so keen on being there when he goes to sleep at night, because I don't want to drive home in the dark. The illumination on the highway is not good, and there are too many dangerously speeding drivers and unexpected hazards (yesterday there was a soccer ball on the road). I have grown considerably more hazard-conscious on my own behalf over the past year or two, I notice.

Monday, August 25, 2014

Most practical problems have a solution. During the past few weeks, like many caregivers, I've had the problem of not getting enough exercise. I do my half hour of morning exercises at home every day, but that's been about it. Walking with Fotis is not much more strenuous than sitting still. There is a gym class I've been to, but he hates being brought along. So this morning I set my alarm for 5:30 and went out at 6:00. I walked down the steep hill, ran for half an hour as far as the Venetian aqueduct and back, walked back up the hill and was home at 7:00, which is when he wakes up. Problem solved!

I can do this practically every day until he moves to the Hjem. After that, I can swim in the sea en route to or from visiting him. Once the summer heat subsides I'll be able to take long walks now and then. The many all-day walking excursions I did in Germany and England were among the very best experiences of those years, even better than the many museums and theaters I went to. I enjoyed them enormously and remember them well. Here in Crete there are some designated, albeit poorly marked, hiking paths and many back roads with little traffic, and there is a walking society that schedules long hikes once a week, going by bus to places one might not manage on one's own. I might take advantage of this.

On another subject, I've been contacted by a relative who cares about Fotis and wants to be helpful. Now, for the second time, he is pressuring me to put Fotis on medication that I don't think is well advised. Fotis' doctor at Harvard shares my opinion on this.

The phenomenon of relatives differing over care of an ill person is not uncommon and can be very destructive. It happens often with end-of-life choices but can arise well before then. I've made clear that I welcome information and thoughtful suggestions, and that I will discuss any issue. It is important to keep things on a friendly and cooperative footing all around, to have consensus to the degree possible, and for the final decision-making power to fall to me. Of course, I defer to Fotis' own wishes and preferences as much as possible and always consult with our daughters—and indeed it was Helen who persuaded me that the Hjem is the best option and that now is the time for Fotis to go.

A few points about end-of-life care. Many Alzheimer's patients finally die of pneumonia, which they get because they can't properly swallow their food, so that bits of it stick in the throat and provoke infection. We inoculated Fotis against pneumonia last year.

At that no-longer-swallowing-properly stage, though, also, many Alzheimer's patients are provided with a feeding tube which goes directly through the abdominal wall into the stomach. This is different from being nourished intravenously, and some people accept one but not the other. The *New York Times* published a feature the other day about how awful and inappropriate these feeding tubes are in an end-of-life situation, and many people with experience of them wrote in to agree. If it comes to that, we will not accept either a feeding tube or an intravenous drip.

Tuesday, August 26, 2014

Yesterday I read Sue Miller's memoir of her father's path through Alzheimer's. I admire *The Good Mother*, the first of her many novels, and expected this to be a worthwhile book, which it is. I could see many parallels to the path that Fotis is on, and she takes the story through to an end that we have yet to see. But she lives in it differently than I do. She uses words like awful, horrible, victim, tragedy... all words that don't come to mind for me. For me, this part of life is OK: different from before, but not better or worse. That seems to be Fotis' impression also.

Thursday, August 28, 2014

It's so thoughtful of Fotis' former colleagues to continue to treat him like one of them. Yesterday I took him to a board meeting of the Onassis Foundation Nobel Prize lecture series. He used to be an active member of the board and they still invite him to take part. He's also been kept on the board of the Fondation des Treilles. There, too, even though they understand his situation perfectly well, people treat him as though nothing had changed.

Behaving with consideration, respect, and affection toward him, as though nothing had changed, is the best thing people can do for him. He doesn't notice the changes that have taken place, so this seems natural to him. He hates being treated like an invalid or a patient, as though his Alzheimer's were the main thing about him, and I sympathize with that perfectly.

At the same time, it's very good that, shortly after he retired from his academic responsibilities, we were able to use his annual personal newsletter and holiday greeting to his colleagues as a vehicle for announcing his condition. I drafted, and he approved (though he later forgot he had done so), a letter in which he said, "My physical and emotional health remain good, but my cognitive health has been affected by Alzheimer's disease." This cleared up some uncertainty and confusion around him and facilitated a very supportive response.

Sunday, August 31, 2014

The local Alzheimer's Association is very active, and will host a conference for the National Association at the end of September. Last year, when we met the head of the local association, who has been very helpful to us since, I wondered aloud to her whether Fotis could play any role as a spokesman for people with his condition. Out of that came a short film clip we made last year, in which he appears looking directly at the camera and saying in Greek, slowly and with difficulty, "In the course of our lives, it's probable that someone close to us, or even we ourselves, will be affected by Alzheimer's disease or some other form of dementia." Fotis is well known and admired in Heraklion and will be identified on this segment. The clip will be shown at the conference and, I believe, broadcast as well.

I feel this is a good, dignified contribution to public education, I'm proud of him for doing it, and I think it will encourage people who see it to respect him, rather than think of him in the third person, as it were. As long as he can speak on his own behalf, I feel, he comes across as living with a condition, rather than being defined by his condition.

We have learned to say that a person "has alcoholism" rather than that he "is an alcoholic," or "has bipolar disorder" rather than that she "is manic-depressive." This is a better way of thinking, encapsulated in a better way of speaking. It allows people with such problems to be seen and treated as more whole.

In a similar vein, I don't like to call Alzheimer's a "disease." I think of it as a set of disabilities that evolve with time. A disability is one thing and a disease is another, so that one can sensibly say that a person with severe disabilities is healthy, not sick. Fotis is certainly impaired, but he isn't ill.

Tuesday, September 2, 2014

The trickiest and most problematic issue in the unfolding of our Alzheimer's experience has been timing. When should Fotis put down this and that responsibility? When should we speak openly about his condition? (Answer: to our family and his close collaborators, immediately; to the wider interested public, once he had put his responsibilities down.) When should he retire? (Answer: once he was no longer functioning adequately, his very supportive personal assistant and I pressed him to take that step. He brought up the question with his university department head, and we arrived at an agreement that seemed appropriate to us.) Should he go into a care environment, and if so, when?

It was during the couple of years when we were still in London, finding our way through these issues, that I was asked at the Poetry Library on the South Bank to name my favorite poem. For a long time I couldn't think of one. At length I remembered the last lines of *Paradise Lost*, which I had last read in college and which came to mind, remarkably, after all that time, intact:

They hand in hand, with wandering steps and slow,
Through Eden took their solitary way.

Friday, September 5, 2014

This week has been busy, with many people coming over to our house or inviting us to visit them. Fotis is sociable and likes to see the people we know, although after two hours or so of being in company he'll get up and say it's time to go. For the past year and a half he's had weekly Skype conversations with former colleagues and students, but lately we have reduced the length of these, from half an hour to twenty minutes, to—most recently—ten minutes; and we are now scheduling just one every two weeks. He has less stamina and sometimes complains that he doesn't want to do it, although when the person appears on screen he is always pleasant, alert, and interactive, though he can't express complex ideas. Much of the time he is content to sit at home quietly, not doing anything, with me present. Occasionally at those times I ask whether he's bored, and he always says no, that he's fine. Sometimes he says he's thinking.

When I first talked with the social worker at the Hjem, she asked me whether Fotis is an introvert or an extrovert. Not certain what to say, and thinking him well balanced, I said that he is sociable and has been a good leader and collaborator but is also content to spend time alone. Afterward I asked him about it, and he said at once, "I'm an introvert." There has been some discussion of this axis in America lately. Extroversion is celebrated and thought healthy, though Susan Cain makes a case for the other side in her book *Quiet*. I myself regard introversion as a strength, the more so since I find myself well over on that side of the spectrum.

Saturday, September 6, 2014

I notice that I'm feeling nervous and frightened at the thought that after tomorrow Fotis won't be here with me at home. I will stay overnight with him tomorrow, and it helps to remind myself that I will still see him every day and can spend as much time with him as I like. I will simply have transferred some of the responsibility for his care. But just giving up that responsibility is an important loss at this point, since I've grown so used to carrying it.

Tuesday, September 9, 2014

Our move has gone smoothly so far. I've hoped that the change to a new environment and routines would not be noticed as such by Fotis, and that seems to be the case. I furnished his room beforehand with things from home, and indeed he doesn't seem to realize that he isn't home. He has adapted very quickly to the "new normal."

One thing that's different is that the nursing staff have taken over from me all of his physical care: getting him up and putting him to bed, helping him eat and so forth. I have been present almost all the time but have kept in the background and let them take over. He doesn't seem to mind this at all, or to find it unusual. He said to me yesterday over breakfast, "those girls are very nice" (the Greek word I've just translated as "nice," "evgenikés," has overtones of "gracious," "refined," and "kind").

Another thing that's different is that lunch and dinner are served in a common space (outdoors, in a beer-garden-like roofed area, except in winter), and that's been harder for him. He has to socialize with the other residents and that is more demanding than just being alone or socializing with me and our friends. However, I hardly think we could have found a more compatible group here in Crete. There are forty residents altogether, of whom ten are men, and most residents have Alzheimer's, but not all. There's a very fit, spry, friendly and helpful, slightly deaf, mentally alert resident whose only reason to be here is that he has no close family and is ninety-six years old. There's another couple, also apparently relatively unimpaired, where the man is a hundred and three. He was a colleague of Fotis' father, and still remembers both of Fotis' parents and that they had sons who were good students and went to America! He intends to live to be a hundred and ten. There is a very charming and gracious woman who does have Alzheimer's, whose son, a professor at the university, is a former postdoc of Fotis' and a good friend of ours.

Right now I am sitting on the balcony of Fotis' room, actually a suite with a large bedroom, small sitting room, bath, and kitchen *sans* stove. This building is in an area of hotels, beach apartments, and people's vacation houses, and was originally constructed to be a hotel: not a glamorous or luxurious one, but I would think a nice, decent three-star hotel. Consequently the architecture conveys a holiday atmosphere more than it does an institutional one. Our balcony zigs around the west and south sides of the building and, being one floor up, is surrounded by the foliage of various trees: an araucaria, an olive, bamboo, and a lemon tree with lemons one can reach out and pluck. Another hotel with swimming pool is just visible through the leaves.

I'll add a few words about practicalities and structure. There is a social worker, a doctor, a nursing staff, a psychiatrist, and a physical therapist, and the director is often here. Required paperwork is minimal, and the residence has no prejudice regarding people's own end-of-life care choices. Fotis' private suite, with meals and all other supplies and services, costs about $23,000 per year. That is a lot for most Greek people to pay. But it is less than a quarter of what we would pay for something comparable in the US, and there are double rooms which are more affordable.

All services are fully included, through to the end of life, and their cost to us will not change with time. At the moment I am looking across to where Fotis is being lathered and shaved by one of the nursing staff. (He's being much more cooperative with her than he was with me when I would shave him with an electric razor.) He has become a very desultory eater and doesn't mind having food put in his mouth like a baby chick; here the staff assist him, putting food in his mouth as needed. In contrast, at a well-regarded place I visited in the US I was told that the regular staff will not feed the residents and that I would have to bring in an outside nurse to do this at my own expense. There is a choking hazard with Alzheimer's people, and the care home is afraid of being sued.

Thursday, September 11, 2014

Ever since I first realized that Fotis might be going to develop dementia—six years ago now—the hardest part has been the decision-making and timing. Carrying out our decisions, once made, and carrying on has not been stressful or difficult.

Now, after five days, our move seems to have gone as well as one could ask. Fotis is comfortable, he's content, and he doesn't seem to miss me when I'm not present, or to miss home. In fact he seems unaware that he isn't home. He likes the staff, and several residents have shown that they like him and want to include him. There is lots for us to do together there: we can listen to music, I can read to him, we can walk on the garden path around the building, we can join in community activities such as reading the local newspaper aloud, and I'm invited to play the piano in the reception area, something that Fotis likes and many of the residents appreciate.

Friday, September 12, 2014

Both Fotis and I have Greek citizenship, and I will shortly have registered us in the Greek National Health system, with status similar to that of Medicare recipients in the US. This accomplishment leads me to share a few observations about why Greece became bankrupt, an event that upset the national economy and the European currency zone and led to our present acute financial crisis.

There were several reasons, but a very important one was mismanagement of the state sector. Greek banks, unlike banks elsewhere, were not to blame for the crash. The Greek state ran up a huge deficit, borrowed hugely abroad, and successfully hid its indebtedness for years. Then the government changed hands, the newly-elected team discovered the state of affairs and revealed it publicly, and all hell broke loose. What had happened?

Many good, competent people work in our government agencies, but they are not organized very efficiently. In order for Fotis and me to obtain our national insurance cards I had to make approximately fifteen office visits to about ten different offices. One of these was in Athens, so we had to ask Fotis' brother to go there on our behalf. It took him three visits on three separate days, traveling an hour in each direction each time, to get the requisite piece of paper. I'd say that approximately one person's normal work week was consumed in this way. In contrast, when we lived as expatriates in London we used the NHS routinely—the care there was excellent—and were not asked for any paperwork at all.

I think this situation has arisen in Greece—and I hear that Italy is worse, not to mention countries like India—because the state apparatus is both a monopoly and a political patronage resource. Uncompetitive private companies and professions depend on state patronage and live with, or work around, the distortions that ensue. Ordinary people rely on patronage to seek jobs and special treatment, and then do their best to avoid and work around the obstacles that an opaque and inefficient bureaucracy puts in their path. The whole thing is dysfunctional, but it serves many people's particular needs in some way or other and so is hard to change. There is now pressure on us from Europe to reform, and this has brought some positive results, but we have far to go.

Sunday, September 14, 2014

I am waiting intently for the outcome of the referendum on Scottish independence this Thursday. This is an example of something I care about, but can do absolutely nothing about.

I feel genuinely close to that world, especially since living in London. Indeed, I'm very keen on all the places I've ever lived. Recent research has found that, if we want to improve our lives, the most effective way to do so is to move to a better place. (Too bad everyone can't do that!) I disagree—I think it's better to improve ourselves and our outlook. (Everyone can do this!) But it is true that place, and social setting, are very powerful and important. I feel fortunate to have lived in good places.

Here in Crete, this has been a good day. I practiced the piano, translated a stanza of Pushkin, made cauliflower soup, spent an hour drawing outdoors, spent two hours visiting Fotis in the afternoon, and had a swim in the sea on the way home, and now it's dinnertime.

I had imagined that I'd spend all day with Fotis every day this month, to help him settle in, but he and I now seem to be doing fine with two hours together daily in the afternoon. The staff provide him with activities when I'm not there, and this is valuable because he seems to have lost the ability to take initiatives of any kind. He's also lost the ability to make decisions and express preferences; he will indicate whether he likes or dislikes something that's happening, and if I propose we do one thing he will say whether he wants to do it or not, but if I offer two alternatives he can't say which he prefers. At the same time, even having lost this much of his cognitive executive function, he is emotionally as alive as ever, and even more so. It's a pleasure to listen to music with him, or just to sit with him in his room and share our loving feeling.

Monday, September 15, 2014

The internet: a marvelous resource when well used. Tonight I made dinner while listening to National Public Radio via my laptop. I'm reading a book on my e-reader, one that I downloaded in a second. What a luxury, in a country where there are almost no public lending libraries, and where the few English-language books in shops are selected for tourists.

Of course I love bookstores and real books. I like to patronize a very good Greek literary bookstore in Heraklion, but how long will it keep going? The owner says his main problem is not competition from e-books; it's that younger people don't read books at all.

Wednesday, September 17, 2014

One thing that Fotis has taught me in the past few years: to improve my temperament and be more relaxed and calm. Helen has pointed out to me how different I am from the way I was five years, or even two years ago. I was happy most of the time then too, but I could get impatient or lose my temper very quickly when frustrated or offended. When I was stuck on hold on the phone having to listen to tinny music, or stuck in traffic when in a hurry, or was treated as though I hadn't understood something when actually I did understand it, I might easily overreact.

Fotis has always had a sweeter, warmer temperament than

mine (though he isn't perfect; he can be obstinate, for example). That doubtless affected me in a positive way generally, but what has especially affected me lately is that he can no longer tolerate it when other people get upset. He's become very attuned to such things, he responds very quickly and accurately to other people's tone and mood, and if someone around him speaks angrily, he doesn't like it. Right away, he gets angry and upset too. It's no use explaining what one is mad about, and that it has nothing to do with him; the only option is to get over it. So I do—and I find that I feel better as a result.

Thursday, September 18, 2014

Today is the festival day of the small church of Saint Evmenios next door, where Fotis and I were married. No women officiate in the Orthodox Church, but here we happen to have two women who are good cantors, much better than the men, and who also read very well from the Byzantine texts. The sermon by a visiting priest was also good. Ritual behavior is stressed much more, and social responsibility less, in the Orthodox Church in comparison with other Christian traditions I'm aware of. On the other hand, the Greek Orthodox Church is not particularly rules-oriented and seems compassionate and tolerant toward its people. Today's sermon stressed the communal, inclusive, tolerant aspect of the culture in a way that I appreciated.

Saturday, September 20, 2014

Yesterday at 2:30 in the afternoon I finished translating the last stanza—the 380th—of Pushkin's *Eugene Onegin*. The entire endeavor took me two years, less a month or so. Here are the final verses:

She's gone. Onegin is reeling
as if a bolt had struck him down.
In what a hurricane of feeling
his heart has begun to drown!
A clink of spurs reaches his ears,
suddenly her husband appears,
and, reader, we leave the scene,
bidding farewell to my Eugene,
as he faces this sad complication
without us, for long . . . forever.
We've followed a route that never
seemed to end. Congratulations
on reaching shore at last. Hurray!
Hasn't it been quite a long way?

Reader, whoever you may be,
a friend, no friend, I've in mind
that our leavetaking be friendly.
Farewell. If you hoped to find
in these careless stanzas here
a wild, tempestuous memoir,
distraction from your labors,
lively images, words to savor,
or some grammatical fault,
may God grant that you found
a bit at least of pleasing sound,
entertainment, dreams, heart,
controversy that interested you.
And so goodbye, farewell, adieu!

So farewell, my strange comrade,
and farewell, my true ideal,
and you, my light task, that led

me constantly. I've known all,
with you, a poet could desire:
a life far from storm and fire,
sweet talk with friends alone.
Many, many days have flown
since Tatyana appeared to me,
with Onegin, for the first time,
in a vague, uncertain dream—
for I could not yet clearly see,
far off, as in a crystal ball,
the contours of so long a tale.

Those others, to whom I first read
my verses . . . some of them are gone,
some distant, as Sa'di once said.
I've finished my portrait of Onegin
without their kind participation.
But she, who gave me inspiration
for Tatyana, my dear ideal . . .
how much, how much Fate can steal!
A man is blessed, who doesn't spend
a long time at life's feast, or sip
the dregs of wine from a full cup,
or read life's novel to the end,
but who abruptly lets them go
as I do now with my hero.

This has been a wonderful project, and it seems worthwhile to
note why it was so good.

It was challenging, yet I was confident from the beginning
that I could do it. The feeling was something like that of setting
out on a very long walk through beautiful countryside. The challenge and reward came in small, steady increments: it took me

sometimes just an hour or two, and at most two or three days to solve each stanza. And the challenge never lost interest: each stanza would seem impossible at first to ever solve, and then I'd find some purchase and would always get there.

It was meaningful throughout. Pushkin's text is on the artistic level of Mozart's music. Each word, each line, each stanza, and the entire felicitous flow of the original was worth studying, dwelling on, grappling with. I always felt that I was engaged in a valuable endeavor, that is, trying to make the best, most accurate, most satisfying and readable rendition into English of a great work of literature, and so to provide access to it to others.

Also, doing the work was convenient and compatible with my life circumstances at the time. I could share it with friends as I went on, and so get some response to what I was doing and benefit from some encouragement. I wasn't under any sort of deadline, but could and did work at will, for pleasure, wholly from inner motivation and without external stress.

Thursday, September 25, 2014

I used to be lonely, for most of my life much of the time, and now I'm not. I don't see other people these days any more than in the past, but I feel secure with them now and that is the difference. What I experienced as loneliness was really a chronic, and sometimes acute, insecurity—not ever with my immediate family, thank goodness, but with friends who were important to me. Now that I don't suffer from this anymore, have I lost something? My kind of loneliness led me to do some generous and creative things. Now I'm less volatile, more stable, more robust, but maybe also more self-contained, more inaccessible than I used to be. Or maybe not. The balance on the whole is very positive, I feel.

We can be lonely because we miss any one of several kinds

of relationship, even when we are fine with the other kinds. It's possible to feel happy and secure in friendship and at the same time lonely in marriage, or the reverse, as Lillian Rubin pointed out long ago in her book on friendship, *Just Friends*. Is there a good book about loneliness? I don't know of one, though there are some good books about solitude, including one by Anthony Storr.

Some older people complain of not being powerful. I actually like this situation, which holds a promise at least of "freedom from," and potentially of "freedom for." It is something like invisibility, which can be a very exhilarating thing. I've reached a point where, while there are surely people who want me around, nobody really needs me, nobody depends on me, everybody in my life can get along very well without me from now on. Fotis is in a safe place, where I visit him every day of course, but where if I didn't visit he would continue to fit in and be supported, and probably, given his condition, he would forget about me, by and by. Our children are grown up and well, and our grandchildren are in good hands with them. "Lightness of being" I think is a good expression for describing this state of affairs. To me it feels good, like an accomplishment; it doesn't feel like loneliness at all.

Friday, September 26, 2014

About injury and loss: this is doubtless a cliché, but it's true all the same to say that trauma itself, bad as it is, in the end is less important than our response to it.

When something good happens, it's good to let it radiate. When something bad has happened or may happen, we should focus on it in order to address it, and once we've addressed it as well as we can it's best to go on and direct our attention elsewhere.

I was told in art school that if we're working on a painting and a particular area bothers us, we shouldn't fuss with it, because that will only make it worse. We should go on with the rest of the picture, and gradually the problem in that area will get less and less important until it disappears. I'm glad to have been given this advice.

The Nobel Prize-winning economist Daniel Kahneman, in his book *Thinking, Fast and Slow*, has made the point that no upcoming life event, or change in life circumstances, good or bad, affects our happiness or unhappiness as much as we expect it will. Our expectations arise from thinking about it, but after it happens we won't actually be thinking about it most of the time. For several reasons including this one, any single event tends to be absorbed into the general tenor of one's ongoing life, just as the problem in the painting gets absorbed into its emerging general tenor.

The worst thing I can imagine happening to me is for my children to be unhappy or in distress, which is fortunately not the case. To be in severe chronic physical pain would also be tough, since that has so much power to command our attention and make us miserable. It would be very bad to lose the ability to work and be creative, but there I feel personally quite safe, since there are so many different modalities available for doing work of some kind. As for things that have happened in the past, there are some things in my life that I would never have chosen to have happen, but several of the worst actually did lead to important real improvement in my life overall, in the long run.

Maybe it's easier to be transformed and recover from bad things that have happened to us than from bad things that we ourselves have done. This was found to be the case in one study I heard of, concerning the children of victims and perpetrators of the Holocaust.

Saturday, September 27, 2014

Our daughter Zoe arrived last night from Virginia to spend ten days. We visited Fotis, and she likes and values his situation at the Hjem but sees how much his abilities have deteriorated over the six months since she saw him last.

Summer is officially over. Today we had stormy weather all day, with occasional thunder and pouring rain.

Tuesday, October 7, 2014

Zoe left this morning for Richmond. She came wanting to make sure that Fotis and I are both OK, and she left feeling satisfied about that. We saw relatives and friends, went hiking in the mountains, took a yoga class together, spent time walking on the beach, talked things over, and visited Fotis every day. I'm very pleased that, like me, she enjoys just sitting with him, being in his company without needing to say very much. In the beginning she wondered whether he recognized her, but by the end she was reassured that he does.

While she was here I contacted a very old friend and so learned that his wife Annie, a really wonderful woman, a gifted poet and dear friend, has Alzheimer's, and that consequently they are preparing to move from Northhampton to be near their children and grandchildren in California. I had been thinking of her as so superbly alive and all there! This abrupt news was more troubling and disturbing for me than any of the times I've had with Fotis, whose condition I suspected early on, and whose trajectory has been so gradual and practically imperceptible from day to day.

Today is a perfectly balmy, windless day, and I've just spent an hour reading on the patio. While sorting through the cartons of books I've moved here from London I rediscovered George

Vaillant's *Aging Well*, which I promptly brought upstairs and have begun rereading. I've long admired Vaillant's studies of the life cycle, and especially his earlier book *Adaptation to Life*, about how people deploy psychological defenses more or less adaptively over time. As he wrote *Aging Well*, the people he was studying were in their seventies: that is, around the age I am now. How were they doing, and what can I learn from them and him?

One thing to take home: What we started out with becomes less and less important as time goes by, while more and more importance accrues to what we did with it. As Vaillant puts it, "It is not the bad things that happen to us that doom us: it is the good people who happen to us at any age that facilitate enjoyable old age."

Friday, October 10, 2014

The literary editor of a journal has just asked me to translate a lyric poem by Pushkin. She needs it right away for her deadline and I did it in a few hours. She is delighted, and it will go in. This is so different from my usual experience of not-very-hopefully sending out work and never hearing back, or hearing that it won't be taken by the agent or journal or publisher in question. The difference is that in this case, there was a strong match between what I did and what was wanted.

In general, I like very much having the freedom to choose my own writing projects and pursue them at my own pace. If the price of that freedom is that it's hard to find a publication outlet for them, then so be it. I do believe the limiting factor for publication in my case is usually not quality: it's the low energy that I put into forming professional connections and circulating work, and it's the match.

Now back to George Vaillant's book and its subject cohort. Those who are aging well have good social relationships, a good attitude, and good habits. These factors seem more important than financial well-being, objective physical health, and any other particular circumstances. Successful older people are able to feel gratitude for the past and hope for the future, and they care actively for other people. They keep on learning new things, they keep on loving and taking love in, they can be playful, and they like to be engaged in some creative project.

That's about it.

Sunday, October 12, 2014

Being a methodical sort of person, and bearing in mind the advice that good habits are key to aging well, I've now scheduled an hour of morning piano practice into my day. I want to play mindfully, for understanding, and the clock helps me focus and do that. I mean to play through the Schubert sonatas, being attentive especially to the key changes and cadences: how are they prepared for, and what do they mean?

Today, after breakfast and piano, I went for a run, and on my way back filled two plastic bags I found by the roadside with other roadside trash. This is a good combination activity from an exercise point of view (lots of bending over and stooping down), and it also provides the satisfaction of leaving the area a bit more picked up, as opposed to the dissatisfaction of helplessly deploring the carelessness of people, stray cats, and the wind.

Yesterday I drove to the village of Stamni and walked around looking for something to draw. Stamni is a shapely small village with two Venetian churches, several tavernas, and a café. Some houses have been renovated and some are derelict; some gardens and patios are full of flourishing plants and some are empty; there is activity and life, but the overall feeling is of a place that's been left behind.

Monday, October 13, 2014

Rudy Tanzi, an Alzheimer's researcher, has made a breakthrough which was reported today in the *New York Times*. Basically, he and his collaborators grew human stem cells into neurons in a petri dish and used genetic engineering to give those cells Alzheimer's: the cultured brain cells, once endowed with the ApoE4 mutation associated with Alzheimer's, produced amyloid plaque, which was followed by the development of tangles of tau. Such dishes of cultured cells can now be used as a quick testing ground for drugs, for which there are thousands of eligible candidate substances. These tests may reveal a substance that can safely prevent amyloid plaque from forming, and may also reveal ways to inhibit an enzyme that seems to be required for the formation of tangles of tau.

Tanzi is an interesting, unusual person, a talented musician and, while being the Rose Kennedy Professor of Medicine at Massachusetts General Hospital, a devotee of Eastern spirituality and ayurveda. We visited him in his office in 2012, and he recommended to us that Fotis take the ayurvedic substance ashwagandha ("Indian Ginseng"), in pill form as a general health-protector and a deterrent to the formation of amyloid plaque in the brain. Fotis began taking it and, although we haven't seen any benefit from it in him, I tried it this month too. I can't perceive any difference in myself, and I suppose will never know whether it does any good or not, but it doesn't seem to do any harm.

In the meantime, this new lab breakthrough does seem very good. It might perhaps reveal a path to prevention of Alzheimer's, and possibly to drugs that can halt the progress of the disease, though I expect that would come too late for those who are already well along the Alzheimer trajectory and whose brain cells have already died. Further, it uses two of the most contemporary resources of biology—stem cells and genetic engineering—in combination in a way that I imagine can be utilized for research and drug testing for any number of diseases besides Alzheimer's.

Tuesday, October 14, 2014

This morning, reading through a Schubert sonata, I'm attending to the transformations of the theme in the last movement. This theme sets out as something very unremarkable and is gradually subjected to twists and darknesses and threats, so that when it reemerges in its fully intact original simple form it feels utterly changed, and like a plain but radiant beam of light.

Thanks to a list of "the year's best books" in the *Economist*, I've discovered the English writer Olivia Laing. I had wondered whether there is a good book about loneliness, and now there is Laing's evocative, beautifully written book *The Trip to Echo Spring: Why Writers Drink*. Loneliness and alcoholism often go together, and this book feels to me like an insider's compassionate reflections on loneliness and fear, well furnished with hard clinical comment about the disaster of self-medicating for these with alcohol. Her forthcoming book will be more directly about loneliness and focused on New York. Seen from another point of view she is a travel writer, doing the kind of personally anecdotal yet searchingly researched travel writing that Geoff Dyer has specialized in; but she pulls on the heartstrings in a way that I've never felt with him.

Thursday, October 16, 2014

Today I visited our friends Dimitris and John. They live in London most of the time, but have renovated a small house in a tiny village in a breathtakingly beautiful part of Crete and spend several months there every year. Dimitris has solved the problem of retirement—what to do in the next phase of my life?—in an inspired way. He was previously a research scientist leading a laboratory at the Medical Research Council. Now he goes to new plays in London with John, and when they see one they like, Dimitris obtains the rights for translation into Greek, finds a theater company in Greece or Cyprus that is interested, translates it himself, and then it is put on. Theater in Greece is very lively and good, and this initiative brings great satisfaction to everyone.

It's interesting to see what sorts of things people think of doing when they retire. A college classmate of mine who was a Foreign Service officer retrained as a Protestant pastor and settled into a small parish in Maine. Wally Gilbert, a Nobel prize-winning biologist, became an art collector and professional photographer. Peter McGhee, after a career of producing major programs for public television, became a carpenter making high-end classic furniture. What might be some further examples of inspired choices?

Sunday, October 19, 2014

Fred Small, known to many in Cambridge, strikes me as a person who made good career choices. He was an environmentalist lawyer who morphed into a professional composer and performer of politically and socially concerned songs, and who later became the pastor of a lively and well-attended Unitarian church.

Bill Gates went from being a monopolist to a philanthropist, like so many robber barons before him. Facilitating such a path for some, there is now a program at the Harvard Business School for corporate executives who've retired and want to take on roles in nonprofit philanthropy. Fortunately, the challenges of achieving generativity and leaving a legacy can be met by most people in ways that don't require great wealth, or much wealth at all.

Sometimes people may feel that potentially attractive new directions are closed to them because there isn't enough time left. I think that there's likely to be enough time left to do a lot, and that many aspirations can be rethought in a way that renders them doable in some form.

Monday, October 20, 2014

Even as I appreciate the poetry and empathy intrinsic to Olivia Laing's book *The Trip to Echo Spring*, which I am still reading, I must not fail to take note of her main point: alcohol maims and kills! This is particularly important for me to be aware of, since I am now living alone. Alcohol is hazardous, and living alone can compound the danger.

I habitually have a glass of wine with dinner, which I enjoy, or else sometimes I have an ounce of ouzo or rakí and don't have wine. I think I'm fortunate to have married into a culture that is not particularly alcoholic, and into a family where people drink very little and it's not a problem. I credit this context for having kept me in good shape, even when I was much younger and had no education and no sense about these things.

Wednesday, October 22, 2014

Having just written a little about drink, I thought I might write something about food. The traditional "Cretan diet" is deservedly famous, even though most people in Crete no longer observe it.

Greek cuisine has benefited from the proximity of Turkey and Italy, both of which have superb culinary traditions. That said, Crete has local culinary excellence based on very specific local conditions. For one thing, Crete produces the best olive oil in the world. The olive tree is said to have originated here, and the very dry climate (no rain in summer at all) and dry rocky soil encourage a concentrated, aromatic oil. We ourselves own twenty-five olive trees, and I'll be here this year for the olive harvest, which takes place in November and December. This should be a good year: the branches are bending under the weight of their fruit.

Crete also produces more species of edible wild greens than any other place in the world, or so I've read at least. Decades ago we used to go out into the fields to gather them; now I buy them in the market. We have greens of one kind or another almost every day, served sautéed in olive oil, salt, and garlic, or else boiled and eaten with olive oil, salt, and lemon.

Beans are a staple, especially fava, chickpeas, dry lima beans, and broad beans. Pureed yellow fava beans and mashed broad beans are best served warm with olive oil, salt, lemon, and thin wedges of raw onion.

In addition to conventional bakery bread, we eat whole-grain bread that has been hardened by baking in a slow oven overnight and essentially never gets stale. We take it from the cupboard, dip it in water briefly, and eat it with olive oil and salt.

Crete produces all kinds of seasonal vegetables and fruit, for local consumption and export. This is a wine-producing region with many vineyards, and we also produce delicious table grapes and raisins. At our house we have several grape pergolas, one of them on the roof. The grape season has just come to an end; now the pomegranates are at their peak.

Cretan yogurt, made by local shepherds, is wonderful, and it's possible to buy fresh cow's milk to boil and drink at home. There are only a few kinds of Cretan cheese—basically four—but they are all good. The most unusual is mizíthra, which when fresh resembles mozzarella and when salted and aged is a kind of white rival to parmesan.

Snails are plentiful and good in stew. They have to be cleaned carefully, though, and I never make them at home. Rabbit is common and is also very good in stew. Chicken, of course. Lamb is classic for holidays. At weddings, in addition to the lamb turned on a spit, a lamb risotto is always served. The beef is good, though not usually raised locally. At the butcher shop, if you ask for ground beef it will be ground in front of you.

Octopus—tenderized by being whacked many times on a rock and then hung on a line in the sun to dry—makes a very good hors d'oeuvre. The best fish, in my opinion, are the small ones. A delicacy is red mullet, about three inches long, fried crisp. Very small fish, called atherína—half the size of one's baby finger—are fried in batches and eaten whole in one bite.

Cretan thyme honey is superb. Many people make fruit preserves—whole dried fruit or chunks of fruit in very sweet syrup—and may bring you some as a present in a little jar. You are meant to have just a small spoonful, together with a full glass of cold water.

Thursday, October 23, 2014

Today the south wind is blowing, so that the air is turbulent but the sea is like glass. A south wind with rain brings down red mud out of the Sahara. The Greek name for it is notiás: others call it the scirocco or khamsin, a troubling, disturbing wind from the desert.

Monday, October 27, 2014

A week ago the weather was warm and bright; I swam in the sea and went on a hike with two friends into a deep limestone gorge very near Heraklion. (Crete has many such gorges, including one, called Samariá, which is said to be the deepest in Europe and is spectacular. The smaller one we walked in for a few hours is also splendid.) This week, though, is rainy and chilly, and it's now fully dark by 6:00.

I've just spent time in my studio painting. During the past five years I've painted almost not at all. Today I took my first step in the direction of getting active again.

Fotis has become quite inarticulate, and I often can't understand things he is trying to say. This afternoon, though, as we were having tea, he brought up an issue and we discussed it for a while. The issue is that he often becomes difficult to deal with when people try to help him with tasks—to dress or shave him, for example. He's not aggressive, but he is very recalcitrant and makes it hard, or sometimes impossible, to do the task. The nurses must have brought this up with him, so that it was on his mind. He asked me again and again whether he'd been acting badly. I said, "maybe," and he demonstrated for me, stiffening his body, frowning and knitting his brow, how cross he can get sometimes. He was very sweet and contrite, and volunteered that he will try to be patient and polite to his helpers. He didn't seem intimidated, just concerned that he might have misbehaved and been unkind.

Tuesday, October 28, 2014

Today is a national holiday, when all schoolchildren take part in a patriotic parade celebrating the entry of Greece into World War II on the side of the Allies. Greece had a semi-fascist dictator of its own at the time, but, when served with an ultimatum by Mussolini, to capitulate or face invasion, said "No!" so this day is remembered as the day of "No." Greece was able to throw the Italian invasion back, but shortly after that was defeated and occupied by Nazi Germany, with very dire consequences for most people. Fotis' family were displaced, were bombed by the Allies while under occupation, and lost one family member to starvation in the winter of 1941, a year when hundreds of thousands of people starved to death. They saved Fotis' father's life by hiding him under the floorboards when the German soldiers quartered next door came to take him to be shot, as sixty-two others were on that day in reprisal for partisan activity in the area.

Wednesday, October 29, 2014

Today I read an article about death and bereavement. My parents died about twenty years ago and I still think of them almost every day. I mourned them deeply, involuntarily, as that came over me, and they are still very alive to me. It pleases me to see continuity between their lives and mine. When I contemplate my own death, I feel I will be content to be remembered as they are remembered by me.

My best friend, whom I met when we lived in Germany and who was German, died of brain cancer ten years ago. I wrote a poem for her and I'll copy the last part of it here. The first part had to do with her personal history—bombed out in Berlin, a refugee three times over, with family members who took part in the resistance to Hitler and were executed when that failed; and, later, living in Heidelberg, liking to work in her garden, where there was a stone copy of a Roman sculpture.

> Time had mended
> much, though not all, when I met you and found
> laughter, music and peace on your home ground.
> You dug your garden while I, beside the path,
> admired the stone shape of a woman at her bath.
> I talked, you replied with a question, a touch—
> I'd never imagined that I could care so much
> for a friend until I knew you. Then you were ill.
> Life is a thread. In the clinic, the hospice, you still
> kept your clear manner, your irrepressible grace
> as we watched the sun go down in a loved face.

Sunlight on pale grass, water tumbling through a weir,
melody of a Schumann song—*Du bist immer bei mir.*

Saturday, November 1, 2014

Yesterday it rained again. I had the idea that, although Fotis' kitchen has no stove, I can bring him an electric kettle and with it we can make tea. I'll do this today; I never would have thought of it were it not for the weather.

He does have a CD player, and we spent our time together in his little sitting room listening to Narciso Yepes playing classical guitar. Fotis is sensitive to music, understands it intuitively, and is very moved by it. He responded with deep feeling to every change in the music and was completely engaged, rapt. In the common area they often play Cretan and Greek music on the radio, and he is always the first one to get up to dance, even though he now can't really dance more than a step or two.

The impact of Alzheimer's on the brain depends on where exactly the plaque and tangles take hold. Some areas are more vulnerable than others; one's sense of direction, for example, is lost early on, even though it was established in infancy and must be profoundly rooted in the brain. The plaque just tends to accumulate there and wipes out those nerve cells. The area for understanding music, in contrast, seems to be one that the disease doesn't reach for a long time. The ability to read is also retained quite well, even as one may be losing the ability to recall what one reads. I'm not sure what other faculties are most robust in people with Alzheimer's and would like to learn more about this.

The likelihood of any of us getting Alzheimer's is quite high, if we live long enough. It's good to practice a healthy lifestyle, and this may delay the effects of the disease a bit, but basically, once we get it we will go down the path. Consequently, I have thought not only about how to stave it off, but about how to prepare for having it. One wants to have made the best possible support arrangements, including buying long-term care insurance and identifying the best professional care options. Beyond that, I think it's important to cultivate one's character and personality in the hope that, even when demented, we will remain polite, kind, gentle, and nice to be with. Most people do retain such traits, even when their cognitive abilities have been damaged, and this can make a huge difference to one's experience of the disease. Further, it is not a bad idea to cultivate one's appreciation for music, since that is likely to be a continuing source of interest and solace.

On another subject, I am having the house cleaned today in anticipation of our daughter Helen's arrival next week. The housecleaner, Mimoza, is from Albania, as are many of the people who work in Greece's homes and fields. The handyman at the Hjem is also Albanian. Albanians began coming in 1990, when the communist dictatorship of Enver Hoxha collapsed. They have assimilated well, despite tensions in the beginning. Mimoza's daughter is first in her class in school!

Monday, November 3, 2014

This evening in Heraklion's central square a local group put on a celebration of Minoan culture. There were dancers in Minoan costume, including a snake priestess with long curling black locks as in the frescoes at Knossos, and also a cooking demonstration: lentils in tripod clay jars simmered on embers in the street, and raisin flatbreads were baked on flat stones propped up an inch above the embers.

What a fine thing, and what fun, to play at bringing ancient cultures back to life, out of the museums and into the streets! The most elaborate such evocation I ever saw was in Tarragona in Catalonia, a city founded by the Romans, where the local people dress up in togas and act like Romans for a few days each year. I now recall that our Latin class put on something of the kind when I was in high school in Palo Alto: a Roman banquet. I didn't do any reclining on pallets, though; I was a slave.

Wednesday, November 5, 2014

This morning I met and talked with a woman whom I found extraordinarily pleasant and engaging. We met over a business matter: she is an examiner for our insurance company and came to the Hjem to assess Fotis' need for care. Why, then, was our interaction so enjoyable? In the first place, her attitude was reserved, yet also friendly and warm, task-oriented and yet person-focused, as though she were anticipating from the outset a pleasant and rewarding time with us. She came across as competent, responsible, self-aware in her role, and not at all anxious or stressed. She didn't dwell on her own personal situation but did tell me at once that she has done this work for a long time (twenty years). She explained clearly what we were going to do, and then asked a few questions, spent some time with Fotis, and gave me a lot of time to explain our situation and my point of view. I think that her ability to not waste any of our time, and yet also to behave as though she had all the time in the world for us, was really outstanding. People say, "I don't have much time for him," or "I always have time for her," as a way of expressing different levels of esteem, and this professional interaction made me appreciate how much it means, and how valuable it is, to be willing to put one's time generously at someone else's disposal.

In the US, long-term care insurance normally provides reimbursement for expenses up to a fixed amount. Fotis does not have any such insurance. His insurance is from a German firm, which organizes payout very differently. There is no reimbursement procedure. Instead, the insurer pays out a fixed amount to the insured directly, year after year. The annual amount is set at one of three levels according to the need for care. It is less than it would likely be in the US (the premiums are also lower), but there is complete freedom as to how to spend it, and it never comes to an end as long as the need continues. The assessor, who is a doctor and not an employee of the company, is charged by law to make her independent assessment of whether an insured person belongs on level one, two, or three.

All this is interesting to me, I expect that we will be treated fairly, and I feel that I've been taught a valuable lesson, which I have yet to absorb, about how to conduct an interaction with a person who is initially a stranger.

Thursday, November 6, 2014

What to say about the disappointing midterm election in the US? Negativity is pervasive, and destructive. The best, and funniest, comment came from Andy Borowitz in the *New Yorker*: "Country On Wrong Track, Say People Who Did Not Vote." President Obama has provided constructive, judicious leadership, but where is the support, the energy for it in the country as a whole?

What if we had a different electoral system? A multiparty parliamentary system might not provide any more wisdom or energy than our so flawed and corrupted system does. Certainly we all need to look after our system, mending it rather than gaming it. Ultimately, a democracy has to rely on the quality of its people, on our understanding of the issues, our participation in substantive policy debates and our careful choice of representatives.

Friday, November 7, 2014

I've been in my studio painting, and am currently reading *Life with Picasso* by Françoise Gilot, the artist, mother of Claude and Paloma Picasso, and, later, wife of Jonas Salk. The book is a fine source of information about Picasso's thinking as an artist, which she greatly respects, as well as a painful, if comical, account of his qualities as a human being. Although she thought of leaving Picasso many times and finally did, and even though he comes across in her version as extremely self-centered and with an emotional age of two, they were real collaborators, and her memoir is, refreshingly, not at all embittered but full of humor and affection.

Saturday, November 8, 2014

I've been reading about Matisse and looking at reproductions of his work. As I understand it, Picasso was a genius draftsman with an astounding ability to reinvent spatial relationships. Matisse was a genius at composition who thought in terms of color. For me, Matisse was the greatest painter of the twentieth century and his pictures are the most beautiful. If you could see the world through the eyes of one or the other, which would you prefer? I'd choose Matisse.

Tuesday, November 11, 2014

Helen is here, and is totally delightful.

Thursday, November 13, 2014

Last night we were invited to dinner by old friends, colleagues of Fotis who are now retired. They've been to see him several times and want to organize a rotation of friends to visit him at the Hjem. His Skype conversations with colleagues world-wide are coming to an end, as he hardly talks anymore and sometimes doesn't focus on the screen. He does respond to visits in person, though, and if such a rota is organized it will be great for him. I am not called upon to take the lead in this. We'll see how it unfolds.

Fotis has now been classified by his insurer, following the assessor's report, on level three, the option requiring the highest level of care. He can no longer do simple things such as sit down in a chair by himself, since he can't figure out the spatial relationship between his body and the chair. Fortunately he can still walk, slowly and tentatively, and I do take him for a little walk every day. The staff do not do this, so he wouldn't get a walk if I weren't there.

Sunday, November 16, 2014

Helen left yesterday. She is very devoted to her husband Stelios' family, who all live here, so we spent some time with them, as well as a lot of time together and with Fotis. On one or two evenings we read aloud from *Howards End*, which I first read ages ago, and we've agreed to finish it together, long-distance.

This morning I went for a walk up the steep slope of nearby Mount Youchtas to the country church of Christ Effendi at the top. Perhaps Forster was on my mind, with his intuition of something larger and more meaningful somewhere behind the daily life that we all live. Maybe it was just the mountain, but in any case I found myself reflecting on how every place we find ourselves, every situation and interaction and experience, is potentially a vessel for the spirit.

Wednesday, November 19, 2014

A monument has been dedicated in Sofia, Bulgaria, to honor Georgi Markov, who was a distinguished opponent of the Bulgarian Communist Zhivkov government. I have just learned this from his widow, Annabel Dilke Markova, one of our best friends in London. Annabel invited us for Christmas dinner every year, vacationed with us in Scotland and Crete, and spent many happy evenings together with us. Georgi was a gifted author and journalist who, in an incident which became known as the "umbrella murder," was assassinated by being jostled and injected with ricin while walking to his job at the BBC World Service. Annabel is a very courageous, kind, and lively person who supported herself and their daughter after Georgi's death by writing novels. Her books, for example *The Inheritance*, are highly entertaining and well done.

Friday, November 21, 2014

I've just read a book, *Dolor y Alegría*, by Sarah LeVine, about women in Mexico who have relocated from the countryside to the city. LeVine's fieldwork is very insightful, her subjects come vividly to life, and many of her convincing observations provide food for thought. Children in large rural families who bring each other up lose their sense of solidarity when living in smaller urban families with greater mother-child communication and intimacy, and develop sibling rivalry instead; girls gain self-efficacy through going to school even if they aren't taught much; macho men want many children with different women, even though they will not reliably care for them; older women, however downtrodden and overburdened, often enjoy a sense of confidence and well-being earned through coping with hardship.

Monday, November 24, 2014

The rotation of visits imagined for Fotis is underway. I'm very moved by a colleague of his who visited, wants to come back every Monday morning, and said, "I really want to do whatever I can for Fotis, he has helped me so much. I love him and look up to him." It is extraordinary how often people say things like this.

Tuesday, November 25, 2014

Fotis had his last scheduled Skype conversation today, with someone who was his graduate student at Harvard twenty-five years ago and is now a professor leading a lab at the University of Wisconsin. Afterward she emailed me, saying, "Fotis is very important to me. He is a beautiful human being, and this has in no way been diminished by his illness; if anything, it has allowed us to see the beauty more clearly." I, too, feel that this is true.

Thursday, November 27, 2014

Thanksgiving. I've just learned that Thanksgiving was established as an official American holiday by Abraham Lincoln in 1863, during the Civil War. Now, roughly a century and a half later, it coincides with the nation-wide protest against racial injustice that began in Ferguson, Missouri.

Thanksgiving is my favorite holiday, but here in Crete I am allowing the occasion to pass unobserved. I've joined a small yoga class which meets on Thursdays, so I spent the morning there. All six or eight participants are women, very fit, around my age (our instructor is seventy-six, and in super shape). All are German expatriates except me, and our conversation is in German. The others have lived here for decades, for various reasons, most often marriage to a Greek man. They have become close-knit and often socialize outside of class, so I'm privileged to have been invited to join.

Saturday, November 29, 2014

Elengo, an old friend, came to visit Fotis yesterday. She did her PhD with him long ago and is now retired and living in Athens, where she has thrown herself into volunteer work to help others. She's co-organized a food pantry where the recipients not only help collect and distribute the goods but are also encouraged to stay and discuss their problems with one another. Recipients include formerly middle-class, currently impoverished Greeks (of whom there are many) and foreigners, especially Syrian refugees. She says there are many unaccompanied Syrian children in Athens and that she has been able to reach some of them. Elengo found it hard to see Fotis in his present condition and was in tears for a while afterward.

Greece is likely to have a general election in the spring. The older political parties have mostly vanished, with the exception of the center-right New Democracy party which is leading the government now. In the present context of acute economic distress, the extreme right has acquired considerable support, in part by creating its own social welfare network to serve ethnic Greeks exclusively. (By "extreme" I mean extreme: the Golden Dawn party uses a swastika-like logo and Nazi-style behavior and salute. Its Hitler-admiring leader has been charged with instigating the murder of an opponent and is presently in prison, as are several of its thuggish parliamentary deputies, one of whom assaulted the mayor of Athens.) On the other side are the left populists, now grouped in a formation called Syriza and led by a man called Alexis Tsipras. It is very probable that Syriza will come out on top in the next elections.

If there are elections, I will probably vote for a new formation of the center-left: To Potami, which means "The River." To Potami is pro-European and favors merit-based reform of our state sector, neither of which can be said of Syriza.

Tuesday, December 2, 2014

December, and still good for a swim in the sea. Yesterday the air was warm, the water was refreshingly chilly but not cold, and there was practically no one on the beach. A friend who swims all year round tells me this will get more challenging in January and February, but so far so good, and the beach will still be walkable if I'm not brave enough to swim.

My life here has settled into a pattern (I won't say routine, since while the form is fairly stable from day to day, the content is always new). In the midst of the contentment this affords, my only serious concern is that I'm not doing anything to help solve larger problems or help strangers in need.

According to the pattern, in the morning after breakfast I practice the piano for up to an hour, then spend half an hour or so doing the exercises on a mat that I've done daily for decades. I've just now found a new way to structure this time: in my practice I play through one of the Beethoven sonatas, a new one each day (I can sight read them; I don't, of course, play them as they should be played) and then, during my exercise time, I listen to a lecture about that sonata by András Schiff. Since there are thirty-two sonatas, this can continue through the month of December and beyond. The lectures, all recorded several years ago at Wigmore Hall and available for free on the web, are superb. Schiff has a marvelous musical culture, he's a wonderful teacher, and the conceptual level is exactly right for me, as I imagine it must be for the average concert-goer.

After that I can do email and various odd jobs until lunch time, and later I can paint if I want until I leave to visit Fotis. One great thing about this schedule is that if it is interrupted and something else happens instead, no harm will come.

Wednesday, December 3, 2014

A friend from the University of Crete came to visit Fotis. He created and directs the optical telescope on Mt. Ida (a good place to put one, since Crete, one of the largest islands in the Mediterranean and relatively well-served with educational and other infrastructure, is also the region's most isolated landmass, with quite high mountains). He told us of people he had met who were candidates to be astronauts. Those who got farthest in the selection process, he said, had one thing in common: they were extraordinarily relaxed, well-balanced, calmly unflappable people.

Thursday, December 4, 2014

Yoga class this morning. Sitting crossed-legged on my mat, focusing on my breathing, what came to mind was the work a potter does. The attention of the yoga student to the breath—for which the word in Greek is also the word for spirit, as in "the holy spirit" and "the spirit has left the body"—seemed to me like the attention of a potter's hands to the clay on the wheel, rising and falling, raising and shaping a jar.

And now another thought from yoga class. When doing each exercise, we are asked to notice how we feel in each part of our body. Toward the end of class we lie down covered up with a blanket and practically fall asleep while music plays. Today that music was the beautiful larghetto from the Mozart clarinet quintet. At the end of our semi-nap we are asked to open our eyes and notice our environment, become aware of where we are. My feeling was, this music comes straight out of paradise. To find it, Mozart must have been aware of such a heavenly world around him.

I know the world is a terrible, anguished place, and Mozart knew that too, of course. But listen.

Monday, December 8, 2014

Plumbing problems have appeared in our house, which is theoretically equipped for winter but where we have never before actually lived in the wintertime. Yesterday, because of a weak link in our hot water system, we had no water at all. This was a small matter and has now been fixed—but it put me in mind of how people lived here not long ago. Many villages in Crete first acquired paved roads, piped running water, and electricity in the 1960s. Fotis' parents, who lived in the city center and were certainly middle class, never in their lives had central heating, running hot water, or an indoor toilet.

Tuesday, December 9, 2014

A political crisis will probably begin when the Greek Parliament fails to agree on a candidate to replace the President of the Republic, a largely symbolic figure whose term is coming to an end. If, after three rounds of parliamentary voting, no candidate has been approved, then there must be a general election. Comico-tragically, no one seems to care who the next President will be. It's up to the government to propose a candidate, but before it does, and without any discussion of who might best serve in that role, politicians are already negotiating and committing themselves to vote for or against whoever it is. The real issue is whether or not the government will fall.

Thursday, December 11, 2014

Our family ties connect us to the whole society. Today I said good morning to a woman I saw on the street and vaguely recognized as someone I've seen before. We began talking and she said, "You don't know this, but your family is very important to me. When I was a baby—now I'm eighty years old but when I was a baby, I was very ill and wasn't expected to live. Because of that, my mother wanted me to be baptized right away, but she didn't have anyone to be my godmother." (To be a godparent can be expensive, what with the cost of the baptismal clothes and small golden cross, and the lifelong commitment to the child that is entailed.) "So my mother carried me to the church of Saint Minas and lit a candle, and then she went to knock on doors in the center of town near the church to ask whoever lived there to be my godmother. At the very first house, your aunt Maria opened the door, and Maria and my mother had been friends in grade school! So my mother explained what she needed, and right away Maria said, 'I'll baptize her,' and she did. Later, after Maria married your uncle George, I would often go to their house. They had such a beautiful garden, so many flowers, it was like a paradise to me. There aren't any gardens like that any more."

Tuesday, December 16, 2014

Today I woke up and saw snow on the mountains. It's not cold outside, though, and today at the beach I was tempted to swim (but refrained, and just took a walk in the gentle surf).

The political situation is getting increasingly dramatic. By the end of December we'll know whether there will be a general election or not. If so, it will come early next year, and our populist party Syriza is expected to win. At present the European Commission, the European Central Bank, and the International Monetary Fund, known collectively as the Troika, are providing our bankrupt government with very large loans to keep us afloat financially while they instruct us as to how to restructure our economy. Our coalition government led by the center-right, though it has managed to soften the terms somewhat, does more or less what they tell it to do. If Syriza comes to power, it may not behave in this way.

The Troika's regimen of financial austerity, which squeezes everyone very hard, has got us into somewhat more sustainable shape domestically, but our external debt remains huge. People are tired, they don't see the light which may be shining faintly at the end of our tunnel, and Syriza proposes to make a leap in the dark. It promises to challenge our creditors, denying them repayment and refusing their demands on us.

Five years ago, a Greek exit from the European currency and return to the drachma was thought to be both legally impossible and potentially catastrophic for the euro. Today it is possible, and the consequences for the euro can apparently be contained. Greece can no longer hold Europe hostage, and if we exit the euro and return to the drachma this will be catastrophic only for us. It may entail leaving the European Union altogether. Already investors are leaving the scene, and Greek people who have savings are sending them out of the country, or else putting their euros as cash into safety deposit boxes at the bank.

Saturday, December 20, 2014

My Mozart epiphany in yoga class was just corroborated and extended by András Schiff saying, "Mozart came from heaven, and Beethoven went there."

Our olives were harvested today. In the past people climbed into the trees and beat the branches with sticks to knock the olives down into a net. Now they stand beside the tree using a hand-held machine which makes a racket like a leaf-blower. In the past the olives were processed in a communal press a few blocks from here; now they are collected in burlap sacks and driven to a larger press half an hour away. This is progress, with its characteristic gain in ease and efficiency and loss of immediate interaction with the natural world.

Sunday, December 21, 2014

The winter solstice is the time of year when the sun is lowest on the horizon and our shadows at noon grow the longest. Today has been a sunny, warm day with no wind, and I was sitting outside on the patio around noon when I noticed the vivid shadow of a cat projected on the wall. Stray cats often come into our garden, and this one had climbed into the grape arbor overhead. I entertained myself watching the shadow for a while, not looking up to watch the cat as it stalked amid the grapevines. Then all of a sudden it jumped down, and instead of the shadow there was a real cat.

Cats don't usually get hurt when they jump or fall from high places. Their spines are articulated in such a way as to cushion the blow that gravity prepares for them. Quite a nice trick!

Monday, December 22, 2014

I've just spent an hour studying Arabic. I began to do this in London, when a friend suggested we do it together and recruited a teacher for us. The person she found, Sharin Habib, is an Iraqi Kurd with a degree in literature from the University of Baghdad. She was given asylum in Britain after fleeing the regime of Saddam Hussein (she had been working for Save the Children, and Saddam had announced that he intended to kill everyone working for that organization). Sharin is a fine individual and an excellent teacher, and she succeeded in bringing us to the level of basic literacy.

I have no compelling reason to pursue Arabic, but it is interesting and I would like to consolidate what I've already learned. Now I've discovered a teacher here and begun ramping up my skills. This teacher, Zoe Segredo, is Greek, from Cairo. Her family lived in Egypt for generations, and after Nasser expelled most of the Greek community they still stayed on. I believe that most people in the Greek diaspora there spoke Greek at home, sent their children to French schools, and didn't necessarily learn Arabic. But her family is evidently an exception; Zoe studied architecture at the University of Cairo. Now, having married and settled in Crete, she is teaching French and Arabic for a living. She says that her other (few) Arabic students have no more practical reason than I have for taking on this rather daunting subject.

Thursday, December 25, 2014

Christmas. I went to see Fotis in the morning and, since it's a mild, sunny day, took him to the beach. We just sat on a bench looking at the sea for an hour. He can't express himself well now, but he was happy and said several times, "It's beautiful."

Two days ago, unusually, he was sad when I came. He tried

to explain why but couldn't. I put on some music (by Theodorakis, passionate and soulful) and he got up to dance with tears in his eyes. Then, yesterday, he was cheerful again, and today was a very good day.

In the afternoon I was invited to Christmas lunch by Fondas (short for Xenophon) and Ruth, who live around the corner. Fondas is Fotis' nephew. He loves the outdoors and makes his living taking people on climbing and hiking expeditions. Ruth is an exercise teacher and trainer, and they have a three-year-old daughter, Marilena. Ruth comes from a village in North Wales, and, remarkably, speaks with Marilena only in Welsh. They are extremely nice people and very good, interactive parents. I think Marilena is having a wonderful childhood, and I loved being with them.

While at the beach this morning with Fotis, I was not thinking about anything in particular, just letting my mind wander. In that way, I began to reflect on how conflict and aggression, such as we all experience sometimes and such as we've seen overwhelm several zones of the world this year, thrive on tunnel vision. The fight-or-flight response, coming out of a sense of emergency, disables our capacity for wider attention. While sitting quietly listening to the sea I felt led toward the opposite of that, an expansive state of open-heartedness and open-mindedness.

Friday, December 26, 2014

For the past few days I've had a mild stomach ache; I'm not worried about it, but perhaps in my sleep I worried, since I woke up this morning with the following thought:

The mathematical physicist Paul Dirac, who is buried in Westminster Abbey, was surely somewhere on the autism spectrum, but had a good life all the same. He was married and was devoted to his wife, but, as I learned from a biography, when his wife once asked him in irritation, "What would you say if I told you I'm leaving you for good?" he answered, "I'd say goodbye, dear." Actually this isn't what I was thinking as I woke up, I remembered it later. My waking thought was, What would I say if I were told I must leave the world tomorrow?, and my answer was, "Goodbye, dear world." I think this was perhaps not a bad response. It's probably best not to get overly upset about the prospect.

Saturday, December 27, 2014

Fotis' former student and colleague Babis Savakis came to visit him yesterday and shared with me his theory of why Fotis got Alzheimer's. This is a puzzle, because Fotis had just about no risk factor at all: no family history of the disease, no lifestyle issue, no physical health issue (head trauma, high blood pressure, high cholesterol, diabetes, and obesity are risk factors), and very good mental and physical health generally (though he did get headaches—not migraines—in the past, and slept poorly sometimes). He still has no illness other than Alzheimer's disease.

Babis has heard that Alzheimer's can be triggered by infection. He remembers that Fotis came down with an acute infection once in Berlin, just a day before he was to give a major speech. Fotis spent the night in the Charité hospital and did speak as scheduled the next day, at an event in support of European science, sharing the podium with Angela Merkel. Babis saw Fotis frequently after that and dates the beginning of his confusion to that time. I wonder whether this is more than coincidence. I tried to follow up online and found only this, from PubMed: "The evidence compiled from the literature linking AD to an infectious cause is inconclusive, but the amount of evidence suggestive of an association is too substantial to ignore."

In today's news, Greece is still twelve votes short of being able

to elect a President. The latest twist is that our neo-Nazi Golden
Dawn party has enough votes to make the difference, and has just
indicated that it could change its vote. Immediately and appropriately, Stavros Dimas, the leading candidate, has declared that he
will not accept the office if he owes it to votes from Golden Dawn.

Sunday, December 28, 2014

Today was devoted to the larger family Christmas that we didn't
have on Thursday. Fondas' parents and brothers and their families,
who were away before, are back in town, and we had an all-day
holiday at Fondas and Ruth's house with them. I brined and roast-
ed a turkey for the occasion. It was all as it should be, with a long
table for all, a fire in the hearth, small children playing . . .

When I first got to know Fotis I saw that he was very attached
to his family, and I counted that very much in his favor. When his
parents were still living and we would come to Greece for a summer
or a semester we lived with them. I knew well Fondas' grandparents,
his parents, and his aunts and uncles and cousins, and the same is
true of another large branch of our family on Fotis' father's side.

Luisa, a woman in my yoga class, moved here with her husband forty years ago. Both are Austrian. They bought a house in
a mountain village ("It cost so little, there was almost no risk"),
stayed, and sent their children to the village school. But they have
no relatives here and, she said, "We are waiting for the day when
our children get married, and then we will have family."

Tuesday, December 30, 2014

About twenty years ago Fotis and I visited St. Catherine's Orthodox monastery on Mt. Sinai, on the site approximately where

Moses saw the burning bush and received the tablets of the law. We met a monk who was at work cataloguing the ancient manuscripts and icons which are kept there and have been saved from destruction through remoteness, fortification, and the arid climate of the Sinai. The monk, it turned out, had studied at the University of Athens and taken a biology course that Fotis taught. He phoned me this morning because he had heard that Fotis was ill and wanted to see him. I remembered him well, as does Fotis, and I drove him out to the Hjem for a very pleasant visit.

Father Nikodemos is here for a church conference. He has retired from his life of work and teaching and lives on Mount Athos, where he is an enthusiastic walker and year-round swimmer. He said that Fotis had been like a beacon to students during the years of military dictatorship, because he was accessible, inspiring, and lifted people's hearts.

After dropping off Father Nikodemos at the intercity bus terminal I parked and walked to the Historical Museum on the waterfront, an exquisite small museum of the history of the past 2,000 years on Crete, to see my dear friend Eva who is its director. Eva's husband Giorgos, also an old friend, is presently in Brussels as a member of the Europarliament, representing To Potami, The River. The environment at the museum stimulated my Greek patriotism, making me feel the more committed to the country now, as we face an election that will be significant for our national fate. My talk with Eva confirmed that there is no knowing what will happen next.

2 0 1 5

Thursday, January 1, 2015

Today's the day to make a new year resolution. I'm reading a book about Pissarro, and propose to take from him the advice he gave in a letter to his son Lucien: "Don't forget that one must only be oneself. But you will have to work at it!"

Today is also a day of wind and lashing rain mixed with sleet. Fearful of driving under these conditions, I didn't visit Fotis. However his friend Stefanos did go to see him and they spent several hours talking and singing together. In the meantime, I went into town with Fondas and Ruth, where we had lunch and spent the afternoon with his parents, his brothers, and their families. Again I was very happy being with them, and I'll see Fotis tomorrow.

Friday, January 2, 2015

I've been studying Beethoven's Opus 10 #3, with its amazing second movement Largo e mesto. András Schiff calls this the supreme musical expression of grief, "a lament for the suffering of a person who is dearly loved." To me it seems also to express, with the greatest nobility and unsparing honesty, the inner experience of a person in severe suffering and pain. It's not in the least stately or somber, like a funeral march, but tender and attentive. There are moments of more intense tension and stress and moments of release, and these deepen and grow ever more intimate and more sublime. Then at last, with only an eighth-note rest—but a rest with a fermata over it—there follows the next movement, the minuet, bringing gentleness and comfort.

In connection with the present political situation, two ancient Greek words come to mind: *talaiporía* and *peripétia*. Both are common in the language of today. *Talaiporía*, suffering, is what Odysseus experienced on his long voyage home. *Peripétia*, reversal of fortune, is the pivot from one state of affairs to another, darker, at the turning point of a classical tragedy. Here in Greece we've endured both of these in the course of the past five years. I'm afraid that we're about to experience them even more intensely.

Saturday, January 3, 2015

We've had cold rain and wind all week, but this morning the sun is shining and the world is crystal clear. I've just swept the patio and also removed some spider webs from around the corners of the house. As I put down my broom I said to myself, "Out came the sun and dried up all the rain!" Then I remembered that the itsy bitsy spider goes up the spout again, and more power to it.

Monday, January 5, 2015

This morning it's raining again, but yesterday was a lovely clear day, not cold, and I went for a three-hour walk on a back road, from the village of Fourní toward the sea and back. Snow on the mountain crests, sheep in a valley and on the road, a few cars on the road, branching paths to ten or fifteen small, historic churches and monasteries beside the road (I didn't stop at them), olive groves with groundcover of clover and various short grasses, views of the sea and of the low, bare islands that echo the shape of the shore.

The groundcover was enlivened by innumerable bright yellow wildflowers: pairs of bell-shaped blossoms atop tall, slender, bare stems. I picked a handful to bring to Fotis. Afterward, I looked them up in my book *Wildflowers of Crete* and learned, to my disappointment, that they are goat-foot oxalis, a weed introduced to the Mediterranean about 200 years ago. One must wait longer for the authentically Cretan wild poppies and anemones to appear.

More than 500 plant species are catalogued in *Wildflowers of Crete*, and of those some ten percent are endemic. Wild trees and plants that I see often and recognize by name include cypress, juniper, pine, plane, holm oak, arbutus, carob, fig, prickly pear, agave, acanthus, oleander, arum lily, borage, caper, cistus, yarrow, chamomile, thistle, mustard, foxglove, euphorbia, dittany, sage, bay laurel, thyme, purslane, cyclamen, asphodel. I intend to carry my wildflower book on country walks this spring, in the hope that I will learn to recognize a few more.

Among the above, dittany is endemic to the inaccessible rock faces of Crete and is cherished for its flavor and medicinal value as tea. Cistus, also an endemic plant, is more common and may have medicinal value which is underappreciated. Friends of ours have used it successfully to cure plantar warts, acne, and sore throat. They gave me a sample which I took to London when we lived there and gave in turn to the head gardener at the Chelsea Physic Garden, a superb botanical garden, initially created as an apothecaries' repository of medicinal herbs, and one of the loveliest places in the city. He took note of my report of this candidate to be the next wonder drug and planted the seeds in the special greenhouse reserved there for Cretan endemic plants.

Tuesday, January 6, 2015

I submitted my Pushkin translation to the Field Translation Series at Oberlin in late September. They responded in December that they can't fit it in. Now I've sent it to the Pushkin Press, a lively young firm with a remit to publish classics and new writing from around the world. They are actually not focused on Pushkin or Russian but one of their editors has a degree in Russian. If they like my translation, I'm thinking, they may also be interested in seeing my unpublished novel. Go, little book! (But I'm not even confident that they will read my email.)

—It's now 3:30 in the afternoon and to my astonishment, I just looked out the window and saw a tornado, or waterspout, a short way out over the sea. These are rare in the Mediterranean, but there it was: a well-defined long dark narrow sleeve reaching from the clouds down to the water. After a few minutes it pulled itself back up into the clouds and disappeared. We've had stormy weather almost every day for the past ten days or so, with hail sometimes and lots of very resonant thunder, and the snow has come down low, enveloping many of the villages on the slopes of the nearby mountains.

—Now it is evening. By chance, reading a collection of essays by Seamus Heaney, I turn a page and there is Elizabeth Bishop's description of waterspouts:

> their heads in cloud, their feet in moving patches
> of scuffed-up white.
> Glass chimneys, flexible, attenuated,
> sacerdotal beings of glass . . . I watched
> the water spiral up in them like smoke.
> Beautiful, yes, but not much company.

Thursday, January 8, 2015

The Charlie Hebdo murders in Paris.

Friday, January 9, 2015

People who commit atrocities of any kind, including this, usually have an ideology, a paranoid notion of the enemy, and personal frustrations and motivations of various kinds. The people who recruit them, though, have an agenda.

There will always be troubled individuals around. Who isn't a troubled individual? But it's the talented recruiters with an agenda—the leaders, strategists, advocates, organizers—who have to be disempowered somehow. The more people everywhere, and especially people in the immediate community, see these destructive and self-defeating agendas as an urgent problem and try to neutralize them, the better.

Whether the virus in question is religious intolerance, ethnic hostility, racism, or something else, some power struggle or other we'd be better off without—I think it takes a village, many villages, and eventually a global village, to build immunity to that.

One may find the cartoons in *Charlie* tasteless and ill-mannered, and I do, but being tasteless and ill-mannered is not a crime. About Islam, in the name of which this crime was committed, an interesting point has been made by Hossein Askari, an Iranian social scientist in New York. Pointing out that Islam is a rules-based religion, and that its rules require not only prayer, fasting, and pilgrimage, but also the creation of social justice and well-being, he's ranked the nations of the world in terms of their performance vis-à-vis specifically Islamic standards of governance. Among the top performers are Ireland and Denmark. Germany comes in at number twenty-six, between the Czech Republic and Israel.

Self-identified "Islamic" countries cluster at the bottom. His paper is informative about core Islamic social values (not the ones we hear most about).

Monday, January 12, 2015

After another week of cold rain, the sun came out yesterday and I took another long walk from Fourní. Now I've spent an hour this morning tidying up the garden. At present we have winter fruit: guava, oranges, tangerines, and bitter Seville oranges, inedible on the tree but excellent in marmalade.

Tuesday, January 13, 2015

Lunch with my friends Natalie and Joseph Ventura. Last year Natalie self-published a book, a lovingly curated chronicle of her family, the Hirshmans, in Latvia in the 1870s, based on one person's surviving diary. Today Joseph gave me his newly self-published memoir of his Sephardic family. As it begins he is a small boy in occupied Greece, where his family are living with false papers that the Greek authorities in Athens provided to the community there. At present, Joseph's relatives, the Venturas and Mizrahis, live in Greece, Istanbul, and Tel Aviv. He's a physicist, a retired professor at the University of Crete. Natalie, who is American, is a poet with whom I often exchange writing and ideas.

From their house I drove on, through pouring rain, to see Fotis. I arrived later than usual and found him sitting downstairs with the other residents around the fire in the hearth. He doesn't socialize with the others, he just sits quietly among them. In fact he now lacks the language skills he would need to interact with them. He was content, and indicated that he wanted to stay as he was and didn't want me to read to him. So I cut up the fruit I always bring, and after a short while I gave him a hug and said goodbye. I've been to see him every day but one since he moved to the Hjem, and there's no doubt that this has been good for him and for me too. But it's also now good to know that he can do all right without my being there.

Wednesday, January 14, 2015

I've just read a book about caring for a person with Alzheimer's: *Keeper*, by Andrea Gillies. She points to the presence of Alzheimer's, not recognized as such, throughout human history—and woke me up to the "senile dementia" of Shakespeare's Lear: "Methinks I should know you, and know this man. Yet I am doubtful, for I am mainly ignorant what place this is; and all the skill I have remembers not these garments; nor I know not where I did lodge last night. Do not laugh at me."

King Lear has lost cognitive abilities, including the ability to make sound judgments, but his emotional life is still as vivid as anyone's. Even when people have been disoriented by the disease, those areas of the brain which haven't yet been affected continue to function as before.

Friday, January 16, 2015

House repairs continue, as I live here through the winter and discover structural vulnerabilities that went unnoticed in summer when it never rains. I've just learned that an exhaust pipe in the basement, one that continues externally up along an outside wall to the roof, is shielded with asbestos.

This house was built in 1990–92; we had removed or wrapped

the old asbestos in the basement of our house in Cambridge long before that. But asbestos standards were not introduced into Greece until after 2000, and up until that point builders here were still installing it. For some purposes, such as the one served by this pipe, there was no substitute available. The contractor never even mentioned this issue to us, with the result that we have been unaware of it until now.

I suspect that European Union regulations, and not Greek ones, are what has brought asbestos awareness to Greece. For this country, an important aspect of membership in the EU has been a general elevation of health and safety standards, together with generous European funding for infrastructure projects such as water management and waste disposal.

Saturday, January 17, 2015

Two of Fotis' old friends took me out to lunch, and afterward we visited Fotis. Over lunch we discussed the upcoming elections. They, too, will not vote for Syriza. Almost all our friends on the left feel the same about Syriza: that it is a reckless, populist party that people have turned to only because it is anti-austerity and anti-status-quo.

In the evening I finished reading yet another book about Alzheimer's, the novel *We Are Not Ourselves* by Matthew Thomas. A very good book, the best one I've read so far. A plain, compelling, honest story, written from the heart in plain, unsentimental, unpretentious prose, about good, flawed, unique, ordinary people. It has true quality and will stay with me for a long time.

Monday, January 19, 2015

In preparation for the general election on Sunday I've read the program of Syriza and spent an hour watching Alexis Tsipras, the leader of Syriza, make a speech. Syriza speaks to people who are poor and in difficulty, and to people who are deeply in debt that they cannot repay. But will Syriza do the right thing for those people, or for the country?

To Potami, The River, which has my vote, is a very new formation that aspires to come in third on Sunday. (It's important who comes in third, and there's a danger that the neo-Nazis will.) The role of The River, if it has one, will be to govern in coalition with the center-right (which has been in power up to now) or the left-to-far-left (Syriza), and to pull whichever party comes first in a pro-European direction and toward the center.

Thursday, January 22, 2015

The painting I'm making now, from memory and imagination, features a Cretan landscape with mountains seen as though from the sea. This morning in yoga class we learned the "mountain pose," where one sits cross-legged with hands raised above one's head, palms joined in prayer position. The body forms a sort of pyramidal mountain shape, very stable-appearing although actually hard to hold. We were instructed to close our eyes and regard the world as though we were a mountain.

I thought of my painting and realized that I had not imagined it from the mountain's point of view. I will now attempt to do this and see whether it makes any difference to the result. Consider Van Gogh. He struggled with the technical problems of rendering an observer's orientation to a scene, even making use of a special viewing device to help him get the perspective right. But he didn't limit himself to that. He also imagined his subject from within, I'm sure, every time. The chair, the peasants' mud-caked boots, the sunflowers, the starry sky . . .

Friday, January 23, 2015

Mindful that it's important to set goals, and that envisioning the future is an aspect of goal-setting, I attempt to visualize myself in the future as a painter. In this vision I am two or three inches taller than I really am and I have grayish-blue eyes, a better haircut, strong hands and upright posture. So far so good! When I go on to imagine the kind of painting I do, though, I can't get beyond what I'm already doing. Maybe that vision will come.

Sunday, January 25, 2015

I got up early this morning to vote. Our polling place is the local public elementary school, and the small first-grade classroom where I voted was well organized and attractive, with simple sums and geometrical shapes cleverly represented on the walls, some tricky spelling rules well diagrammed, and cutouts of swallows higher up on the walls with wings outstretched.

Our yoga group climbed Mount Youchtas recently and went out to lunch afterward. Today it rained buckets on and off, so rather than climb Mount Stroumboulos as planned we just walked for a few hours along the municipal waterfront promenade. We passed many derelict buildings along the waterfront; this is a common sight all over Greece, not only because of the economic crisis but also because the legal status of derelict property is often unclear.

Monday, January 26, 2015

Syriza has beaten every other party by a wide margin, but doesn't have quite enough seats to govern alone. The River is fourth, very slightly behind the Nazis who are now our third-largest party, and barely ahead of our unreformed, hammer-and-sickle Communist Party. Rather than cooperate with The River, which it considers too "soft" on the core issue of repudiating our commitments (known as "The Memorandum") to the European Union, Syriza has chosen to govern in a coalition with the Independent Greeks, a small, clownish right-wing party which rejects the Memorandum. This is not a good sign. The River is focused on reform of our underperforming public sector; the coalition would rather blame all our problems on Germany and Europe.

There are some deadlines which now press upon us: one in February, when we will need an injection of cash from abroad, and several in the summer, when tranches of Greek government bonds will fall due. Syriza will negotiate with the EU over these. Tsipras has announced that his government "does not recognize" the so-called Troika of European Commission, European Central Bank, and IMF that has been supervising Greece via the Memorandum. But he will have to find an interlocutor within the legal framework of the EU.

I have little confidence in this government, but I am an incorrigible optimist about the world. Perhaps we will be respected by our creditors, will gain some helpful relief, and will actually go forward with the kind of reforms the country needs. Maybe Europe as a whole is being prompted, in part by the Greek financial crisis, to get its act together better.

I do feel confidence in the capacities of the Greek people. Some unhealthy attitudes are widespread and deeply embedded, but a great many people are generous, hardworking, well-educated, and honest. Many are creative, collaborative, and entrepreneurial. In the arts and sciences our contributions are distinguished.

Friday, January 30, 2015

The thermometer got stuck in our twenty-year-old VW, and it overheated just as I was passing an auto repair shop on my way home. That was really lucky: suppose it had happened on the highway, in the rain, where I'd been driving fifteen minutes before! I'll have the car looked over properly and serviced, even though it hasn't gone 500 miles since the last time.

We have a second car, a Volvo, which was shipped here from the factory in Sweden ten years ago, and which was expensive because, even though Greece is a member of the EU, we had to pay half of the purchase price all over again in Greek tax when it was delivered. Despite our having paid the import tax, the Heraklion registry of motor vehicles then refused to register it (did they want a bribe?), so we couldn't use it until last year, when we finally managed to get license plates issued in Salonika. I use it for highway driving; it's very comfortable and feels very safe. But it's unsuitable for city driving in our narrow streets, and since I had needed to go into town beforehand I didn't take it on the drive to visit Fotis as I usually do.

Saturday, January 31, 2015

Since January is the month to make self-improving resolutions, the *New York Times* has published an article on the subject of why so many of them fail. The writer claims that we don't stick to our resolutions when they are not congruent with our existing values and lifestyle. He suggests that we each create a personal mission statement incorporating those values, and to help us with that task he provides a set of questions. I thought this was worth doing and did answer the questions for myself, though I didn't then go on to write a mission statement.

How do you want to be remembered?
How do you want people to describe you?
Who do you want to be?
Who or what matters most to you?
What are your deepest values?
How would you define success in your life?
What makes your life really worth living?

These are my personal answers:

I want to be remembered with affection and as a source of values to live by, just as I remember my parents.

I hope people describe me as reliable, resourceful, and enlivening in company.

I just want to be myself, and true to the values I hold for myself.

My family and my work matter the most to me. I aspire to be honest, creative, and always growing in understanding. I have to add that I also value safety, stability, comfort, and general good health and well-being, particularly now that I'm older than before.

"To love things that are worthy of love, and interact with them positively." This is not my own formulation—I've borrowed it from the philosopher Susan Wolf—but I can't improve upon it.

Success in my life is when I have realized my goals, and the people I'm connected to are also successful.

Everything about life makes my life worth living.

Sunday, February 1, 2015

A mild and misty morning. I've had breakfast outdoors on the patio while reading *The Making of the Cretan Landscape*. The title recalls W. G. Hoskins' classic *Making of the English Landscape*, as well as Francis Pryor's *Making of the British Landscape*, both of which I have on my e-reader. I've turned to these for their intrinsic interest, but also because I've been painting landscape from memory and imagination and am thinking about it.

I've also been reviewing my Arabic, using a textbook which lists hundreds of Arabic phrases and sentences opposite their English equivalent. I look at the English, then write out an Arabic translation, then look at the textbook Arabic and compare it to mine. My efforts are almost always approximately OK but never quite right. Arabic spelling is phonetic, but so far my ear isn't up to the challenge.

So whether I'm painting or studying Arabic, I use an iterative process. I put down my version of what is out there, then attempt to improve upon it by looking at and learning about the real thing, then try again. This is what we do every few seconds when we draw. In the case of painting I'm not interested in replicating the real thing with any exactness, but I do want to be aware of what is out there. (I also, of course, look to other painters and their ways of expressing visual ideas, no matter what the subject matter.)

A very good thing about this kind of process is that we begin with what we already know. When teaching geography to children it's helpful to have them draw their own maps first, putting in everything where they think it is, and then proceed toward greater accuracy. It's when we're involved in the material from the outset that we learn most quickly, correct our imprecisions and mistakes, and have the most fun. Learning, in this mode, is a constant back-and-forth, one could say an ever-renewed reality check.

Thursday, February 5, 2015

I'm painting from memory and imagination the beach landscape where I usually go to swim, complete with a seagull, beach umbrellas, and a seaside café. When working in my studio I always begin with abstract imagery and then discover what I'm going to represent, my abstraction consisting mainly of linear doodles that divide up the canvas and create odd incidents. This time I've given equal importance to color areas that I intuitively set down as I try to see what my picture will be of. These are two complementary ways of seeing, one relying on the rods in our system of vision and one on the cones: in effect, two different ways of thinking that overlap.

The northeast of the US is experiencing huge snowstorms, while in Crete the temperature is seventy degrees and strawberries have appeared in the market. They are grown in the inland plain of Mesará, in shallow trenches where they're protected from the wind. (There are also greenhouses in Mesará where a small variety of banana is grown year-round.)

Crete is one of the most prosperous parts of Greece, since we have tourism, agriculture, higher education and research, and even some industry. The economic crisis and depression are present, but not very noticeable, here. They are much more evident in Athens, where the quality of life has deteriorated a lot, and in other parts of mainland Greece.

Friday, February 6, 2015

This week the Syriza leadership has been visiting heads of government around Europe. Some of its demands, such as the one for simple debt forgiveness, were rejected immediately. But there is a lot of sympathy for us internationally, and there is general recognition that the austerity program we've been in is too hard on too many people (even though it had some success on its own terms, in that we did achieve a primary budget surplus, the economy grew a little last year, and growth in 2015 was projected to reach three percent before the election of Syriza intervened).

Syriza now proposes that our repayment obligations be suspended, reclassified in various ways, or linked to growth in GDP.

The Nobel Prize-winning economist Joseph Stiglitz and a few others have endorsed this last idea, saying, "If Greece does well, its creditors will receive more of their money; if it does not, they will get less." That would be nice, but it seems unlikely.

Saturday, February 7, 2015

The American ambassador, commenting on our predicament, has just said, "Greece should continue to make administrative and structural reforms and exercise fiscal prudence." I find this to be rather stilted, but essentially good advice. The US government wants a happy end to our present standoff and has sent a team here to advise us in our negotiations and help us avoid an adversarial meltdown.

Sunday, February 8, 2015

Today is a beautiful day, clear and cool. I painted in my studio and then went for a run. The back road where I run is within a few hundred meters of Knossos, and as I'm jogging by I can see the upper walls of the palace. It was not built on a high ridge, like an Iron Age fort or medieval castle, but is nestled in a river valley. Much archeological evidence leads one to think that Minoan culture, which was sustained by trade, not conquest, was not only among the earliest, but also one of the most pleasant varieties of European civilization.

Monday, February 9, 2015

Europa was a Cretan moon goddess. She took the form of a beautiful Phoenician princess, and Zeus, who fell in love with her, took the form of a bull and carried her off to Crete, where they had two sons, Minos and Rhadamanthos. Minos became king of Knossos, around the corner from here. The bull is remembered in the Minoan bull-leaping game where male and female athletes take a bull by its long horns and somersault over its back; also in the cult of Mithra, the bull, which contested with Christianity for the status of top religion in early Europe; in Spanish bullfighting, of course; and in the sculpture of a bull which stands outside the headquarters of the European Union in Brussels. If Greece were to leave the EU, Europe would lose a crucial component of its founding mythology and Greco-Roman cultural heritage.

More seriously, not only would Greece outside of Europe be friendless and undefended in a dangerous neighborhood; not only would every Greek person be deprived of an invaluable opportunity for travel, study, work, and economic and cultural inclusion; we would also be separated from the cultural and civic heritage of the European Enlightenment, our most important import from abroad. Yet there are quite a few people, on the left and right of the Greek political spectrum, who seem not to care about this. That does worry me.

Tuesday, February 10, 2015

My interaction with Fotis is very much the same now from day to day. I visit him every afternoon in his room. I bring him fruit and nuts, and the Hjem brings him tea with halva, rice pudding, or another traditional sweet. We listen to music (today it was Kathleen Ferrier singing *What Is Life?*, *An Die Musik*, and other beautiful songs). I ask him how he is and he says he's fine. I ask him whether anything has happened in his life and he doesn't answer. I give him news of friends and family and ask him whether he wants me to read aloud from Kazantzakis and he says yes. After that (we're halfway through Kazantzakis' novel, *Christ Recrucified*) we go downstairs, and if the weather permits we take a short walk around the grounds. Then I find him a place to sit with the others near the fire in the hearth and tell him goodbye. That's all. But we do have a good time, he does understand these things and he's very sweet to be with, he's moved by the music and he's interested in the story.

Wednesday, February 11, 2015

"O my brother! Do not leave the water tap open. Do not write on the wall of the house nor throw the waste paper and peel of the fruits except in the waste-paper basket." This is one of the short English passages in my textbook that I've been translating back into the original Arabic. If only everyone here would heed this saying! We are not likely to leave the water tap open, but we do litter a lot, and we completely cover the walls of the house (other people's houses, that is, and the stone walls of public buildings) with casually scrawled graffiti. What is written there is almost always obscenities, insults, and extremist political slogans.

The ubiquitous and disfiguring graffiti amplifies the feelings of a small fraction of young men, and can't be assumed to reflect the public mood in general. But no one removes it. Public authorities and private householders rarely even try to scrub it off or paint it over.

This leads me to an observation that I'd rather not make: people here, when stressed, are liable to react either with passive fatalism or in aggressive and passive-aggressive ways. We are very inclined to blame others for our problems (conspiracy theories are popular), and we can be very tolerant of irresponsible behavior that we should be working to control.

Now I sound like a prig and a scold. I hope that's not what I really am; but it's very much what people faced with passive-aggressive behavior tend to turn into. There arises a reciprocal dynamic with the power of a magnetic field.

I'm sorry to say that I think this dynamic has become quite salient in the present interaction between us and our European partners, especially Germany, at a time when what is needed is mutual respect and support. There are several sides to the way Syriza approaches our partners, and among them is one that's very pointedly passive-aggressive, that is, "You are to blame for our difficulties, so stop interfering with us, but also help us, or else we will crash our country and damage you as well." This is only an undertone, but it is certainly there.

Another aspect of Syriza's approach is simply humanitarian: "We have suffered too much, and it is the mission of our government to alleviate the suffering of our people." This is valid, and it's true that Syriza has more solidarity with people on the lowest economic levels—including, much to its credit, immigrants and asylum seekers—than any other political party here. Since in fact the austerity program we've been in is generally recognized to have created much more collateral damage than anticipated, this tone of voice might create a more positive dynamic and may lead to an improvement in the situation of all. I hope.

This evening our government is going into serious talks with our interlocutor, which is now known as the Eurogroup, and people are again filling Constitution Square in Athens to demonstrate against austerity. But nobody has ever demonstrated in favor of staying in the Euro and the EU, even though that is an existential issue with very serious economic consequences, including for the people who think they have "nothing to lose." And nobody has ever held a rally in favor of our paying our taxes.

Thursday, February 12, 2015

Today is the first day of Carnival. When I arrived at the Hjem everyone was dressed up in funny hats and a party was underway. Fotis was wearing a blond wig, and those who could do so were dancing to loud music. The whole thing was charming, silly, and poignant.

Sunday, February 15, 2015

In the film *Rebel Without a Cause*, a high-school student played by James Dean is pressured into playing a game of chicken. He and his opponent, "Buzz," are to race a pair of stolen cars to the edge of a cliff: the first one to jump out of his car loses. But Buzz loses everything when his jacket gets caught on the car door handle and he can't get out in time.

Now our government is playing chicken with Europe. Asked in an interview what we will do if our discussions come down to the wire and no agreement has been reached, our finance minister, Yanis Varoufakis, said, "I don't know. I have no idea. I don't intend to be doing this forever anyway. I can always go back to writing my book."

Monday, February 16, 2015

Many people are emptying their bank accounts, for fear that their euros at the bank will be turned into drachmas shortly. This morning I, too, got up early, went to the bank, and withdrew all but a few euros from our account. This was prudent, since I will need to spend all the cash I have on monthly fees to the Hjem plus the replacement of our asbestos pipe and completion of repairs to our roof. The money will stay in the country, in other people's bank accounts or in their pockets.

The larger problem is that, in the present climate, hardly anyone will invest money in anything here. Deflation discourages investment and consumption and is a looming problem for Europe; but acute instability, such as we've had in Greece since the end of last year, is even worse for productive investment.

After leaving the bank, where the scene was calm, I went for a walk, since the weather is splendid today. On my way I passed an old one-family, one-story house such as were the norm in cities until the 1960s, when apartment buildings began to go up all over Greece. We once rented and lived in such a house in a working-class district in Athens. Because this one was derelict and collapsing, I could see the building material of the walls beneath the plaster, and it was not stone or brick. It was sun-dried mud brick and straw: adobe.

This evening it's raining again, and intensive talks in Brussels have led to nothing. Our government's unyielding insistence that the Memorandum be abandoned or revised has very strong backing at the moment within Greece: a recent poll registers eighty percent support overall. One notable result of the poll: among all political parties across the spectrum, there is one whose voters now support Syriza even more than Syriza voters themselves do, at ninety-seven percent rather than ninety-six. This party is Golden Dawn (Nazis).

Tuesday, February 17, 2015

All eighteen other countries in the euro currency zone say firmly that Greece can't continue to receive financial support without conditions. We have been asked to specify which of the existing conditions we accept and which we seek to change, but we haven't responded to this request.

Is it because of my age that I see Greece heading for the rocks and am alarmed, while most Greek people seem to be saying "full speed ahead"? It's true that my views have changed over time. Decades ago, my thinking was in some ways close to that of Syriza today. Subsequently, I've learned to take a more considered view of the many factors involved in economic development or failure to develop, and now I think that good government and public administration, and competitiveness of some sort in the international economy, are crucial development strengths.

We older people have more experience to draw upon than before and may see things more in the round. If we don't get cranky and crabby then we may become wise. I don't claim this accomplishment for myself, but I do think it's the right way to go. Look toward the future, and take the long view.

That is where I think Syriza falls short. Its vision for the future is unclear. Syriza wants to lead all of Europe out of its austerity trap and into a future of fairness and growth. Good! But it can't do this just by defying the rules of collaboration and mutual expectation that are already in place. It can hardly do it by seeking new loans from Russia and China, as is happening now. Nor can it do it without a forward plan for Greece, and this seems to be lacking. Syriza is reactive. Regrettable things have happened in the past and up until today, it's true, but reacting against those things is not the same as knowing what to do next.

I went early this morning to visit Fotis at the Hjem because I received a phone call saying that he had a light fever last night and has a cold. I brought zinc pills, because I believe that taking zinc within twenty-four hours of getting a cold ameliorates the symptoms. However, I found that he's losing the ability to swallow a pill; he chews it a bit and spits it out. I've heard that one can mash powdered pills into applesauce for people who have difficulty swallowing, so I will try that.

Thursday, February 19, 2015

We are still at loggerheads with Europe, and, if there is no agreement, Greece will exit the euro. This seems to be what the left caucus within Syriza wants.

People here seem remarkably calm and relaxed despite the situation. As far as I can see, everyone is just going about daily life as though nothing special were happening. I visited my friend Natalie yesterday evening, we talked for almost two hours about art and poetry, and neither of us mentioned the crisis. That doesn't mean we aren't aware of it, though.

Friday, February 20, 2015

I continue to study Arabic. It's a good way to pass the time indoors during the very cold, blustery weather we've had this month. Arabic is Semitic, unlike other languages I'm familiar with. A key aspect of it is the central role of three-consonant roots in creating vocabulary. A large number of words of different kinds—noun, verb, adjective, what have you—may be built, according to established grammatical rules, from each root, so that each root learned is a big step forward.

The news tonight is that we may be getting closer to a deal on our debt. In the meantime, one billion euros were withdrawn from Greek banks today. The home of a Syriza MP was burglarized, and it came to light that he had hidden 10,000 euros in cash under his mattress.

Saturday, February 21, 2015

We seem to have an agreement. We have guidelines, which the Greek government must fill in with draft specifics by Monday. Essentially, Syriza has accepted the framework that was in place before the election. It has continuing obligations to its partners and must meet targets, but has gained some flexibility with regard to how exactly it will do this. I'm glad to see the concluding sentence in the agreement: "We remain committed to provide adequate support to Greece until it has regained full market access as long as it honors its commitments within the agreed framework."

This has been a turbulent and stressful period. In the course of it our generation of Greek politicians has left the scene. The next generation has taken center stage. New political formations—Syriza, the Independent Greeks, The River—are in place. The old, battered, creaky, and corrupt order has stepped aside.

The European Union ignored the high level of dysfunction in Greece for a very long time. There was a sensible reason for this: the principle of subsidiarity, according to which problems should be addressed at the right level. European bureaucrats in Brussels can't be charged with monitoring every member country; that should be the task of each national government. However, the Greek government has failed to meet its responsibilities; it is clear that we need help, and I hope we get some.

This evening, our daughter Zoe arrived for a week-long visit. We had a lovely talk, and she went to bed early following her long flight here from Virginia.

Sunday, February 22, 2015

We went to see Fotis in the afternoon. He recognized Zoe immediately and was very happy and sweet in his quiet way. He's over his cold, but there is a new concern: he's become quite stooped over when sitting or standing, and now he also bends his body toward the right. That has only been true since this morning, and it may just reflect some muscular stiffness. Or it might be the result of lost brain cells; people with Alzheimer's sometimes develop physical asymmetries as a result of the disease.

Wednesday, February 25, 2015

We visited Fotis, then drove on a short distance to Mália. The Minoan palace there was one of the grandest, in a superb setting where snow-crested mountains come down very close to the beach. We walked around the excavation, where we were the only visitors, and the beach, where some men were fishing and a few people were exercising their dogs. We'd brought swimming suits and plunged for two minutes into the sea: it was ice-cold and brilliant!

Fotis is no longer bending to the side, but there is a new issue. Although he is very calm and sweet most of the time, he can be very uncooperative when being bathed or shaved. The staff find him hard to manage at those times, and they have suggested medicating him to make him more compliant. We have rejected this idea in the past, but now they've brought it up again. Zoe and I will go in the morning to be present while he's being bathed and to problem-solve about this. Zoe is a medical social worker, and her advice on this and everything else has been very helpful.

I've begun reading *Why Nations Fail*, by Daron Acemoglu and James A. Robinson. This is an influential book with a very clear thesis, namely that the main prerequisite for economic development throughout human history has been stable, inclusive, pluralistic government, and the main impediment to development has been extractive, parasitic, authoritarian government. Greece is by no means in the worst category world-wide, but is at the bottom of the class in Europe, together with Italy and Romania, in terms of government transparency and efficiency. The question is, will Syriza improve our performance or will it make it worse? Things could go either way. Many people in Syriza haven't been in government before, so they are not tied into old networks. But new elites often step into the shoes of old ones they have displaced and behave just as before or even worse. This has been called "the iron law of oligarchy." Syriza's rhetoric has been all about undoing reforms and going back to old ways, and that is what people voted for. Yet now they are being asked to bring reform.

Thursday, February 26, 2015

We will not resort to medical management with Fotis. Instead, I will go to the Hjem on the mornings when he's to have a bath and will help out and try to keep things calm.

Saturday, February 28, 2015

It's 6:30 a.m. and I've just dropped Zoe off at the airport for her flight back to Virginia. We've had a wonderful time.

The view from the house at this time of day is magical: the sea and sky are blue, the snow in the mountains brilliant white, and the streetlights still glittering in the white city below. I went for a run and saw the first wild anemones of the year. Roses are blossoming in our garden and there are oranges and lemons on the trees. Despite our tribulations, I think this must be one of the very best places in the world to live.

Sunday, March 1, 2015

I look forward to my life here continuing more or less as it is now. This is an appealing plan, and if I remain healthy then I can see no obstacle to it.

I expect Fotis to live for five more years. My guess could be off by a few years. I hope his life will continue for as long as it has value for him.

If he were not living, I expect I would spend more time—up to six months each year—in Cambridge, Massachusetts, with my family and friends. Probably I'd also travel somewhat more, to parts of the world where I already feel some connection that I would like to deepen.

The neurologist Oliver Sacks has terminal cancer. He wrote an op-ed piece about it in which he said, "I feel intensely alive, and I want and hope in the time that remains to deepen my friendships, to say farewell to those I love, to write more, to travel if I have the strength, to achieve new levels of understanding and insight." Amen.

Today I attended a lecture in memory of Stelios Alexiou, who died last year. He was a director of the Archeological Museum of Crete, an editor of classical and Renaissance Greek texts, a poet and translator. He was also a friend of Fotis' family, and I'd known him for over forty years. When I was about twenty-five years old, he read a translation I'd made into English of a poem by Cavafy, and whenever I saw him afterward he would tell me what a good job that was and that I should translate more poetry. After the lecture, questions were invited, and one audience member after another got up to say how much, and how effectively, Stelios had encouraged him or her in whatever endeavor was dear to his or her own heart.

If there's one thing I would add to Oliver Sacks' agenda, I think it would be this: to encourage other people to do whatever it is they have in them to do in life. That would be a legacy!

Saturday, March 7, 2015

Vangelis Alatsatianos, who looks after our garden for us, is here today with his hand-held electric saw to prune our trees. He's a neighbor in the village and we have long known him and his family. His uncle, Michalis, used to bring milk from his goat in a bucket every summer afternoon to give to Fotis' mother, who would boil it on the stove while Fotis' father and Michalis sat in the garden discussing this and that. We were related, I don't know in what way exactly, but someone baptized someone, or was best man at someone's wedding, so that Michalis was always known to us as "O Kumbaros O Michalis," that is, "Michalis our Godbrother."

If only more people were like Vangelis! Highly intelligent and educated (with an advanced degree in agriculture), very pleasant and helpful, well-informed and capable in every way. I'm always glad to see him. Whenever I tell him of some difficulty I have, he says cheerfully, "That's not a problem," and tells me how to fix it. He works in the government agricultural service, has his own fields where he grows grapes and vegetables and keeps sheep (he imported his own select sheep from Scotland), and helps us and some others in the village with our seasonal garden tasks.

Vangelis' family, like most in our village, came here in the 1920s as refugees from Asia Minor. Most of the earlier residents of this village were Muslim and therefore regarded as Turks (though they may have been local converts to Islam), and so were deported to Turkey according to an arrangement for the exchange of minorities after a period of upheaval and war. Greeks from the other side were brought into the empty spaces that the old inhabitants left. "Alatsatianos" is not a family name; back in Turkey most people didn't have family names. It's derived from the name of the village near the city of Izmir (then known as Smyrna) that Vangelis' family, and other families now living here in Fortetsa, come from. They are survivors of a particularly savage massacre back in Alatsata, which took place in the course of the events always referred to here as "the catastrophe."

Monday, March 9, 2015

Helen, our older daughter, will be flying in this afternoon for a week-long visit. We are looking forward to a lovely time together. Time with each of our daughters is a great happiness for me.

As for happiness, I've just glanced at a book on the subject edited by Daniel Kahneman. From it I learn that social relationships, and especially marriage, are an important source of well-being. Unemployment has a strong negative effect, but retirement, and leisure activities, a positive one. Income above a certain minimum, and increased prosperity, have little effect on happiness, but declining prosperity, and invidious comparison of one's situation with that of others, diminish it. These results are by now well known. It surprises me that the effect of children or grandchildren on happiness is not discussed. Some points made—the one about marriage, for example—may be contested (but who wouldn't agree that it's good to live in a committed relationship with someone we love?).

Questions remain. What is the happiness quotient of a clear conscience? Of freedom from resentment? Of freedom from fear?

Wednesday, March 11, 2015

Yesterday Helen and I drove to a nearby town so that she could visit a close friend of hers who is in jail awaiting trial. The issue is a misunderstanding that arose in connection with drugs. Use of heroin and other hard drugs is widespread among young people here; in summer, addicts and dealers from around the city have made use of the small park next to our house. This particular person is not herself involved in drugs at all. She had gone to visit her ex-husband, who was in jail as a dealer, bringing him what she thought were his clean clothes. When the clothes were inspected at the entrance to the jail, residual traces of some drug were found in them, and as a result she was arrested. Helen talked with her for a long time and gave her excellent support.

I didn't enter the jail, but I saw it from outside. It looks very scary, with two high, concentric barbed wire fences around it and guard towers on four sides. Helen reports, though, that most of the staff inside are considerate and kind.

This situation put me in mind of a bad situation in which I found myself two summers ago. I was driving in the countryside with Fotis, stopping to look in on a few small medieval chapels along the way. At one point I left him belted into the passenger seat while I went to see whether a particular small church was locked before helping him out. The road was almost level, but not quite, and I had pulled the handbrake but left the gear shift in neutral. Evidently I didn't pull the handbrake hard enough, because when I'd taken about four steps the car began to roll backward. I turned and ran after it, but it picked up speed and there was no way I could reach it. There was a stone wall on one side of the road and a ten-foot drop on the other. The car veered, thank goodness, toward the wall, hit a utility pole, and was stopped dead, its rear end crumpled and rear windshield broken by the impact. It was drivable, and I was able to get back in and drive it home.

Suppose it had veered the other way? Fotis might have been killed as it went over the drop and rolled on down. I might then have been charged with his murder: a spouse worn out by caring for her disabled husband who decides to do away with him! My trial would by now have taken place, and I might today be sitting in that very jail, or a much worse one, serving out my time.

Thursday, March 12, 2015

Quite a few people here seem to think we are "at war" with Europe. I've heard people say that our financial crisis was engineered by Germany in order to ruin and take us over. Greece suffered terribly under Nazi occupation. Nothing of the kind is taking place now, but the narrative has power.

What will happen, now that people who half-believe in that widely-shared narrative are running our government? One thing is that the government is demanding war reparations from Germany.

Another is that the fate of undocumented migrants in Greece has been given a new meaning. Syriza is the party that has expressed most compassion for these people, and has just announced that it will open detention centers where some 10,000 people are being held. No sooner did it do so than Pavlos Kammenos, our right-wing Minister of Defence, reconfigured those refugees as an unconventional weapon aimed at Germany. If Germany "strikes" us, he said, we will "strike back": we will give papers to those migrants and send them into Europe. Among them are "ISIS jihadis," he went on, who will head "straight for Berlin." Our government has just threatened Germany with a terrorist attack.

Such confrontational posturing does nothing to address our core problems of low productivity and institutional dysfunction. But it pleases the—evidently large—segment of Greek opinion which is hostile to Germany, Europe, and the West.

System change is hard. This is true for behavior change in individuals, just as it is for social and political systems. A thousand threads hold things in the shape they are in. An intervention from outside is liable to provoke "riot"-type behavior, in individuals and in society. This is an aspect of what is happening here now.

Friday, March 13, 2015

I'm enjoying writing this journal.

I've had one core ambition in my life, and that was to be a writer. I committed myself to it when I was ten years old, and although I have done some other things, they never displaced that core commitment. Once or twice I've thought, Why should I feel bound by a decision made by a ten-year-old child? But I've never really deviated.

Now it seems to me that I've actually come a long way toward meeting my goal, despite the fact that I still have an infinite way to go. I've produced a history book, a book of poems, short stories, a novel, criticism, letters, translations, a memoir, and now this journal. I've never done any travel writing, but perhaps this journal could be considered that, even though I'm not traveling but sitting still. I've also liked editing other people's work. To this extent, I've lived the life I chose for myself and have done what I set out to do.

Monday, March 16, 2015

Helen left yesterday. We had a lovely time together, as always, and she and Fotis spent some happy hours, mostly just sitting together not doing anything.

As I drive to the Hjem I've been listening to the Haydn string quartets. They get better and better, and today I found that rather than simply enjoy the shape and sound of the music, I was appreciating, most of all, the way the four members of a quartet listen to each other and play interactively together. That relationship!

Fotis and I listened to Brahms' "Four Serious Songs." I had been unaware of the text to these. This morning's *New York Times* featured an article about assisted suicide for the terminally ill, which is now legal in a few states. I was struck by the relevance of Brahms' music to this. The text of the third song is taken from Koheleth / Ecclesiastes:

> O death, how bitter is the remembrance of thee to a man that is at peace in his possessions . . . and that still hath strength. O death, how acceptable is thy sentence unto a man that is needy and that faileth in strength, that is in extreme old age, and is distracted in all things, and that looks for no better lot, nor waiteth on better days! O death, how acceptable is thy sentence.

I continue reading aloud to Fotis from Kazantzakis' highly dramatic novel. At the close of today's stirring episode he said, "There aren't any people like that anymore." He may not remember the story, but he does understand it as it unfolds.

Wednesday, March 18, 2015

Lenya, Katia, Effi, and Maro, who were classmates of Fotis from the first through the twelfth grade, came to see him today. He clearly remembered the other classmates and friends that they mentioned to him.

Home again, I find the following report in today's *New Yorker*: "Studies have shown that when people keep a journal they tend to fare better emotionally, recover more quickly from negative experiences, and achieve more academically and professionally." What's more, the highest benefits come from writing entries that are open to comment. I circulate this journal to a few family members and friends, and I always feel good when they write back to comment.

Friday, March 20, 2015

My yoga group celebrates birthdays by going out to lunch, and yesterday we went, appropriately for yoga, to a small Indian restaurant. Appropriately, but remarkably; foreign cuisines are very little represented in Crete. There is pizza everywhere, of course, and Turkish kebab. But as a rule Greeks, who eat out a great deal, prefer and are limited to Greek fare. This is a good thing in a way.

Sunday, March 22, 2015

The vernal equinox, the beginning of calendar spring, was on Friday. Doves are cooing, the almond trees are decked out in pinkish-white blossoms, the fig trees are putting out their first crinkled leaves like tiny hands, and the air is aromatic.

I listened online to a short, charming TED talk by Adam Leipzig, "How To Know Your Life's Purpose in Five Minutes." He asks how what we do makes us useful to others (actually—more powerfully—he asks how what we do changes other people's lives), and so has prompted me to ask myself, "What do people need from me?" or more generally, "What do people need from other people?" There is an unlimited number of answers to this question, but it took me less than a minute to arrive at what I think is the general answer.

They need to know that I'm OK and that I love them.

I think this is what children need from their parents and also what parents need from their kids. It's what we need from our friends and, eventually, from everyone we're involved with. Of course, "I'm OK" doesn't mean that I have no problems, just that I'm handling the problems I have and accepting help with them. And of course, "love" includes an infinite spectrum of benign attitudes.

I think that when we have this basic, general awareness of each other, then we are each free to live our lives in the best and fullest way possible.

Monday, March 23, 2015

American movies come to cinemas here, and last night I went with my yoga group to see *Still Alice*. As the film ends, Alice is in exactly the stage of Alzheimer's that Fotis is in now. She can't do much, but she's still able to walk, she can be read to, and she still has understanding, as is shown very touchingly—and believably—in the final scene.

In a previous stage of Alice's disease, she is instructed, via computer file, by her earlier, already diagnosed but still quite functional self, to kill herself. The earlier Alice has created a simple test—"What is my older daughter's name?" "What is my address?"—and tells the later Alice that when she can no longer answer the questions she should go upstairs, find the bottle of pills at the back of the dresser drawer, and take them all. The later Alice is able to grasp the instructions, sort of, and finds the pills, but then is interrupted and spills them on the floor.

The early-stage, still-functioning Alice thought that her life would not be worthwhile once she didn't know her daughter's name. But it's our experience that the value of Fotis' life, to him and also to us, remains very high. He doesn't know his address, and hardly knows what happened an hour ago, but he is certainly still himself and can not only report that he is happy, but asks me whether I'm happy too. He still has dignity, responds to other people, and enjoys life.

Wednesday, March 25, 2015

Greek Independence Day. I've just finished a painting of Heraklion harbor, based on memory and imagination. It includes an icon that often appears in my paintings—the Greek flag—and although it doesn't look much like the real harbor, I think it conveys the spirit of the place and is recognizable as the place.

I think my painting is improving. If I want to improve I can't be timid; I have to take risks and try new ideas which may ruin the work I'm engaged in. This makes the process more stressful and also more fun.

Some guidelines: Be intuitive. Use visual form-logic, not rational, practical, real-world logic. Don't worry about making sense. Keep experimental and loose. Draw on accidents for ideas. Don't get caught up in detail; always act according to what the whole picture needs.

Thursday, March 26, 2015

Natalie has written sixty poems she wants to put together as a book manuscript. She's given them to me to try my hand at arranging, and she will make her own arrangement independently. Once we've both done this, we will see what themes and relationships seem to emerge.

Sunday, March 29, 2015

After visiting Fotis I went for a run along the seafront. There I came upon an organized 5K race with several hundred participants, all running to support people with autism. I ran the distance and was surely the oldest one doing it. The youngest runner I saw was a twelve-year-old girl whose time was rather better than mine.

This has been a good weekend for joggers. Our twelve-year-old granddaughter Sophia completed her first 10K in Richmond, Virginia, yesterday. Bravo!

I'm starting a new painting and, as I do so, am thinking about the commonalities between music and visual art. In both media, there is a crucial step to be taken from linear thinking to larger pattern-thinking and building.

There are so many analogies. Dynamics, from *pianissimo* to *fortissimo*, in music, are comparable to tone, the degree of light in each pixel of a black-and-white photograph. A key in music is like a colorist's palette. Rhythm is rhythm, in any medium. Drama is drama, and so forth.

Monday, March 30, 2015

This morning I took a walk on Youchtas. There were beautiful vistas of olive groves and vineyards with the sea in the distance, and I discovered a discreet, almost invisible botanical garden. A 10,000-kilometer European hiking trail, the E4, begins in Spain near Gibraltar and continues through France, Switzerland, Austria, and the Balkans (it gets a bit sketchy there) on down through Greece, and traverses all of Crete from west to east. (There also exist an E1, E2, E3 … E12; one could spend one's entire life walking these.) The E4 winds around Youchtas, and beside it there's a small area dotted with little six-inch signs identifying thirty different species of endemic plant. They are all growing naturally on the hillside, but you wouldn't notice them normally because some are so common and others so small. Once I began looking I saw many more sorts of plants that were not even signposted.

Monday, April 6, 2015

"A history in the making where the next step is totally unclear." This is an apt comment on the Greek situation from a person to whom I've been sending my journal.

Syriza entered government in the hope that, with itself in the vanguard and with others such as Die Linke in Germany, Podemos in Spain, and Sinn Fein in Ireland at its side, it could inspire a continent-wide revolt against neoliberalism in Europe. But the question right now is, Can Greece pay its next installment to the IMF, which will fall due on Thursday? The government is preparing to do so by moving the unspent funds of every public entity in the country, including the municipalities, the health services, and the universities, to the Central Bank of Greece.

Last week, some anarchists disrupted Parliament. As they were leaving, they defaced a marble statue of the poet Kostis Palamas. In 1943, the funeral of Palamas was the occasion of a mass demonstration against Nazi occupation, but our young anarchists seem not to know that, or not to care.

Wednesday, April 8, 2015

This is Easter week, the most important holiday in the Orthodox calendar. For the past twenty years, Fotis and I have spent this week on holiday with Greek friends on some island: Kithera, Sifnos, Samothraki, Patmos, Amorgos, Chios, Kefalonia, Kerkyra, Zakynthos, Tinos, Syros, Skyros, Evoia, Karpathos, Mytilini . . . There are more—Paros, Mykonos, Spetses, Naxos, Kalymnos, Andros, Aegina, Hydra, Poros, Santorini—that we've visited at other times. The names alone are beautiful, and each island is beautiful in a different way. Actually, though, it's fortunate that we're not taking that holiday this year, since the weather—very unusually for April—is stormy, windy, rainy, bleak, and cold.

A much more serious problem than the weather is affecting our islands: the stream of desperate refugees coming across the Mediterranean. Greece and Italy are the most accessible points of entry into Europe for these people. Many of them are losing their lives at sea, and those who manage to get here receive minimal support or none.

Saturday, April 11, 2015

Yesterday was Good Friday, and some friends called to invite me to the evening service with them. We drove up a steep and winding mountain road to the Convent of Savathiana, attended the liturgy, and went out to a taverna afterward, as is the custom, for a meal of the kinds of things that are acceptable during this Lenten period (no meat, and no fish, but shellfish, olive oil, and wine are all right unless you are really devout). I thought of the many other times I've been present at this service, including in Central Square in Cambridge, where the Greek and Syrian Orthodox Christians choreograph their street processions around each other.

Sunday, April 12, 2015

Though not a believer, I appreciate the cultural and community aspects of the church, and I think that my attitude in this is perhaps similar to that of many Greeks. (Probably many are believers, in some way or other, some of the time.) Despite that appreciation though, I didn't have the stamina to stay up for yesterday's midnight service, when the congregation sings the triumphal hymn "Christ Is Risen from the Dead" and lights candles in the darkness. I went to bed early, expecting to be woken up by the firecrackers—not endorsed by the church—that boys always set off, but I slept right through them.

Today, Easter Sunday, is a lovely day, mild, sunny and warm. I'm happy for all the people sitting outdoors right now tippling raki and roasting lamb on a spit. You would never think that three days ago, the wind was wild enough to make one's car veer on the road and to rip a fixed screen off a window of our house.

I'm not roasting a lamb, but I have invited Fondas and Ruth to lunch, with chicken in the pot and kokorétsi (lamb innards) roasting in the oven.

Monday, April 13, 2015

The waterfront cafés that were closed for the winter have opened their doors. Today is a holiday, and suddenly hundreds of people have appeared where, all winter long, there was almost no one.

Thursday, April 16, 2015

Half an hour ago I was sitting at my writing table when it began to sway a little. I thought briefly of getting under the table or under a doorway, but decided instead to go outdoors, where I stayed for a little while. Then I came back inside and looked up the event online. We have just had an earthquake, 6.1 on the Richter scale, its epicenter in the sea east of Crete near the island of Kasos.

The ceiling and roof of this part of our house form a barrel, a half-cylinder. This is unusual in Crete, where houses have been roofed with flat terraces for thousands of years. Flat roofs are great for hanging out laundry, drying fruits and vegetables, and sleeping out on hot nights, and also good if you intend to add another story to your house someday. We chose the barrel design for aesthetic reasons, but it's also thought to provide some earthquake protection. In nearby Santorini, which is a volcanic island (as Crete is not) and where there was a devastating earthquake in 1956, many houses are built with barrel roofs.

Looking up that 1956 earthquake now, I learn that it was accompanied by a tsunami thirty meters high! I'd had no idea such things ever happen in the modern Mediterranean.

Looking back on my own earthquake response, I realize that it wasn't very good. I went outdoors (good), but then sat in my white plastic chair just a few feet from the house until I got cold and went indoors again. If the house had collapsed, I would have been crushed just as surely as if I'd been in the kitchen. Next time

(next time!) I should take that chair, which is very light and porta-
ble, up into the olive orchard.

Friday, April 17, 2015

This morning after visiting Fotis I drove to the plateau of Lassithi,
an hour away. Walking above Lassithi, where goats were my only
company and spring meltwater was rushing in the culvert beside
the road, I could look down on a green saucer-shaped alluvial plain
with white villages at its edges and mountains all around. Good
agricultural land, and good cycling country! I returned via the far-
ther, eastern side of the mountain, which was beautiful but where
the thousand-foot drop from the road's edge prevented me from
duly appreciating the scenery. Then, safely back on the coast, I had
a chilly swim beside the archeological site of Malia and returned,
tired but happy, to Fortetsa.

Saturday, April 18, 2015

Fotis' birthday was on Thursday. He is seventy-five, and he responded with pleasure and understanding to this news. My birthday is next week—I'll be seventy-two—and Helen has given me a
sachet of bath salts as a present. My gift is especially appropriate,
I'm thinking, because I've announced my retirement. This is a joke,
since I have never worked for a living, and I've clarified the point
by stating that I've retired from being a Stoic and am going to be
an Epicurean.

That is in fact a good idea, and I believe I have really done it. I
will never be a hedonist, despite the bath salts, because hedonism
doesn't interest me enough. But to be an Epicurian, to live mod-
estly and simply, to care for the world and be able to live within it

in a state of relative tranquility and relative freedom from fear: this does appeal to me as a way to a good and happy life.

Sunday, April 19, 2015

I phoned this morning to see what was happening with the case of Helen's friend who was in jail. I called her mother's number, since it isn't possible to phone a prisoner (it's also not possible to visit a prisoner unless you are a relative, which Helen could successfully claim to be since she is a god-relative, having baptized her friend's three-year-old daughter). To my relief, that friend answered the phone herself. She has been released and is waiting to enter a drug rehab program, a condition of her release even though she herself is not an addict. She can now be together with her daughter, who was cared for by relatives during the months she was incarcerated.

Two articles in today's *New York Times* provide some notes on creativity, in general and in older people. One, "The Other Side of Boredom," is really about creating free, relaxed mind-space in which new paths can be explored. Sitting doing nothing, staring, for example, at a blank page, can be strenuous work but key to mental integration and creativity. The point "is to allow our…minds to wander freely and to pay close attention to where they go."

The other story, part of a series on retirement and titled "More Older Adults Are Becoming Inventors," points out some strengths of the older population in this regard. Retired people can more easily afford to take risks when investing their time. The aging brain doesn't calculate as quickly, but can detect patterns better than before. Women, the article claims, are particularly creative because they perceive a need, imagine the benefit of a product, and then work backward to make it.

Monday, April 20, 2015

Vangelis and his helper came this morning to plow beneath our olives and around the fruit trees in our garden, a necessary annual task which leaves the earth bare and brown where it was green before. Yesterday evening I went with our old friends Petros and Sonya to visit Fotis. The three of us went afterward to a seaside tavern where there were tables for over a hundred people but we were the only clientele. We discussed family and personal life and also politics. Petros and Sonya have always been active in the democratic left, and Petros was imprisoned for a period by the right-wing military dictatorship of 1967–74. They too feel apprehension about Syriza, which—in tandem with its unsuccessful attempts to strong-arm our creditors—has been behaving clientelistically, just like its predecessors, filling the government bureaucracy with its own supporters regardless of merit.

We discussed the neo-Nazi Golden Dawn, whose leadership is about to go on trial for criminal activity. Petros thinks they will continue to draw six to eight percent of the vote, because there is a reactionary, authoritarian element in the population and that element has been stimulated by the current influx of immigrants who are not being absorbed. He thinks their share of the vote will not go beyond this. But on the other hand, it is not their intention to come to power through the vote. They are a paramilitary, street-fighting organization with some support in the military and police, and they intend to come to power by force. If we leave Europe, then Golden Dawn will see its chance.

Is it remotely possible that the situation of Greece could evolve from here into a Hugo Chavez-type predicament, or into a Pinochet-type predicament? Nobody expects this (except Golden Dawn), but it is, remotely, possible.

Tuesday, April 21, 2015

I've been reflecting about what happened in Chile. The election of Allende's coalition came as a surprise to most people; they themselves hadn't expected to win. They had run for office on a radical program, and once in government they felt honor-bound to carry that program out. This provoked a backlash, with ultimately tragic consequences.

Syriza did expect to win its election, it was no surprise, and in this the two situations are not the same. But Syriza campaigned on a program that promised impossible things. It won power by making those promises, and its leaders now claim to be torn between their European contractual obligations and their electoral mandate to repudiate those same obligations.

Or perhaps the Syriza leadership is torn between a desire to keep the country whole and in Europe and its fear of its own intransigent left wing, without whose support it might be unable to remain in power.

I think that people in Syriza do genuinely care about the welfare of the poorest strata of the population. I also think they are right to point out that the "austerity" formula backfired and sent Greece into depression. If only they were really on a path to address these problems and help us go forward!

Sunday, April 26, 2015

Yesterday I went to see our friend Irini, who is ninety and not too well. She is a very intelligent, generous person, and her story is an exemplary one. During the German occupation she was a courier for the resistance. In Greece, the war was followed by a five-year, on-again-off-again civil war between left and right which took a terrible, terrible toll on the country. The Communist Party had provided leadership to the resistance during the war, and as a result many fine people, including Irini, were committed to the Party. The civil war was soon over in Crete, but in the 1950s, throughout the country, anyone associated with the left was persecuted: you couldn't get a driver's license, a passport, or a government job, and you might very well find yourself in prison. Irini and her husband both went to prison for years. They could have been released if they had been willing to sign a statement repudiating their communist ideals, but they both refused to do so.

Once out of prison, they began to import lumber from Russia and Scandinavia. There was a building boom (many people had moved from the country to the city to find jobs, or to escape the civil war), and they became quite well off. They helped a lot of people, and when a university campus was created in Crete they were prominent supporters; their house was always open to young academics coming to create a forward-looking model for education and research in Crete.

It happened that Irini and her husband had children, but no grandchildren. There was always a cook in their house making meals for everyone who would drop in. Their Greek cook moved on at a time when Greece had a labor-recruitment arrangement in place with the Philippines. Many Filipina women came as contract domestic laborers for a defined period, and Irini hired one of those women, Suzanna. Suzanna got involved with a Bangladeshi immigrant and conceived a child, but didn't want to marry the father. Irini arranged for Suzanna to stay in Crete, and she and Suzanna have been bringing up that child together. The child, Mary-Grace, is now fourteen and beautiful, a straight-A student and talented in music and dance.

I asked Irini what she thinks of the current political situation. She has remained, life-long, passionately on the left and a committed public citizen, though no longer a partisan of the Communist Party. She is as concerned and apprehensive as everyone else

I've talked with. She sees Syriza as a collection of irresponsible ideologues and opportunists.

Tuesday, April 28, 2015

I discussed the political situation with a friend. He feels that it was appropriate for Syriza to try to negotiate a better deal for Greece, but that they should have moved more quickly to that point and then moved on. As it is, the uncertainty they've brought about has cost the country more than any negotiations could have won for it.

Wednesday, May 6, 2015

"The road to character is for every one of us who is trying to become a better version of ourselves." This citation is from the *New York Times* columnist David Brooks. I like the phrase, "a better version of ourselves." It resonates with *Happier*, the title of a helpful book by Tal Ben-Shahar.

Our house and garden recently became a better version of themselves, as I got help last weekend with cleanup inside and out. The weather here also became a better version of itself, miraculously calm, peaceful, clear, and warm (but not too warm).

How might I become a better version of myself? Perhaps, in whatever I do, I can become more calm, peaceful, clear, and warm, like the weather today.

Thursday, May 7, 2015

I am hosting a lunch for the members of my yoga group. Each of us does this on the approximate date of our birthday.

A birthday can be an occasion, like New Year's Day, to institute some new practice. I didn't do this on the day, but I've now thought of beginning to keep a gratitude journal. The idea is to take a few minutes every day to write down five things that one is grateful for, and to focus on and reimagine those things as one does so. This practice is recommended as a way to improve one's attitude and quality of life. I'll try doing it each morning and see how it goes.

Saturday, May 9, 2015

I've now kept my gratitude journal for three days, and I notice that each day is focused on a theme, even though I haven't intended this. Day one: five chance encounters that have made huge differences to my family, and without which we wouldn't be here. Day two: five ways I have of practicing active awareness. Day three: wellness in the life of each person in my family.

Sunday, May 10, 2015

This morning it took me just five seconds to write down five things I'm grateful for. Part of the exercise is to meditate on and reimagine those things, and I can invest infinite time in doing so with this list:

sunlight
the moon
the sea
rain
sleep

SARAH KAFATOU

These are bedrock, dependable things. Each one is inexhaustible and awe-inspiring.

Monday, May 11, 2015

The social safety net, such as it is, seems to consist largely of our age group, in that many pensioners are now supporting their unemployed working-age children. Our age group, for better or worse, is a larger segment of the population in Greece than in any other European country. But this sort of safety net is not self-sustaining, obviously, and with the government running out of cash and the real economy in a coma, there is no telling from month to month whether pensions will continue to be paid. If we crash out of the euro, of course, everyone's savings and pension entitlements will become more or less worthless.

Tuesday, May 12, 2015

People continue to visit Fotis. Two of his former classmates will come on Thursday, and his older brother Antonis will come from Athens to see him on Friday.

Last weekend I got back in touch with an old friend, Kiki. She grew up in a village near Kalamata in the Peloponnesus and moved here when she married her Cretan husband. Her husband, Euripides, was the head of a private school here, but he died and the school, where Kiki was working as a teacher, eventually failed. What, then, was she to do?

Kiki had been happily married and devoted to Euripides, and she loved teaching elementary school and was very good at it. What she did was to redirect her energies into counseling parents on how to bring up their children. She is excellent at this, loves doing it, and is in great demand. She organizes consultation circles for parents in the countryside, sees parents by appointment in her office, and has by this time published three or four books on her subject. I have one of them, titled (in Greek) *Cut the Lecture, Mom*. Kiki is about my age, full of energy, and delighted with her life.

Wednesday, May 13, 2015

I spent the morning in my studio, beginning a new canvas and touching up some old ones. I've completed eight studio paintings this year, about one each month. They go slowly, because I invent each one from scratch and it takes time to figure out what I'm doing. Painting "sur le motif" outdoors goes much faster, and the result is of comparable quality. It's a good deal of trouble to set up, though, and not practical in bad weather. This summer I will go out more to do drawings and watercolor, for practice in seeing and to make studies I can use in the studio.

I am pleased with the pictures I've done. Each one is unique, but the style is coherent and they look good together.

Saturday, May 16, 2015

Fotis' brother Antonis is here. The two of them are so different! Fotis lived with a wide horizon, took bold initiatives, and was at ease with leadership. Antonis has lived a more circumscribed life, and has been loyal and responsible, sometimes frustrated, but also comfortable within its boundaries. I appreciate Antonis greatly for his loyalty and attachment, and the unqualified affection and admiration he feels for his brother. "My ears pricked up," he said as we were talking last night, gesturing with both hands around his ears as he remembered praise of Fotis he had overheard in the past. Antonis also is a very good raconteur and mimic, with a great sense of humor and marvelous memory for detail. These two brothers complement each other and have enriched each other's lives.

Sunday, May 17, 2015

I spent the morning in my studio. Looking back at the drawing of a street corner on which I based a picture of a room overlooking the sea, I remembered how I'd copied the drawing onto my canvas, but then rotated the canvas by a half-turn and made it into something totally different. Only a few guidelines from the original drawing remain. This was a good, fruitful procedure. The original drawing should be compositionally sound and eventful enough, and my subsequent transformation of it into a painting should be a new departure, "deconstructing" and then reconstructing in a new way the formal information that the drawing provides.

Tuesday, May 19, 2015

I've written a short review of a book of poems by Jane Duran, *American Sampler*, and sent it to Christina Thompson at the *Harvard Review*. My procedure in reviewing is to read and reread, making excerpts and notes, and then review my notes, put my observations together, and edit them. A "bottom up" procedure, not a "top down." My aim is to discover qualities and themes that emerge with close and attentive reading, and if possible to point out strengths and felicities of which even the writer of the book may be unaware. It's a process rather like teaching.

I continue to keep my gratitude journal, and each day so far has had a theme. I write these down after the fact (for they, too, emerge "bottom up") and so far my themes have been, in order of time: chance encounters well prepared for, awareness, wellness, bedrock things, gadgets, teamwork, lived values, learning, daily exercises, meaning, emotional connection, some individual people, and group belongings.

After seeing Fotis this afternoon I told him that I won't come tomorrow because I'm taking a trip and that I'll see him again when I come back. He accepted this. I asked him whether he would wait for me and he said yes. I'd told him last week that I'll be away for two weeks, and that seemed to make him sad, though I'm sure he's forgotten it, so I didn't mention the time frame this time. In fact he has practically no sense of distance or time; two years ago he thought that his brother could drop over from Athens to visit us in Cambridge and be home again the same day.

Saturday, May 30, 2015

I'm always glad to return to this journal, but haven't done so since arriving in Massachusetts because I've been so busy with family time, errands and tasks, and my fiftieth college reunion, which ended yesterday. Cambridge is beautiful, with fine weather and every garden blossoming after the hard winter. This reunion, just like the previous ones, has reinforced my admiration and love for many classmates and enhanced my awareness of our extraordinarily varied and still unfolding accomplishments.

The main thing I got out of college, aside from the people I got to know and the support I was given for taking my next steps, was the thrill of being presented with suitable challenges. I came out with a sense that some large accomplishment was expected of me, and for a very long time I thought of my accomplishments, such as they were, mainly in terms of individual achievement. But our reunion activities this time around have brought home to me, more than ever before and at long last, that achievement is all very well, but the real question is, how much have I contributed—to my family, my communities, society? How can I contribute now?

I think that maybe the tone, the ethos, of the university itself has changed. Maybe an element of competitiveness, combined with insecure self-satisfaction, that was formerly so evident at Harvard has evolved into something better: into a shared culture of commitment to do better for others and the world. Maybe, if this is true, it has something to do with the migration of women and minorities into core positions in the academy. Including rather than excluding, fostering more than demanding, and encouraging us to look beyond ourselves so as to become our best selves: it's been good to see those values, central as they are to the idea of education, celebrated this week.

Wednesday, June 10, 2015

Every day I spent in Cambridge was filled with appointments, meetings, my college class reunion, and time with family and friends. All wonderful, and leaving me no time to keep this journal.

Back now in Crete, life goes on much as before. I had worried that Fotis might be different—would he still recognize me?—but find him much the same. He was pleased but not excited to see me. He seems content. He's lost some weight, walks more slowly and tentatively than before, speaks a little less. I know a number of people came to visit him while I was away, but he doesn't seem to remember that. Yet though quiet, he's not apathetic: he understands what I say to him, he can join me in a happy mood, there's still a vivacious sparkle in his eye.

Thursday, June 11, 2015

Downtown doing errands, I found the city pleasant and bustling as usual, without any obvious sign that Greece continues to stand on a precipice and is moving closer toward the edge.

In the evening, I attended an event to mark the publication of a book by a local author, Manolis Dretakis, professor emeritus at the Medical School of the University of Crete. In July 1943 a hundred prominent citizens of Heraklion were arrested by the Gestapo and sent on a grueling month-long journey to the concentration camp of Mauthausen in Austria, where most of them died. Dretakis' father was among them and perished there. He had been a lawyer, a profession which lost one third of its members in that or a similar way.

Friday, June 12, 2015

I told Fotis that "The Fotis Kafatos Prize for Excellence," for an outstanding young Greek researcher in biology, is being established in his honor, and he was mildly pleased at this news. I asked him whether he had missed me while I was away and he said he hadn't, though he is clearly happy to have me here once more. After visiting him I stopped at the beach for a wonderful swim and a classic taverna lunch of mashed fava beans with field greens.

Then I had a look at my paintings. For composition, it's a good idea to look at one's work from every possible point of view: close up, far away, upside down, in the mirror . . . I tried looking at them through my sunglasses, and in that way discovered areas in each that can be improved.

I'm reading an entertaining, intelligent novel about a fictional painter: *Notes from an Exhibition*, by Patrick Gale. There are not very many books of this kind. John Updike wrote a nice one called

Seek My Face. Gale's includes a cameo appearance by Barbara Hepworth, and Updike's main character is based on Lee Krasner, with Jackson Pollock just offstage.

I myself have written a novel about painters, and although some readers have liked it a lot, others have found it wanting. Most recently I was told that my characters don't develop, which is rather true. They are well-differentiated and go through various crises and relationship changes, but only a few of them develop except in terms of their art. If I ever write another novel, I will make sure that my characters make use of their struggles to develop and discover unsuspected aspects of themselves.

For me as a reader, the most important thing in fiction is the style: the writer's way of thinking, observing, structuring, and formulating things. For me as a writer, by far the most important thing in fiction is the characters: they become like real living people in my imagination. Their existence is my reward for the work I put into creating them.

Sunday, June 14, 2015

While I was away in Massachusetts, Fondas and Ruth had a second child. I've now been over to see them and their tiny sleeping baby Sophia. We discussed their wish to move their three-year-old daughter Marilena from her good, but expensive, private nursery school to a public one. It seems that while admission to the public nursery is supposedly by lottery, in fact it helps to have "meso," the Greek term for someone who can intervene with an authority on one's behalf.

Fondas and Ruth are unwilling to apply meso, as a matter of principle. This nursery school issue is a small example of precisely the kind of corruption of public goods that got Greece into its present predicament. I suggested that the lottery could be held in the presence of the candidate families, to eliminate the possibility of tampering, but I doubt that this will be done.

It takes courage to advocate for such things. One may view Greek society as permissive, in that a lot of rule-breaking is tolerated, on the road and in many other situations. But I don't think this is tolerance in the liberal sense of "live and let live," so much as it results from the fact that the potential price for confronting a rule-breaker may be high. People tolerate inconsiderate behavior because they don't want the other person to threaten or harm them.

Monday, June 15, 2015

An authority on Pushkin has just sent my manuscript to the Yale University Press with a note saying, "Her rendering of *Onegin* captures, I believe, better than any of the existing translations, the conversational manner, the syntax, and the novelistic qualities of the original."

A reason it does so is that I have maintained four beats to a line while freely varying the feet (the term for this is "accentual" meter) and have preferred off-rhyme to full rhyme, whereas other translators have used perfectly regular meter and rhyme, producing a sing-song effect that has a cost in terms of naturalness of diction and that tends to muffle every shift in emotional tone.

I am proud of my translation, and, in terms of the evolving meaning of my life, this moment has its particular point. I have long said about the course of my life, and it's true, that I've done what I wanted. I can't think of much I've done that wasn't at my initiative and according to my own preference at the time, and fortunately, though I've sometimes been disoriented, I haven't made any really bad choices. But it now occurs to me that, in the long run, I've also done what was expected of me. My teachers, and also my parents and in particular my mother, instilled in me the idea that I was expected to do something worthwhile, to use my talents to accomplish something. Now I believe I have, and I find that this sense of having lived up to expectations that were held of me is just as satisfying as is the awareness that I've done the things I wanted to.

Wednesday, June 17, 2015

Tsipras walked out of his most recent talk with our creditors, and another meeting tomorrow is said to be our last chance (but we've already had quite a few deadlines and "last chances").

Thursday, June 18, 2015

Pension reduction will be the sticking point in the negotiations that will probably fail today. It's understandable that the government is holding out on this. According to the *Guardian*, almost half of Greek families rely on pensions as their main, or only, source of income. This is partly because of unemployment, and partly because, although Greeks work long hours, they retire early. Some scandalous corruption has been eliminated from the pension system, but it is still costly and, in our present circumstances, not sustainable. This point is being made by the Europeans, who want further cuts. But the average pension is now less than $1,000 per month and the lowest is half that, which is barely enough to pay one's rent.

Friday, June 19, 2015

It is hard to hold two competing world-views at once. They oscillate rather, the way the famous Rorschach inkblot oscillates between looking like an aged woman in profile and a young woman wearing a hat. In the world-view of the European (and American) governments, enormous support has been provided to Greece and more support will be forthcoming, but the Greeks must do their part and pull their weight. In the world-view of Syriza, a neoliberal international elite, in tandem with a corrupt domestic oligarchy, have exploited and pauperized Greece, disregarding the will of the people, and Greeks must do all they can to resist their domination.

Alexis Tsipras, who will ultimately decide which way Greece will go, seems himself to oscillate, first posing in a relaxed, friendly, and confident way with European leaders, then returning to Athens and playing the role of an angry, defiant tribune of the people, using words such as "pillage" and "criminal" to refer to the European rules that those leaders represent.

No one can know what he will finally do. I suspect that beneath the ambiguity, he does in fact want a break, and that is what will happen. But I don't know. The process of decision-making in this government is highly opaque.

Tsipras has developed a literary side. He told the Europeans that they should read Hemingway's *For Whom the Bell Tolls*. He also said that Greece may finally speak "the big No." This could be a reference to our patriotic day of No, celebrating our defiance of Mussolini. Or maybe he was referring to a phrase in a poem by Cavafy, "*Che fece . . . il gran refiuto*," about the day when a person must speak "the great Yes or the great No . . . He who refuses has no regrets. Ask again, and he'll refuse again. And yet that No—the right No—crushes him for the rest of his life."

Ambiguity, oscillation, obscurity, suspense.

Saturday, June 20, 2015

Today I heard my first cicada of the year, alas! Until today the sounds in the air—apart from those of traffic, hammering, church bells, etc.—were of birds twittering and doves cooing. But soon there will be the scratchy rattle of the cicada, which will deafen us until the end of summer. They burrow underground in winter, then emerge to perch on trees and sound their raucous call all day long. They love olive trees particularly, and since our house stands in an olive grove there will be no peace from them.

Sunday, June 21, 2015

Today is the International Day of Yoga. As I did my morning sun salutation (twelve repeats) on the terrace I reflected on whether yoga is for me a spiritual practice, just a set of exercises, or what. I decided to dedicate my sun salutation to Apollo, god of light, reason, moderation, healing, and the arts. (He has negative attributes too, but I won't dwell on those.)

Fotis' younger brother Menas and his wife Susan, who live in California, were here this week. We visited Fotis together several times, and they had the idea of hiring a companion to keep him company and get him up for walks during some of the hours when I am not there. This seemed a good idea, since the nursing staff don't have time for such things and his interaction with the other residents is minimal.

We brought up this idea with the social worker at the Hjem, and she thought right away of a young musician who lives nearby. I've now met that person, Sophia, and she seems a good fit for Fotis. I think she will be able to sustain a good rapport with him, entertain him with music on her instrument—the oud—and take him for little walks around the building.

Monday, June 22, 2015

Our friend Anne, her husband, and their son have been here on a visit. I took them to Knossos, and because their son Alexander studies archaeology at Oxford we were invited to visit a newly discovered archaeological site hidden nearby. My habitual jogging route is only about fifty meters from this dig, yet I was unaware of it until today. We walked out onto scaffolding from which to view the complex remains of 2,000 years of continuous human habitation: Minoan, Mycenean, Hellenistic, Roman, and so on. The task of teasing out and identifying these elements, layered to a depth of ten to twelve meters, is being carried out by a Greek team of about twelve people. Notable among the many identifiable structures are two kilns whose shelves held hundreds of small ceramic jugs, a stone altar where the remains of a jeweled dagger were found, a large hall, and a number of small rooms where a necklace bead was found and a vanished wooden door has left its imprint in clay.

Meanwhile our national crisis approaches an inflection point. Two competing demonstrations are taking place in Constitution Square in Athens today: one in favor of our staying in Europe and one, in which some Ministers of Syriza are participating, in favor of our leaving it.

Tuesday, June 23, 2015

At eye level above the kitchen sink this morning I discovered a perfect spider in a perfect web. Small, grayish, with all her eight hands on the transverse threads, she sat quietly in the exact center of sixty or so gossamer rings that encircled her like an iridescent, transparent LP record. An hour later, when I looked again, she had folded her tent and vanished completely, as though she had never been. What a refined, neat, clean creature!

Friday, June 26, 2015

Arkas is a Greek cartoonist who has been publishing his jokes for thirty years. Apparently he has just closed down his column in the face of threats from Syriza supporters. A recent cartoon of his was captioned, "As we leave Europe, don't forget to turn out the lights of civilization. We can't afford the electricity."

As negotiations over our national future approach convergence, but then stall and break down, I've been rereading the classic *Getting to Yes: Negotiating an Agreement Without Giving In*, by Roger Fisher and William Ury. I wish Tsipras had followed the sensible advice in this book! Instead, he turned what should have been a cooperative problem-solving process into an adversarial one. He made the threat of mutual assured destruction his main—almost his only—negotiating strategy. He stuck rigidly to prior positions rather than pursuing our national interest or seeking to enlarge any areas of common interest. He talked past our interlocutors rather than focusing on the issues at hand, and tried to apply inappropriate pressure (raising a demand for German war reparations, questioning sanctions on Russia over Ukraine). He undermined trust, denouncing our partners' motives, and even misrepresenting their positions, for domestic consumption. He escalated disagreement by turning it into a contest of will and prestige.

In the meantime the other side just held still, keeping rigidly to a narrow, technical focus on financial sustainability. If we could have reached agreement on that, then I think the Europeans would have become more flexible in terms of debt renegotiation; but they wouldn't give in on the debt without credible assurances regarding financial housekeeping from us.

Saturday, June 27, 2015

This morning I sat in on a session with Sophia, who will be coming regularly to play the oud for Fotis. He enjoys this, and I learned a little about the makam, a Turkish and Arabic way of organizing music which differs fundamentally from the classical European way. Meanwhile, Tsipras walked out of the talks at the very last minute and is going to hold a referendum in which we will vote up or down the European negotiators' final proposal to us. Syriza rejects their proposal and will campaign for a No vote, which if it wins will take us out of the euro.

Sophia, the musician, shared her thoughts on the referendum with me. She will vote No, she said, because she identifies culturally with the legacy of Byzantium and believes in our Orthodox Christian brotherhood with Russia. Further, she adheres to the worldview and believes the wild prophesies of Father Paisios, a monk of Mount Athos who died twenty years ago and was canonized this year. Apparently his apocalyptic predictions are widely disseminated and taken seriously by quite a few people in Greece. Paisios prophesied that there will be a World War very soon, perhaps next year, and that in this war Russia will totally destroy Turkey. As a result, Greeks will recover our lost heritage in Asia Minor, including Istanbul, which will become Constantinople once again. Sophia, who's unemployed, is now living quietly in what she regards as a safe place while she waits for those events to come about.

Sophia has an ideological reason for voting No. Many people will vote No for other ideological reasons, such as that they feel pride in an independent Greece or that they regard the European Union as undemocratic and an instrument of class warfare. (Sophia may have these reasons also, as they are not in conflict with the first.) Some people will vote Yes because they believe in the European project, or feel Greece belongs in Europe, or are sure we can't get out of trouble by leaving the euro, or because they dislike

Syriza. Some will vote Yes out of dislike of turbulence and fear of the unknown. Many people will vote Yes or No without knowing what the consequences of either will be. I will vote Yes.

Monday, June 29, 2015

This morning I picked the last fruit from our plum tree. As I did so I remembered lines by Sappho:

> Like the sweetest apple on the highest bough,
> the highest twig, that the harvesters forgot
> —no, didn't forget, but they couldn't reach it.

Tuesday, June 30, 2015

Greeks trusted Syriza with political power but not with our money. Tsipras' impulsive, snap decision to hold a referendum at the very last minute has triggered bank closures and capital controls. All suppliers here and abroad are now demanding to be paid up front. Greece imports most of what we consume, and there are tight controls on transfers of money out of the country, which makes it difficult to import goods, raw materials, spare parts.

Wednesday, July 1, 2015

Our friend Anne was here again for a day. What a fine thing is a long friendship founded on mutual admiration and love.

Thursday, July 2, 2015

Tsipras seems to have good manners and social skills and to be personally likeable. His self-presentation as a public speaker is attractive, and his care for the people he represents seems genuine. But he is a demagogue. Not, however, a demagogue with a plain, simple message; his messages are typically ambiguous and unclear. Presently he is insisting, implausibly, that a No vote is a vote for our continued membership in the eurozone under better terms.

Sunday, July 5, 2015

I voted at 9:00 this morning. The polling place was calm and not very busy; I queued for two minutes, more or less.

Polls have revealed that the older one is, the more likely to vote Yes. Evidently Tsipras' claim to be defending the welfare of pensioners has failed to convince. Young people, and students most of all, will be voting overwhelmingly No. Yesterday I talked with a friend, a professor at the University of Crete and an excellent scientist, whose son graduated from a magnet public high school and is beginning graduate study in the United States. Our friend sees the situation much as I do, but his son will vote No.

—10:00 p.m. Participation in the referendum was ample. The vote is sixty to seventy percent No in every single region of Greece (except for Athens, which is closer to fifty-fifty—but this is misleading: the poorer neighborhoods in Athens voted up to eighty percent No, and the better-off up to eighty percent Yes). Crete, and Heraklion, voted seventy percent No. This is a landslide, a stunning win for Tsipras.

Tuesday, July 7, 2015

Yesterday was the first day of an annual week-long advanced biology workshop at the University of Crete. The principal speaker, John Gurdon, was awarded a Nobel Prize for his work in reprogramming cells. He prefaced his talk by expressing appreciation for Fotis, whom he had long known as a colleague and who he said has contributed enormously to modern biology in Greece and around the world. Gurdon's talk itself was a model of clarity, taking us through the process of cell specialization in the embryo and then into his own work in getting mature cells to de-differentiate back into a pluripotential state. The interest of this from a medical point of view is that if we can ever grow replicas of the cells of our own organs from our own cells (from skin cells for example), then we can receive them as transplants without risk of immune rejection.

Wednesday, July 8, 2015

Today I had the interesting experience of getting a flat tire. It was quickly dealt with: I found someone to replace all four worn-out tires on my twenty-year-old VW with four slightly better used ones that I'd been keeping in the basement. I paid ten euros, with no receipt and no sales tax included. Many simple tasks like this are done quickly and well by people operating on the margins of the system, actually in the black economy.

Major tasks such as home renovation are also in the black economy. I have learned that in addition to fixing our roof, I need to see to the reinforced concrete columns that support our house. Just about every building constructed in the past seventy-five years has these, and the iron rods inside the columns gradually rust. I have a proposal from a contractor who can drill down to the areas affected and treat these rods. What I have just learned is that many building teams, including his, are not insured, and that if any workman should happen to be injured I will be liable. Apparently this is normal. The national insurance scheme allows building crews to insure themselves piecemeal, job by job, so of course when they are short of funds, as everyone is now, they often leave this step out. I will try to make arrangements to cover workmen's compensation insurance and pay the taxes due on the work, but this is unusual for small jobs such as mine.

Friday, July 10, 2015

This morning when I went to visit Fotis, the director of the Hjem, Marco, was there. He told me that he's been preparing since the beginning of the year for every contingency. Families who can't get access to their bank accounts are managing to bring in amounts of 200 or 300 euros toward this month's fee, and Marco has some cash in reserve. He has also stocked up on food and has a two-month supply of medicines on hand. In addition he has arranged with staff that in the event there is no gasoline they will come in for week-long shifts and eat and sleep there so that the Hjem can continue to function.

This afternoon we will see whether or not the Greek parliament approves the agreement that Tsipras has proposed to the Eurogroup. His proposal does exactly the opposite of what our No vote called for. In fact, this agreement makes even more concessions to our creditors than the agreement we've just voted down did. The Greek term for this is "kolotoumba": somersault. For the past half year we've been waiting to see whether or not Tsipras would perform a somersault, that is, abandon his campaign promises and embrace reality. He has taken a very long time to do it, but he just did.

Saturday, July 11, 2015

The Greek parliament has overwhelmingly endorsed Tsipras' proposal, with more or less only Syriza's Left Platform not voting in favor. Will the government ministers from the Left Platform now resign?

I am practicing the piano, reading through the preludes and fugues of Bach's *Well-Tempered Clavier*. I have a procedure to help me avoid mind-wandering, when one's fingers are playing the notes on the page but one's thoughts are somewhere far away. I read a commentary on a passage. Then I play it, trying to apply what I've read. Then I listen to a CD of Angela Hewitt playing it. Then I play it again with her performance in mind.

On another note, I've become aware of something that happened a few weeks ago, but that I hadn't heard about until now. Tim Hunt, a distinguished English biologist and recipient of the Nobel Prize, has put his foot in his mouth. He had been asked to make a dinner-table toast at an international conference of science journalists and made what he thought was a light remark, saying that things can be tricky when men and women work together in the laboratory because "you may fall in love with them, they may fall in love with you." Now it was unwise of him to say that, but in my opinion not wrong, since what he said is demonstrably true. Among our own friends I can think of eight happily married couples that were formed in that way; in three of those the more senior partner was a man, in two it was a woman, and in three both had the same status at the time. Tim unfortunately then went on to say that women in the lab "cry when you criticize them," which may reflect an experience of his but is a regrettable example of gender-stereotyping. He then said, "Now, seriously . . ."

As a result of these remarks, which were taken out of context (without the "now, seriously") and quickly tweeted around the world, Tim has been forced to resign from his professorship at the University of London and his responsibilities at the European Research Council and the Royal Society. Do you think that is right? I understand the negative impact of what he said, and I think that, given a culture of science that is less than perfect, some of those hearing it may feel that this is the last straw. But I don't think those words represent his presence in the world of science—much less his whole character, as far as I know—and I don't think they should have led to this consequence. I've sent him a consolatory note.

Sunday, July 12, 2015

It's long been true that when I daydream about how my life might be different, I'm not likely to think of new and wonderful things that could become part of it. Instead I usually think of how little I need to live and still be happy. This defensive mode has its merits: I feel free when I imagine that my needs are few.

The future of Greece is still in limbo. Tsipras' proposal was not accepted as is, and a meeting of all European heads of government scheduled for today has been canceled abruptly. In this context I find myself thinking of how I will manage if we go over the cliff. Even if there will be no gasoline (suppliers have said that stocks will last until October or so) or if, as is likely, it is rationed for essential tasks, I will still be able to visit Fotis, assuming that the Hjem is able to carry on. Not only is there an intercity bus service, but I estimate that I can get there in four or five hours by walking on the secondary road. Or maybe I could cycle.

Tuesday, July 14, 2015

We have an agreement, thanks in part to the fact that one individual who would have made it impossible—Yanis Varoufakis, Syriza's minister of finance—was not present at the final negotiation.

Many people have worked long and hard to help us reach this semi-conclusion. But Varoufakis could have wrecked it. He has just said publicly (in an article in the *New Statesman*) that right after the No vote in the referendum he proposed to the central committee of Syriza that the government take over the Bank of Greece, which is designed to be independent, and begin issuing IOU's. His proposal was voted down six to two and he resigned.

As for Tsipras, I seem to have underestimated him. It's impossible to judge whether he has any goal in mind other than enhancing his own personal political standing, but he has succeeded in that. He has become the most prominent politician in Greece. Now, rather than break away from Europe and the eurozone, he has staked his career on keeping us in.

Friday, July 17, 2015

Wildfires arise here every summer. I've lived through one frightening one and walked through acres of ashes from another, but never seen anything like what is happening today. There are huge wildfires raging uncontrollably around Athens, in the southern Peloponnesus, and in several other parts of Greece. At least one seems to have been deliberately set. Arsonists are often private real estate developers wanting to encroach on public forest. According to the law, public land cannot be privatized after being burned, but in practice this law is often ignored.

Saturday, July 18, 2015

Helen and her family are here, and Zoe and her family will arrive tomorrow. We visited Fotis, who was very sweet, cheerful, happy in our company. It's good to see that, although his cognitive horizon has contracted, he is not confused. He understands correctly what he is able to understand, and he expresses his thoughts and feelings appropriately. This makes it easy to form a rapport with him.

Monday, July 20, 2015

We all, except for Fotis, are spending a week in the small village of Sougia, on the southwest coast of Crete, where we have vacationed every year as a family for more than forty years. We drove here yesterday afternoon along the coast and through mountains, a beautiful route, and have spent the day swimming, reading, greeting old friends, and socializing together. The sea is as always: cool, calm, clear, and deep. Due south from here is a small island, and then nothing but open sea between us and the coast of Libya.

Tuesday, July 21, 2015

We all got up early and hiked for three hours in the spectacular gorge of Saint Irini, which begins in the mountains and ends in a dry riverbed near Sougia. Its sheer walls, studded with aromatic herbs and often stained rust color, tower like a limestone version of El Capitan on both sides of the narrow strait the path runs through. The sun illumined the heights but did not penetrate into the cool, shady streambed where we walked.

Wednesday, July 22, 2015

A quiet day of swimming, resting, and socializing. I am reading *Being Mortal*, by Atul Gawande, a book that our daughter Zoe brought with her. It's about end of life care, and makes the important point that if we want to maximize quality of life toward the end, then a medical, disease-treatment approach can't be the whole story. Instead we need to take a holistic approach to the question of what makes life of value for the person concerned. We should be careful to support whatever enables integrity, all-around well-being, and an experience of meaning and purpose.

Thursday, July 23, 2015

We all got up at 6:00 this morning to hike through a wooded gorge, across a plateau and down a steep stony path to the archeological site of Lissos, which was once a Hellenistic city and where one can still see the mosaic floor and massive squared stone walls of a temple to Asclepius, god of healing. A stream bordered by mint, now dry, used to flow beside it. I thought of lines from W.H. Auden's "In Praise of Limestone":

> ...where everything can be touched or reached by walking
> ...what I hear is the murmur
> of underground streams, what I see is a limestone landscape.

There is a charming small Christian church there beside the sea, built of stone and incorporating small broken pieces of the ancient temple in its walls. It's apparent how poor and primitive Christian settlement in Lissos has been, compared to the ancient civilization that preceded it.

Our twelve-year-old grandchildren George and Sophia got off the path on their way down and were lost on the mountainside for half an hour. That particular slope is not very hazardous, but the mountains in general can be dangerous, and inexperienced hikers who've gone off the beaten path have perished in them. George reports that, "I was worried, but I didn't panic," which is characteristic of the way he handles things. I remember the time he got lost bicycling to Harvard Square a few years ago, and how he handled that well, too.

Saturday, July 25, 2015

We first discovered Sougia in 1972, and in 1973 we spent a month. A handful of families, more or less related to each other, lived there then and are still there now. The road to the village was unpaved. There was one café and a hotel with one room. A few German hippies were camping under tamarisk trees near the shore, or in caves above the beach; otherwise there were no tourists. In the tiny port with its few fishing boats there were some large abandoned canisters stamped "Wehrmacht."

Sougia had been occupied by the Germans during WWII. There was some guerilla activity in collaboration with the British, and the Germans in retaliation burned the village of Koustogerako in the mountains just above. They tried to massacre the women and children of that village, but most managed to escape and spent the rest of the war homeless in the mountains. The lovely man whose simple guest rooms we stay in helped the resistance, stepped on a landmine, and was evacuated to Egypt by the British; he recalls that before being evacuated, when he was lying on a cot at home, a German soldier risked punishment by stealing bandages from the German army dispensary to dress his wounds.

Before that, when there were no roads in this part of Crete, Sougia was a market depot. Ships unloaded goods to be conveyed inland by donkey, and in exchange took aboard local produce such as olive oil, carobs, and gypsum from the nearby now-abandoned quarry.

Monday, July 27, 2015

We are back in Heraklion after our very peaceful and relaxing week in Sougia. From now until the end of August ten or twelve people will be living together in this house where I lived alone all year. We've turned Fotis' former office into a dormitory for the children, who seem to have settled in happily.

Tuesday, July 28, 2015

A French architect couple came by for a visit and to take photos. They produce books on architecture and run a bookshop-plus-school-for-the-arts in Marseille, and are preparing a book on the work of Dimitris and Suzana Antonakakis, the architects who designed our house for us. Their book will complement existing books on the Antonakakis published by the MIT Press and by Rizzoli.

Classical Greek architecture is superb, Byzantine architecture is extremely fine, and traditional Greek vernacular architecture, with its hand-made and community characteristics and in its setting, is very lovely. Italian Renaissance classicism and Bavarian neoclassicism have also inspired fine, stately public buildings here. Now, post-Bauhaus, Greece has produced quite a few excellent modern architects; this is one of our continuing cultural strengths, along with poetry, music, and theater. It's a shame that our cities and towns do not better reflect this. Most of our existing structures—apartment buildings especially—have gone up haphazardly, often illegally, and on the cheap. The ensemble can be lively and satisfying, and I think that's true of Heraklion, but individual buildings often lack distinction.

For myself, I enjoy living in and taking care of the house that Dimitris and Suzana built. It is a fine work of art. But we lived for many years in just the sort of minimal two-rooms-and-balcony or semi-basement that most people have, and I liked that too. In fact I felt very happy to be there because that was what I had chosen, it was my life.

Tuesday, August 4, 2015

Today we had a visit from very old friends, Will and Annie, who've come to spend a week in the town of Sitia in Eastern Crete. Annie, a poet who founded the very successful Poetry Center at Smith College, was diagnosed with Alzheimer's disease in 2012. She is not nearly as far along in the trajectory as Fotis, but already she needs to have someone beside her all the time. She has always been a wonderful person, and it seems that, like Fotis, she will sustain her wonderfulness as things progress. Like him, she is very responsive to beauty in her surroundings. The disease seems to facilitate this, as it makes everything more immediate for the affected person. Annie kept saying how beautiful the flowers were around us, and how beautiful the colors of the sea. They brought with them a copy of her most recent book, which she dedicated to me on the spot, Will helping her to write in the date and so forth. Where he instructed her to write With love, she interrupted authoritatively to say, With *much* love, and wrote that.

Saturday, August 8, 2015

Since Tsipras' recent turnaround our relationship with Europe has grown calmer. The leaders of the Left Platform have left the government and Tsipras has the support of most Syriza parliamentarians. Under these conditions, stability has become more probable, although not assured.

Friday, August 14, 2015

August so far has been hot and enervating. In accordance with their annual cycle, the cicadas are beginning to disappear. Ordinarily the meltemi, a strong wind out of the Caucasus, blows during August, freshening the air and slamming doors, but this year and last the meltemi has been weak-to-nonexistent.

When not out on beach trips or trips into town, the children have been good at organizing themselves. Sophia (twelve years old) and Anna (nine) have created a make-believe café on our veranda, with a menu of make-believe drinks and sandwiches. We adults can relax there as patrons of their open-all-day enterprise, paying with make-believe money for our make-believe fare.

A few days ago, municipal road work caused city sewage to back up into our basement. This was fairly quickly addressed, we've cleaned it up, and we're now upgrading our own effluent system. The end result will be an improvement, but in the interim the yard beyond our kitchen patio is a construction site, alas.

A high school classmate of mine, Karl Schonborn, has published a memoir, *Cleft Heart*. Karl was born with a severe cleft palate which had to be corrected by repeated surgery. As a child he demonstrated remarkable resilience and determination to be a normal healthy person, and in that he succeeded. An aspect of his story is that he was bullied and abused repeatedly at school because of his unusual appearance and voice, and that he refused to reveal this at the time or to denounce the boys who tormented him. After high school he went to Yale on a scholarship and to medical school at Columbia, but then moved to graduate school to study violence as a public health issue. Violence and its prevention have been the focus of his professional career ever since.

Wednesday, August 19, 2015

I drove with Zoe and her family to visit friends in their ancestral village, now the beach resort of Agia Galini on the south coast. Lunch was prepared by our friend Mary's mother Chrysi, who is my age. Chrysi, Mary and her husband Peter, Mary's brother, his wife and their two children, Mary's uncle, his wife, their son and his wife, another cousin, and the five of us were all present, for a total of seventeen. This is evidently a normal number of people for lunch at their house in the summertime.

My daughters are joint godparents of Mary and Peter's daughter Christine, who graduated from Cornell and spent two years as a volunteer in Teach For America before entering medical school, where she is now. Teach For America has been much celebrated for putting highly selected recent college graduates to work in the public schools, but also criticized for its supposed amateurishness. The program itself uses the proportion of its graduates who go into teaching as a career as a metric for its success, and I learned that Christine, while volunteering, earned a teaching credential in the state of Illinois. Particularly now, as the US is facing a shortage of teachers overall, Teach For America seems like a splendid idea to me.

In the harbor of Agia Galini a derelict ship was moored. Gray, rusted, and depressing-looking, it had been used to carry refugees trying to enter the EU via Greece. Most such people— over 200,000 this year so far, mainly young men, most of them from Syria—come in small inflatable boats via Turkey to the Greek Dodecanese islands off the Turkish coast, where they are registered and then herded about from place to place. Very few get to Crete. I've read that it is illegal to help them, for example by giving them a ride from their arrival point to a registration point several days' walking distance away, but that on Samos volunteers have nevertheless formed a car convoy for that purpose, and that on other islands such as Mitilini (Lesbos) and Kos the locals and tourists have also been volunteering to help. Governments are reluctant to take responsibility for these people, who have lost everything. In the case of the ship I saw, its passengers got safely to shore and the captain was arrested. The ship is to be auctioned for scrap, but has been awaiting that end for over a year and will probably wait for several more years as legal issues are sorted out.

Thursday, August 20, 2015

As the recent heat wave has ended and fall will soon begin, several members of our family are coming up with projects and goals for the year to come. Our grandson George has the ambitious goal of watching every match played by his favorite soccer team, Liverpool. Zoe, who has been an active amateur runner but was held back last year by a foot injury, aims to get back on track with that. I, too, inspired by our friend Mary who does half-marathons and triathlons, want to devote plenty of time to yoga, walking, running, and swimming. I also need a book project and have felt a bit at sea in recent months for lack of one. Now I think I might undertake some sort of historical novel set in Greece and Rome. I have some wisps of ideas about it and if I can develop those, then no matter how well or poorly it turns out it will provide a meaningful activity for me.

Sunday, August 23, 2015

In yoga class we are asked every so often to pause after a series of poses and stand still. The word for this in Sanskrit is "tadasana," and the essence of it is just to relax while standing up with good posture.

The last visiting members of our family will leave Crete on Wednesday morning. It will be quiet here before the next phase of life begins. Between one activity and another, one phase of life and another, it's a good idea to stand still for a moment.

A defining discovery in American poetry of the twentieth century was to keep the form of one's work open, loose, breathable. Just so, it's a good idea not to fill one's life with activity just for the sake of keeping busy. The standard advice to a bereaved spouse is not to make any major life changes for a year. Similar advice may apply no matter how great or small the transition in question. Let things settle. Stand in tadasana.

Thursday, August 27, 2015

Yesterday, in the local minimarket, I overheard a man saying that he had voted for Syriza but now was disgusted with all politicians and was going to vote in September for Golden Dawn—the Nazis—to "smash everything." The vote for Syriza has been above all a protest vote, and that man was evidently moving on to the next available vehicle for his protest.

Saturday, August 29, 2015

Fotis has been growing very gradually quieter. He can still walk holding my hand, recognize people, understand what we say to him, smile warmly, and laugh at a joke. But he does everything with less energy. He isn't agitated or upset and is seldom sad, but he's just neutral more of the time.

Monday, August 31, 2015

Oliver Sacks has died. He was a delightful person. I saw him in person once, in Heidelberg, talking about his book *Uncle Tungsten*. My main impression is of how much fun he was having. He was someone who, while acquiring wisdom, never forgot what it was like to be a little boy. He did a chemistry experiment on stage, and though I don't recall what principle was being demonstrated I remember vividly his mischievous delight as smoke began bubbling up from his beakers.

This morning I went back to my studio after a summer hiatus. I began two paintings over a month ago and had been feeling frustrated because I couldn't figure out what they were of. I begin painting by scribbling aimlessly, building up material which should become an idea. But if it doesn't become one? I'd stared at both of those canvases a number of times and not been able to see what to do. Today I pulled myself together, said, "After all it doesn't matter," and began fooling around and having fun. Two hours later I have an idea for what each one will be.

Thursday, September 3, 2015

The most urgent unresolved issue in Europe is now no longer the Greek crisis, but the enormous number of refugees coming to Europe, mainly through Greece. To quote Julia Ward Howe via John Steinbeck: "He has trampled out the vineyard where the grapes of wrath are stored." Thousands of these desperate people are being found dead in trucks, in ships, and in the sea, and hundreds of thousands are struggling at every checkpoint and every national border to keep moving, toward Germany, toward the UK, toward …

Friday, September 4, 2015

As I continue to practice the piano, I keep looking for ways to keep myself alert and focused on the music. I once heard Michiko Uchida give a master class. She told us, "Performance is a never-ending attempt to discover what the music is about." The Schumann Fantasy, she said, for example, is about how to find the tonic C. The piece is in C, but most of it is not in C. Throughout the piece we are asking, Where do I go—which path to take— where do I go next?

I remembered this today as I was practicing the *Well-Tempered Clavier* II no. 20 in A minor. The prelude, I thought irreverently, is like a game of snakes and ladders: the weeping downward-tending theme turns itself upside down, that is upward, every so often and sets off from a new starting point, the mood changing accordingly. And the fugue? It's like dancing a quickstep on a very slippery floor.

Saturday, September 5, 2015

Today I completed the task of getting a new hubcap for our old VW. One of the four was missing, and I've replaced it at the cost of twelve euros and about an hour of my time. The item had to be shipped from an old parts repository in Germany, and while waiting six weeks for it I wondered whether this task was really worth doing. Investigating online, I found out that hubcaps are in fact unnecessary, but also discovered some good advice from Click and Clack on *Car Talk*: you don't need them, but if you leave them off then the appearance of neglect can lead to real neglect. "That is exactly how the Roman Empire fell. One hubcap fell off Titus' chariot in around 150 AD, and it was all downhill from there."

Monday, September 7, 2015

I continue to research the subject of older age. Jane Miller, in her book *Crazy Age*, says, "I like being old at least as much as I liked being middle-aged and a good deal more than I liked being young. There are lots of bad things about it, but then there were lots of bad things about being young." Her self-report is consistent with the well-researched finding that life satisfaction tends to follow a U-shape: relatively high at the beginning and up again toward the end.

I'm reading a lot right now, since I'm home alone and it's been too hot to get out and do much. Following up on my idea of spending imaginative time in the ancient Greek and Roman world, I've downloaded Wheelock's *Latin Grammar* and am reviewing it. I find this enjoyable, since I don't have to memorize anything, only to refresh my memory of what I already know.

I've also picked up a book about ancient Chinese ways of solving problems and organizing life. The first point it makes is that in Chinese tradition, the idea is not to set a goal, envision some kind of pathway or blueprint for it, and then implement that. Instead, Chinese strategists such as Sun Tzu preferred to rely on what *Times* columnist David Brooks calls Metis, that is, "the ability to see patterns in the world and derive a gist from complex situations." A kind of observant, wise passivity may facilitate insight into how such patterns are evolving and, perhaps, how we might encourage them to evolve.

I'm interested in this sort of thing in part because I've had training as a life coach. I took this up while living in London. Although I haven't done anything with it professionally, I benefited, and I think my non-paying clients benefited, from the practice coaching I did to earn my diploma. Life coaching is not psychotherapy: it's very present-focused and future-oriented, and a purpose of it is to help one's client identify and achieve his or her goals. What I found, though, in talking with people was that many of them, while being high achievers, did not like to think of their activities in terms of setting and reaching some goal or other. They would say that they just liked to get on with what they were doing, without thinking too much about what might come next. Goal-setting can be very helpful, even essential in many situations, but I think that those people were on to something, too.

The poet Adrienne Rich may not have thought about Taoism, or maybe she did, but in any case the titles of her books seem to evoke a Taoist sort of progress: *A Change of World . . . Diving into the Wreck . . . A Wild Patience Has Taken Me This Far*. A point about these titles is that they refer to outcomes which were not foreseen or planned for in advance; they represent milestones in self-discovery.

The distinction I've drawn here is that we in "the West" are encouraged to review our past and design our future, whereas the practice of "the East" would emphasize honoring the past, paying close attention to the present, and greeting the future with ever-closer attention as it approaches us. In terms of human development, while both ways are valuable, the "Eastern" one may be the more powerful of the two. How can we plan when we don't know what to plan for? Can a ten-year-old know what will be important to his or her thirty-year-old self, or a sixty-year-old anticipate what his or her priorities will be at ninety?

Thursday, September 10, 2015

Yesterday I phoned our friend Stefanos to suggest we watch this evening's debate on TV. The leaders of the main seven or eight political parties will be speaking. There is a parliamentary election coming up in ten days, and the old, establishment, center-right New Democracy party and Syriza are at a dead heat in the polls.

Instead, Stefanos invited me to a dinner he was hosting for Angelos Chaniotis, a historian and archeologist with special expertise in epigraphy. At the dinner, Angelos impressed us with his command of the sweep and detail of Hellenistic history and contemporary scholarship about it.

Angelos and Stefanos both have the good fortune of being completely committed to what they do and enthusiastic about it. A difference is that Angelos' professional trajectory has seemed extraordinarily swift and smooth, from the University of Athens, to Heidelberg, to New York University, to Oxford, and to the Institute for Advanced Study at Princeton, whereas Stefanos has met significant difficulty on his way. Stefanos grew up in a poor, fatherless family in a small village in the south of Crete. He was an outstanding physics student in Athens and went to graduate school at Harvard. While there he became preoccupied with the situation in Greece, which was then a military dictatorship, and after brilliantly passing his PhD qualifying exam he fell out of touch with his Harvard department and never completed his degree. He returned to Greece, couldn't get an academic job, and decided on his own initiative to write a textbook on quantum physics in Greek. That took him years, during which time his marriage fell apart. Once he'd finished writing his book he had the idea of editing a series of books about science, and he fortunately found support from the research center of the University of Crete for that. Eventually, over thirty years, the university press he founded and went on to direct has become one of the best and best-run publishing houses in Greece. Now he's focused on creating online courses in Greek, and Angelos had come to participate in that project. Stefanos today has a family he loves and work he loves, and I think he's a happy and satisfied man.

Friday, September 11, 2015

The River has published its list of candidates for the upcoming election, and I am delighted to see at the top of it Nikiforos Diamandouros, who is a friend. Nikiforos was the ombudsman for Greece, and then was the ombudsman for Europe until two years ago. He is incorruptible and extremely qualified to bring about improvement in our public administration.

Sunday, September 13, 2015

The refugee exodus from the collapsing areas of the Middle East continues unabated. It is mind-boggling to see news photos of groups of families with young children and babies fleeing across the European continent on foot, as though they were people on pilgrimage. It is also remarkable to witness the leadership and follow-through of Angela Merkel's Germany in this issue, taking in over a million refugees while other countries squabble over how little they have to do.

In my personal life, I am on holiday in Eastern Crete. It takes about six hours to drive from one end of Crete to the other, not a short distance, so it's natural that the far eastern and western ends are the less developed and therefore in many ways the most attractive. I have a room overlooking the sea in the small, tranquil, pleasant town of Sitia and have been exploring the arid, gently mountainous countryside by car and on foot.

At dinner in a taverna I overheard an old-fashioned, completely formulaic telephone conversation at the next table, as follows: "Hello, Sympethera (one's sympethera is the mother of one's son- or daughter-in-law). Congratulations on your name day! May you live long. Yes, we are well. You have greetings from Cousin X, Cousin Y, and Uncle Z. Yes, we would like to see you, too, but . . . Yes, we are all well. We wish you many happy years. Now here is A who wants to talk to you . . . (passing the phone) . . . Hello, Sympethera, congratulations on your name day, etc." I'm afraid that I myself tend to neglect these rituals, but they are a thing that holds society together.

Tuesday, September 15, 2015

Highlights of my holiday: Walking through the garrigue, on an uphill path dividing various species of aromatic, thorny plants, and gazing across olive groves toward the sea. Swimming in pellucid blue water on the site of ancient ports in Itanos and Zakros, where Phoenicean and Egyptian traders would once come. Listening to the surf crashing below my window as I fell asleep.

On the drive home I stopped to visit Fotis. He was in good spirits but seemed weak. With difficulty we took our usual walk around the building; I asked him whether he was comfortable walking and he said, "not." I'm presently reading to him from a novel he liked when he was young: *Argo*, by Giorgos Theotokas. Today we came to the following bit of dialogue: "Don't you read the papers? The Greek state is collapsing . . . and the foreigners don't want to give us any more money." *Argo* was published not today, but in 1936!

On the next page a character exclaims, "I want to live life to the full!" I asked Fotis whether he thinks the most important thing is to live life to the full, and he said yes.

Thursday, September 17, 2015

The cicadas are quiet. Before I went to Sitia they were still noisy. Now they are almost gone.

How can I write things like "the cicadas are quiet" when places just across the sea are in murderous disarray and refugees are entering Greece by the thousands every day? Some small, immediate first-line support is being provided to those people, but not much. My friend Annoula has an excellent idea that goes to the root of the problem: "Take away all the weapons. Just don't sell any more weapons and don't let anyone have any."

Monday, September 21, 2015

We have an election result, and Tsipras together with his previous coalition partner will be in power for the foreseeable future. A significant novelty is that a Greek vote, having become less relevant to the fortunes of others, is no longer front-page news around the world.

Tuesday, September 22, 2015

I visited a friend in the village of Gouves, near the Hjem, who's created a labyrinth around a tree in front of her house. The paths are bordered with stones scavenged from the beach opposite, and because it's not possible to mow the grass where the stones are, those borders have turned into a sort of low grassy hedge. The whole thing looks like a work of art of the kind meant to be viewed from above. The design is a traditional one, and very successful: there are no culs-de-sac in it, but it leads one toward the center and then subtly away from it again just as one thought one was about to reach the tree. I tried it, and although the diameter is not great and I was walking briskly, it took me over ten minutes to get completely in and out again.

Thursday, September 24, 2015

A friend alerted me to an article about the English biologist Richard Dawkins and his arguments for atheism. I, too, do not believe in "god," and understand that people have been led to think and do many good or wonderful, but also often bad or terrible, things by their desire to believe in something.

I notice, among the books Dawkins has written, one called *The Magic of Reality*. I'm reminded of the title of another book, by Ursula Goodenough, a non-theist biologist: *The Sacred Depths of Nature*. The point of these titles is that nature, reality, our universe, everything, is to be appreciated as a wonderful, awe-inspiring, inexhaustible phenomenon. We continue to gain—partial, tentative—knowledge of it and how it works. We ought never to lose the ability to be moved, inspired, and made humble by the astonishing world in which we live.

Saturday, September 26, 2015

Today I spoke briefly, in my capacity as significant other of someone in a care home, as a panelist at the annual Alzheimer Society symposium. Others discussed aspects of treating the disease from early to late and very late stage. Images of the latter—ulcerated bedsores, choking on food—were disturbing. At what point does life begin to seem less worthwhile?

We will do our best, at least, to avoid the worst, and continue to hope for the best. I think a turning point looms when one can no longer walk, and so am particularly motivated to keep Fotis walking as long as possible. He is growing slower, though.

Monday, September 28, 2015

This morning at breakfast I listened to András Schiff play the Brahms Handel Variations. In his performance, each single variation is its own completely distinct concept, its own world. That is exactly what I fail to achieve when I practice the piano! I've been practicing the preludes and fugues of the *Well-Tempered Clavier*, and much as I try to develop the individual character of each one, they all come out sounding more or less alike—that is, like an intermediate piano student plugging away at reading music. Whereas, when a real musician plays, every single phrase comes multidimensionally alive.

Sunday, October 4, 2015

This weekend I drove to Fotis' ancestral village of Monastiraki, in the very beautiful and unspoiled mountain valley of Amari at the foot of Mt. Ida in the center of Crete. I took our eighty-four-year-old cousin Hará with me, and together we tramped around several small fields that belong to our extended family but not to anyone in particular. Our aim was to identify these and arrive at some arrangement by which their ownership can be settled. In tandem with that, we can try to simplify the ownership of the ancestral house, presently in ruins, of which five families have each inherited a share. The hope is that eventually we will restore the structure. It's a traditional small vernacular family house, several centuries old, and we want it to be preserved and habitable even though none of us needs it now.

Hará grew up in Monastiraki, in the days when our family lived on what they could grow. People would make a bonfire and cleanse their linen by soaking it in a solution of ash, then wash it at the communal fountain. The leftover ashy water would be used to scrub the floor. Hará remembers all that and still knows many residents of the village, since its population consists mainly of old people who were always there.

Our visit included an unhappy interlude in which a very drunk man, uninsured and lacking a driver's license, drove his dilapidated truck into the side of my car, creating a large dent. He lives in the village; Hará knows him, and she says that all his siblings are fine but he has always been a problem. He emigrated, like many Greeks, to Australia, was deported from there, and returned with a long-suffering Australian wife, a hairdresser, with whom he has three children. After our smashup, he provided his neighbor's name instead of his own. The police came, we all went to the station, I did my paperwork and then Hará and I left. At the station I emphasized to the police, who know him well, that the man is a serious hazard and shouldn't be allowed on the road with his truck, but they said the law by itself can do nothing about that. Did I want to lodge a formal complaint against him? I didn't, partly out of compassion, largely because it would involve too much hassle for me with remote court dates and so forth, and also because I sensed that if I were to intervene in the village social fabric I would soon find myself out of my depth. Indeed, the very most important point is this: if you live in a village or are connected to one, then the one thing that you never, ever want to do is find yourself in a dispute with another person who lives there too.

I stayed with Hará overnight in her house in the city of Rethymnon, and in the morning walked in the narrow streets of the old town, which is a bit like a poor quarter of Venice. Many walls were disfigured with graffiti, but one person had painted swallows in flight on the façade of his or her small house and further decorated it with sayings such as "Every problem brings a hidden gift." A lemon tree in front of the house bore this handwritten sign (in Greek): "Thank you for being a good person and paying attention to what you see. With love, the tree."

Monday, October 5, 2015

My auto accident was not serious. Unfortunately, I've just heard that a close relative—Helen's brother-in-law Alexis—and his partner Ritsa have been seriously injured in a car crash. She has to be immobilized for a spinal injury and he must be operated on for a broken hip. I learned that the hospital in Heraklion is so cash-strapped that families must bring in medical supplies as well as food for their hospitalized relatives. Her immobilization involves a very expensive brace which the family must purchase now, in the hope of being reimbursed by insurance months from now. Capital controls, which are still on, make everything like that more difficult.

Wednesday, October 7, 2015

I visited Alexis in his eight-bed hospital room, where a friendly, convivial atmosphere prevailed among the different people there looking after their injured relatives. Alexis' operation was successful and he is expected to recover well. Ritsa, though, is badly off. She was not wearing a seatbelt when she lost control of the car, and she was very knocked about in the crash. She must wear her brace for three months at least, possibly five.

Here, the belief, and indeed the reality, is that if you are hospitalized you must have relatives and friends come to look after you. I've mentioned the need to bring supplies. It's also believed that you will not be cared for unless you can use some personal connection—meso—to get the attention of the professional staff. In addition it's very well known that some, perhaps many, doctors will accept a bribe in an unmarked envelope in exchange for scheduling a procedure.

Thursday, October 8, 2015

In response to my musings about Taoism, a friend mentioned the practice in psychoanalytic psychotherapy of "evenly hovering attention" on the part of the therapist toward the client. A valuable skill, not easily attained. The sheltered environment of a psychoanalytic session, like that of a concert hall, facilitates calm, attuned attention. In the hurly-burly of daily life, with unanticipated events erupting around us all the time, we need to work to sustain such disinterested attention. I know I myself am far from achieving it.

Friday, October 9, 2015

Alzheimer's is said to be a disease of memory, but we haven't experienced it as that, primarily. Today I brought Fotis a copy of a scientific paper describing the genome of a certain species of mosquito. Fotis pioneered a decades-long effort to elucidate mosquito biology as an approach to controlling the malaria parasite of which it is a vector, and the authors of the paper write, "We would like to dedicate this paper to our friend, colleague and mentor Fotis Kafatos on the occasion of his seventy-fifth birthday." There are some thirty authors, of whom I personally know about half, and I imagined the same would be true of Fotis. I read him the names, asking him each time whether he knows that person or not. He nodded yes or no, and his response was according to my expectation every time.

Sunday, October 11, 2015

A south wind is bringing in showers of warm rain, and quinces, lemons, oranges, and persimmons are ripening in our garden. I've finished two paintings I began last month, continued to read in Latin, and read my way through the *Well-Tempered Clavier*.

Thursday, October 15, 2015

Composition by field: this was a term liked by poets, such as Charles Olson and Robert Creeley, who were associated with Black Mountain College in North Carolina in the 1950s. It came to mind as I was looking at, and wondering how I can improve, one of my paintings. The abstract, impulsively designed grid with which I begin every painting in the studio is a "field," and I could see that the specific details of my painting please me best when they are nestled into some strategic location in the field. I always, as I proceed, supply representational shapes, so that the painting when finished will be readable as representing something. In order to resonate well, those shapes need to fit well into the field.

Friday, October 16, 2015

The idea of undertaking a historical novel has not left me, and I've been looking at several with an interest in how they are done. John Williams' well-made epistolary novel *Augustus* gives us the life of the Roman Emperor Octavius through fictional letters written by people relevant to him; this is a lively way of conveying information and may or may not allow us to get very close to any character. David Lodge, in *Author, Author*, which is about Henry James, and in *A Man of Parts*, which is based on the life (especially the sex life) of H.G. Wells, keeps a sharp, selective focus on his protagonist and writes in the sort of cool, dry, rational, third-person voice that would be the normal choice of a conventional biographer; the result is lively and insightful. Hilary Mantel's *Wolf Hall* seems, as I begin to read, a very empathically imagined work. The focus is on the passions and intentions of her Tudor English characters, not on their historical setting as costume.

Saturday, October 17, 2015

I've been rereading *The Art Spirit* by Robert Henri, a good, gutsy artist and great teacher of painting. Some hundred years ago he wrote,

> Art when really understood is the province of every human being.... It is not an outside, extra thing. When the artist is alive in any person, whatever his kind of work may be, he becomes an inventive, searching, daring, self-expressing creature.... He can work in any medium. He simply has to find the gain in the work itself, not outside it.
>
> It takes wit, and interest and energy to be happy. The pursuit of happiness is a great activity. One must be open and alive. It is the greatest feat man has to accomplish, and spirits must flow. There must be courage. There are no easy ruts to get into which lead to happiness.... It beats all the things that wealth can give and everything else in the world to say the things one believes, put them into form, and pass them on to anyone who may care to take them up.

Monday, October 19, 2015

Even more than "talent," all good musicians have the desire to study and practice. Many have very musical parents and are immersed in music practically from birth (Bach, Mozart, the Jacksons, Bobby McFerrin). Bonnie Raitt, the daughter of a fine musician, dropped out of college to sing but went back to school in mid-career to earn a PhD in music. It makes sense to me that music is about feeling and about learning, and sharing what you feel and what you learn.

Friday, October 23, 2015

I had dinner with our friends Rea and Elias, who live in Athens. Rea is a novelist, here in Crete for a panel discussion of her latest book, and Elias is a professor of biology at the University of Patras in the Peloponnesus. They are relieved that the drachma-preferring Left Platform has left the scene and expect that Syriza will eventually evolve into a normal center-left, social democratic party. I, too, hope that this will be the case.

Fotis grows ever quieter. His vitality, more than his physical strength, has diminished greatly. Last Sunday there was a party at the Hjem with live Cretan musicians and dancing. A year ago he would have been the first to get up and dance, but this year he sat expressionless through most of it. I brought two friends to see him, but he hardly acknowledged their presence or mine, and I couldn't get him up out of his chair to walk as we usually do.

Tuesday, October 27, 2015

I had tea with Gabriele, an Austrian friend. She earned a PhD in art history, was employed in the French cultural bureaucracy in Paris, and has lived in Crete for decades and brought up her children here. Unusually, she and her Greek husband live together but are legally divorced. They decided to separate their finances when his shop went bankrupt, and that was the only way.

Her purse was snatched on the street around noon one day last month, and as a result she's had to replace all the official papers that were in it. When she went to replace her Greek ID card she was told she must revert to her maiden name, since that is the rule in Greece for divorced women. This was news to her, and a bit of a shock, she says.

Friday, October 30, 2015

Alexandra, who has Alzheimer's, came to live at the Hjem early last spring. She is about seventy, I guess, physically trim and distinguished-looking, always well-groomed and well-dressed in tasteful natural-fiber clothing, with a warm and authoritative manner and a habit of approaching people with an air of interested concern. She is Greek, but bilingual and bicultural, having been a professor of psychology in Germany. She is quite bewildered as to where she is and where she ought to be, realizes she is confused, and is not shy in asking for directions and help. I hadn't seen her for several weeks, so today I asked about her and was told that despite her appearance of relative competence she has not long to live, as she has lost the ability to eat and drink; she no longer understands how to swallow. Her husband has decided to take her home for this last phase of her life, so we will not be seeing her again.

Saturday, October 31, 2015

Halloween! and I've just come home from a costume party across the street. Most of the attendees were around six years old, and at the beginning there was bobbing for apples, which I think I did as a child but don't remember for sure. Soon everyone was dancing, children, parents, and me, to a rock or a Latin beat, welcoming in the dark half of the year.

Costume? I found in my closet a Japanese robe and a fan, and practiced keeping a straight face in the mirror while singing a few bars of Madame Butterfly's aria "Un Bel Di." Only three bars, because my voice has a range of about five notes and the vocal part of that aria very quickly reaches beyond an octave. In the end I didn't sing at the party, since more than enough was already happening, but did have many laughs and a good time.

Tuesday, November 10, 2015

One of the local cultural associations has been planning an excursion to Alexandria and a few other points in Egypt over the Christmas break, and I'd thought of perhaps joining in. I've never been to the opposite side of the Mediterranean, except for short trips to Israel and to St. Catherine's monastery in the Sinai. However the excursion has been canceled due to the situation in the region. The last straw was the downing of a Russian plane flying out of Sharm Al Sheikh.

Thursday, November 12, 2015

The political situation in Greece is normalized, in the sense that people are no longer grappling with existential issues, but instead are arguing over particular ways in which fiscal goals will be implemented. To fulfill one target, for example, the idea of a tax on beef was floated, but then rejected (why?) in favor of a tax on private education. That tax was then scrapped when the government realized that aspirational poor and middle-class families all rely on private after-school schools, the public ones having failed in their mission of preparing students for the national school-leaving exam.

Friday, November 13, 2015

The weather this month has been beautifully sunny, clear, and mild. I went for a walk downtown in search of scenes to draw, but ended up just looking, framing impressions in my mind. Heraklion was once completely surrounded by a high, deep stone wall—actually two walls, with a wide space between them which now contains a theater, sports field, park, parking lot, and other things—and there are splendid views across the city to be had from atop the walls.

I've enjoyed my project of painting cityscapes from memory and imagination, and they've had the welcome result of helping me to see. I feel I've improved a bit at seeing the world in terms of composition and design. When I try to draw from nature, my deliberate effort goes into making marks that are approximately accurate, with everything about the right size and in approximately the right place. When I look at my drawing afterward though, accuracy no longer interests me very much. What I care about then is whether or not I've succeeded, more or less unconsciously, in making an interesting design.

Saturday, November 14, 2015

The news this morning is of the mass shooting at the Bataclan in Paris. I sent a message to our friend Catherine, and she wrote back that her family are safe and that they are giving blood.

It is very difficult, but surely important, to have some access to the psychological world of people who perpetrate such things. To me, it seems that the otherwise intelligent and often apparently normal people who shoot up elementary schools, or perpetrate atrocities at sports events and concerts, as in Boston and Paris, are likely to be in the grip of what psychologists call reaction formation, that is, hating the thing you are attracted to. Loners who feel excluded from a society they long to join, or puritanical jihadists encountering "permissive" Western culture, may well have this hang-up. Many other important factors are involved. But I think it likely that this is a factor. If that is so, then what can be done about this—very human—response to experience?

Sunday, November 15, 2015

I was invited to lunch in town and afterward went for a walk out to the end of the very long pier that reaches out from the small-craft harbor into the sea. I passed two young women there walking arm in arm, and this sight transported me back in time to when the Volta was still a custom in Greece. Until some point in the mid-1960s, people went for a stroll up and down some thoroughfare in every town and village every afternoon, the young women on one side going one way and the young men on the other side going the other way. That was the afternoon's entertainment. I had forgotten all about the Volta, and about being harassed on the street because I was an unaccompanied young woman, and about being served almond milk to celebrate an engagement . . .

Thursday, November 19, 2015

I've been reading *SPQR*, Mary Beard's entertaining new history of Rome. She speculates that it was the expansion of the territorial reach of the empire that led to the end of republicanism, simply by concentrating exponentially more power and wealth in the hands of a few. In our day, too, this is an important issue.

Saturday, November 21, 2015

This morning Aristides, who owns the olive grove across the street from our house, was there scattering grain by hand from a sack. His plot once belonged to Fotis' grandmother. She bequeathed it to Aristides' stepmother, who lived in this village and used to help our family with the housework. The olive trees—there are twelve of them—are older than anyone I know. Two years ago, when many people were unable to afford heating oil, Aristides cut them down for firewood, being careful to leave a green sapling growing straight up from the center of each trunk. All of his trees are growing back nicely.

After visiting Fotis I stopped at the beach, for the second time this week, to have a run on the sand and a swim. The water was cool and very calm and there was almost no one there. Two or three people were out on the water doing the local alternative to surfing or punting: standing upright on a plank and propelling themselves with a long paddle. This is tricky even on a calm sea, and the practitioners kept capsizing and getting up again, having a good workout and enjoying themselves.

Monday, November 23, 2015

Last fall I thought I might join an outing of the Heraklion hiking club sometime, and yesterday I did. It was great! We took a chartered bus to a point in the foothills of Mt. Ida and walked ten miles, ending in the small village which everyone still calls by its old Turkish name of Yení Gavé, even though its official name has long been changed to something blandly Greek.

The club schedules a hike somewhere in Crete every Sunday, and anyone can sign up to come along. On Sunday our group included one high school student, some college students and young people, and quite a few fit folks in their fifties and sixties; I was probably the oldest of all. The leader of the day's excursion took us down unpaved roads and paths no hiker could have followed alone. His family came from there, and he pointed out to us the ruined stone house in a deserted village where Kazantzakis' mother—a cousin of his own grandmother—had lived before she married. On our way we also saw the well-kept stone square of a village whose only remaining resident is a man in his nineties, and a well-kept, but half-ruined, rural monastery whose abbot, and almost only resident, is a Palestinian Christian.

Wednesday, November 25, 2015

Fotis doesn't talk much anymore; usually just one word, or maybe two, in answer to a question. He does understand a lot that's said to him, though. I don't keep him fully informed about contemporary events; I shield him from learning about wars and other catastrophes, for example. But today I told him about the current controversy over whether or not Woodrow Wilson's name should be removed from Princeton University buildings. I explained that Wilson was a very rigid, stubborn person who did a great deal to transform both Princeton and the US government for the better, and who committed himself heart and soul to a visionary, though impractical and failed, plan for peace and an early version of the United Nations, but who held a racist view of African Americans, supported the Ku Klux Klan, and excluded black Americans from the civil service during his presidency. "Do you think his name should be erased, or not?" I asked. Fotis' answer was yes.

Saturday, November 28, 2015

Helen and her daughter Anna have just arrived to spend a week here: the happiest possible Thanksgiving week for me.

Saturday, December 5, 2015

Helen and Anna have been here for a week. I'd been looking forward to playing with Anna, and this works best when she can take the initiative and be in charge of the agenda. One morning she got the three of us to play a game of "Mother, May I?" in which she claimed the first turn as Mother. Another day she created an indoor bowling alley with empty plastic water bottles for pins and a crumpled-up piece of paper for a ball, and we had a lot of fun competing at that (she kept score).

Monday, December 7, 2015

I went on yesterday's organized hike in the mountains—five hours of trekking, with a visit to a Byzantine monastery at the beginning and a swim in the Libyan sea at the end—and have signed up for next Sunday's outing.

My seatmate on the bus was a doctor with a second degree in alternative medicine. In addition to herbalism, she told me, this includes things like aroma and color therapy. I have no interest in the idea that certain parts of the light spectrum influence certain chakras in the body, as color therapists claim. But I'm sure we are affected spiritually, emotionally, even physically, by color.

I think our ability to find beauty, harmony, and aesthetic interest in our environment characterizes us profoundly and is of great importance to our happiness and health. As a painter I strive to compose in color, and my project is to get better at that. Think of cathedral windows, of Van Gogh, of Matisse: marvelous color is balm for the soul.

Matisse said that he would imagine himself within the picture, its colors and space a medium surrounding him. Of his paintings with windows, he said that there was no difference in them between inside and outside.

Wednesday, December 9, 2015

I've been thinking about the problem of economic inequality and have just read the sociologist Robert Putnam's book *Our Kids*. He finds, and illustrates through both individual portraits and statistics, that the hourglass shape American society has been assuming is reflected in all the conditions that influence our lives. The nuclear family is strong in the upper economic tier but disintegrating in the lower, neighborhoods are cohesive in the upper tier but dysfunctional in the lower, and so on. These phenomena have also been noted by the social theorist Charles Murray, but unlike Murray, Putnam doesn't believe that people are being sorted according to ability. He simply shows that our economy, and consequently our society, is failing too many children.

I once heard a talk by a woman whose vocation it is to promote the participation of women at high levels in the work world. She said that when she would go to a CEO and raise issues of empathy and fairness, that would go only so far. She got the most traction, she said, by telling a CEO that his organization was losing out on resources. What you need, she would say, is talented personnel. "You scour the globe for it, you're prepared to pay the price. But you've been losing your talented women: they're dropping out. Your pipeline is leaking!"

That got their attention. I think the same sort of argument

can be made about the economically divergent society Putnam describes. Every time a child—or an adult—fails to realize his or her potential, society loses. We're wasting our children!

Thursday, December 10, 2015

I should add, though, that some large government anti-poverty programs have been effective and successful long-term. I think particularly of Social Security and Medicare (for seniors exclusively, though), Medicaid, Head Start, the WIC program for pregnant women and small children, and the Earned Income Tax Credit. One will quickly think of more (food stamps, school lunches—though the quality of nourishment could be improved), and innumerable pilot experiments are underway. Cheers to those who are tutoring schoolchildren in Cambridge!

Monday, December 14, 2015

Our hike yesterday began in thick fog in the mountains, clearing up as we walked downhill toward the village of Anogia. Today, for the first time this year, there was snow on the peaks.

With Fotis, it's been demonstrated yet again that some faculties remain robust while others are lost. Numbers have long ceased to mean anything to him; when I last asked him—a year ago—how old he is, he said, "four." This morning, as we were sitting with linked hands, I began counting our fingers out loud, and the total naturally was ten. Then I asked him how many toes he has, and he couldn't answer at all. So I asked him, "Enough?" and he laughed and said Yes. He got the joke.

Tuesday, December 22, 2015

A friend writes in her holiday letter, "The ratio of funerals to weddings on our calendar is now skewed in the wrong direction." On Thursday I will attend the funeral of a school classmate of Fotis whom I knew. In the same unlucky week, Vangelis, who looks after our garden, slipped on wet grass in a field where he was harvesting olives and broke his leg. I've been to see him; he was cheerful as usual, but in pain. Besides that, our cousin Evmenoula was hit by a car while walking on a street downtown which, like many, lacked a sidewalk. She didn't break any bones, though, and, although bruised and shaken up, has invited me to Christmas dinner on Friday.

I learned to read Turkish when we were living in Germany because I fell in love with it. It's a very architectonic, expressive language with a very attractive literature, and it opens the window onto a different, large part of the world that has overlapped a lot with Greece. Right now I'm reading a Turkish novel called *Git Kendini Çok Sevdirmeden*, that is (in my translation), *Go Before You Make Me Love You Too Much*. The protagonist is a middle-aged woman whose only child has died in an accident. In one passage, she comments that she's been avoiding people so as not to be distracted from her grief. Then she says, "but at one moment I realized that I wouldn't ever lose my pain, that I would always have it, and so I felt less fear of losing it and I could go on."

Sunday, December 27, 2015

I went with Joseph and Natalie Ventura to see a new Greek film, *Ouzeri Tsitsáni*, set in Salonika under German occupation during WWII. Part of the story is concerned with Greek collaboration and resistance, and part with the fate of the Jewish community. Of roughly 46,000 Jews living in Salonika at the time, almost all were deported to Auschwitz; only about 2,000 returned. The film ties the two histories together by having a Greek Christian boy and a Jewish girl fall in love, but in fact the two strands were by and large separate. Greek partisans were fighting Greek collaborators and the army of occupation, while the deportation of Jews from the city was managed by the SS, with little involvement by Christian Greeks apart from a few individuals here and there.

Some of Salonika's Sephardim were saved from deportation because they had retained, or were able to obtain, Spanish passports, and some Jews whose ancestors came from Livorno were saved by the Italian consul, despite the fact that Mussolini's Italy was officially under the Nazi race laws. I learned this from Mark Mazower's excellent history of Salonika, which I just reread after seeing the film. Something the film brings out very well is the terrible anxiety and uncertainty suffered by everyone, as no one could be sure what to believe, whom to trust, or what would happen next.

Wednesday, December 30, 2015

The year 2015 approaches its end, and I reflect that I've now lived alone for over a year. In this journal I try to bring out issues that come up for people in my age group, and that is surely one of them. How do I feel about it? I find I can live this way very well. It helps—it's essential—to have structured activities that I've chosen for myself, so that I'm never at a loss for something to do. It helps to have commitments, such as keeping up this journal, for example. It's good to face some manageable challenges and have to do some problem-solving. It's certainly important to see family and spend time with friends.

It's important for me to be with Fotis, as long as I can.

Fotis and Sarah's house in the village of Fortetsa, *photo by John D. Niles*

The garden, *photo by John D. Niles*

Sarah Kafatou, Bird Mirror Balcony, oil on canvas,
photo by Chrysostomos Stefanakis

Sarah Kafatou, Heraklion: Bakery Awning, oil on canvas,
photo by Chrysostomos Stefanakis

Sarah Kafatou, BOATS AT REST, oil on canvas, *photo by Chrysostomos Stefanakis*

Sarah Kafatou, SUNSET WITH MOONRISE, oil on canvas, *photo by Chrysostomos Stefanakis*

Fotis and Sarah in Crete, 2009

Sarah in her studio, 2016, *photo by Zoe Kafatou Bunnell*

2 0 1 6

Playing Mozart this morning, I try to pay attention to every note within every phrase: an infinite undertaking. He is the composer who can instill the most meaning into a single simple note. The feeling tone can change from delight to sadness within a fraction of a second. One thinks of the lines from Keats' "Ode To Melancholy,"

> . . . Beauty that must die,
> And Joy, whose hand is ever at his lips
> Bidding adieu . . .

As an amateur music appreciator, I sometimes think in shorthand of Mozart as the quintessential master of the appoggiatura—that poignant moment just before a resolution and new departure—or of the young Beethoven as master of the dramatizing seventh chord, or of Brahms and the hemiola, or Stravinsky and ostinato, syncopation, and so forth. These are extremely simple ideas, but they do have something to do with style.

How is it that we can so often instantly recognize an artist through his or her individual style, the way we recognize a face?

Wednesday, January 6, 2016

Today is Fotis' name day, and several old friends came to see us at the Hjem. One's name day takes precedence over birthdays in Greece and Russia, and I suppose in Eastern Christianity generally. It's the special day of the saint, or the event in the church calendar, that one is named after. The name Fotis comes from the word for light (photon, photography), and the day on which Jesus was baptized, according to the church calendar, is the Day of Lights.

If your name isn't in the church calendar (and names such as Artemis and Aristotle are not), then you don't have a name day. But if you do have one, then it's customary for people to phone or visit you on the day.

Thursday, January 7, 2016

In doing a thing, we want to challenge ourselves in certain ways while taking it easy in others. The ability to direct our attention and concentrate, or relax and not concentrate, appropriately, is crucial, I expect, to doing most kinds of things well.

A friend who reads this journal wrote that she finds it "restful and stimulating all at once!" which I took as a very fine compliment.

Sunday, January 10, 2016

I went with the hiking club to the very hilly wine country south of here, where we walked for five hours. The air was cool, and the slopes were a challenge but not dangerous; the hazard on these walks is of slipping and falling on wet rocks, and we weren't on that kind of terrain this time. The countryside is green and beautiful, and I was tired and stiff at the end.

One's mind wanders while walking, and as this is the beginning of a new year I found myself thinking—not of making any self-improving resolutions, but of the experience of holding on and letting go.

Wednesday, January 13, 2016

Our friend Stefanos' mother, who was in her upper nineties, died this winter. I thought of these lines by the Greek poet Miltos Sachtouris,

> With her arthritis
> Mom can't walk downstairs
> so every night in my dreams
> I go upstairs to see her.

Friday, January 15, 2016

Stefanos gave us a short book he's written about the lives and work of great physicists of the twentieth century. The scientific and biographical gist is very well summarized and selected, and much of it is new to me. I hadn't known, for example, that Max Planck composed music, including several operas, and almost chose music over physics as a career. Nor did I know that he lost one son in World War I and another who was executed by the Nazis for plotting against Hitler. I hadn't known that Niels Bohr was a fine technical rock climber and excellent soccer player, although not as good as his brother, who played in a match where the Danish national team beat the French 17-1! In fact these little chapters are so good that I've begun reading them aloud to Fotis, even though one wouldn't ordinarily think of discussing quantum physics or the special theory of relativity with a person who has advanced Alzheimer's.

Fotis pays attention and enjoys them. When we finished the chapter on Einstein I said, "But I still don't understand how it can be one time in one place when it's another time somewhere else, do you?" and he laughed and said no.

Sunday, January 17, 2016

Today another five-hour walk, this time partly in the rain, high above the sea near the spacious and serenely beautiful Gulf of Mirabello with its many upscale houses and resorts. A woman I met on the walk has the unusual name Electra, and I asked her about it. Electra is famously the woman in ancient Greek tragedy who recruits her brother Orestes to murder Clytemnestra, their mother. She told me that no, she wasn't named after that Electra, but rather after a young woman, Electra Apostolou, a communist and leader of the resistance to German occupation, who had been captured, tortured terribly, and executed. She explained that her own parents had been militant communists and were among those who, when their side was defeated in the civil war which followed the world war, fled into exile in the Soviet bloc. Her family went to Romania, where she grew up, and they were not allowed to return to Greece until 1975. Electra studied medicine and became a pediatrician.

Electra said that the political stresses of the last few years have been, at least partly, in her view, a replay of those events of over a half century ago. How long must it take for such conflicts to be dealt with, assimilated and forgotten? We have come a long way. I believe the English seventeenth-century civil war has by now receded into the past. But how far is Spain today from its traumas of civil war and aftermath? How far has the United States come toward healing the divides that broke open in our civil war?

Wednesday, January 20, 2016

I've just talked with our tenant in Athens, where Fotis bought a house when he was still in graduate school. The house had belonged to Fotis' father's brother Manolis, who died of starvation in German-occupied Athens in the winter of 1941, and after that to his widow. It dates back to 1925, has three rooms, a small kitchen, a patio, a small garden, and a roof terrace, and is in the center of town, near the Acropolis, in a quiet neighborhood where many artists and intellectuals live. We always imagined we might live in it, but we never did. For many years we had one tenant, the writer Kevin Andrews.

Since Kevin's death in 1988, our tenant has been a composer, Vassilis. In 2012 Vassilis' wife left him, taking their two daughters and all their furniture except for his piano, a bed, and a frying pan. We happened to move from London that year, and I was able to ship enough of our belongings to Athens to fully refurnish the house. Vassilis continued to pay a market rent—around 400 euros, that is, about $500 a month—through 2014, but since then he hasn't been able to pay anything. There is the crisis, times are hard, and for an artist they are particularly hard. I would like to keep him on without a lease, as a caretaker essentially, and in exchange have occasional access to the house myself. I hope this will be satisfactory all around. I plan to spend some days in Athens in March to test the idea out.

Monday, January 25, 2016

Ursula, a founding member of our yoga group who is German but has lived here for fifty years, including the several decades since her Greek husband died in a traffic accident, invited us to her apartment for a New Year's Feuerzangenbowle (a kind of punch where you set fire to a large lump of sugar that flames blue and melts into a bowl of warm red wine and black tea). There was also dinner, and we continued to socialize until after midnight. The women in our group are all committed to living in Crete, though they also remain connected to Germany or Austria. They all manage their lives very well and are good friends with one another, and it's a pleasure to be with them.

On the next day, Sunday, I got up early to go out with the hiking club. We tramped around on a frigid, wet, and windy day, ending up in the village of Agios Thomas which is partly hewn out of, and partly built of, stone, on a site that's been inhabited for 3,000 years. There are Roman chamber tombs, elegantly hollowed out of the rock, and large wine-pressing floors considerably older than the tombs, also carved out of rock. Much of Crete is limestone, a hilly landscape with many outcroppings and innumerable caves and underground streams, varied and providing good opportunities for human habitation, as in this very old village.

After the hike we had a party in the "cultural center," a long room next to the village church, with roast pork and other traditional winter foods, music, and line dancing. Traditional Cretan music and dances are unique to this island and continue to be popular here. The most distinctive sound is that of the brisk, keening Cretan "lyre," a small stringed instrument which is propped upright on the player's knee, held with one hand around its neck and bowed with the other hand. In addition, we had an oud and an askomandoura or Cretan bagpipe, whose bag was made of goatskin with a mottled pattern of black and white goat hair. Practically everybody got up to dance, and we all had a happy, wonderful time.

Thursday, January 28, 2016

Recently I discovered that my Austrian friend Gabriele, whom I knew to be fluent in French and Greek, speaks flawless English as well. She used English to communicate with her husband, she told me, until she learned Greek. She would like to read more, so I lent her two collections of short stories, one by William Trevor and one by Tobias Wolff. Afterward I thought about the two books. Trevor is Irish, and in the world of his stories people live narrow, repressed lives, yet manage to bring a bit of color into them at times. Wolff is American, and his world in contrast is one in which constraints don't function and loneliness and chaos threaten at every turn of the road.

In my own reading, I've been enjoying two English literary biographies: Hermione Lee on Penelope Fitzgerald, and Michael Barber on Anthony Powell. I once asked an English friend what it takes to be a good gardener, and she said, "Well, in the first place, it helps to be English." I think this is as true of literary biography as it is of gardening. These writers about writers—and others I've come across, such as Michael Bloch on James Lees-Milne—find exactly the balance of curiosity, collusion, and distance necessary for superb portraiture.

Anthony Powell is not much read in America. I've read several, by no means all, of the twelve volumes of his dryly hilarious *Dance to the Music of Time*. It's a taste I'm still acquiring (the biography has helped me with this): a bit, one person said, like the English predilection for cold toast. His world of dysfunctional upper-class English people is lively, barren, well-observed.

Friday, January 29, 2016

The Iowa caucus will take place on Monday. Today I read a column by Nikos Konstandaras, of the Greek center-right newspaper *Kathimerini*. His piece focused on the ability of populist politicians to attract support in Greece and Europe. This is a disquieting result of the discomfort many people experience when having to adjust to a rapidly changing world in which formerly reliable supports have deteriorated. It strikes me as pertinent to the long-term deterioration of the Republican Party and rise of Trump.

I've registered to vote absentee in US elections and will vote in the Massachusetts Democratic primary. In the 2008 Democratic primary I supported Obama over Hillary Clinton, and in 2016 I intend to support Hillary and not Bernie Sanders. I will miss Barack Obama, for I feel his values are right and he has done an admirable job in the face of utterly unreasonable opposition.

Saturday, January 30, 2016

Balmy weather is returning to Crete, and also to the east coast of the US. A difference is that the balmy weather here is about twenty degrees warmer than it is there. I feel privileged in another way, too, beyond the weather. My thoughts and impressions go out every month to a few people who read them, and in return, often enough, I receive responses that nourish my spirit.

Monday, February 1, 2016

I've begun a new routine, for the days that leave time for it. I sit at the window for an hour and do a writing meditation. That is, I just let thoughts pass through my mind at random and write down whatever I feel like writing. This is quite enjoyable, but the result was quite incoherent the first couple of times. Today I looked out and saw laundry hung out to dry on a nearby roof terrace, and I wrote about that.

Something about education in the Turkish Republic crossed my mind as I wrote, namely that until recently, schoolchildren did not say a prayer or salute a flag, but instead recited a pledge beginning, "I'm a Turk. I'm honest. I'm hard-working." Also that Turkish children of the early Republic were taught, "Dirty clothes are shameful. Patched clothes are not shameful."

Another thing that came to mind was a chapbook, *Laundry Lines*, that I came upon some years ago at the poetry festival in Aldeburgh. This was an anthology of poems from several centuries about doing laundry and hanging it out to dry. It conveyed a charming and wholesome environmentalist message, since clothes dryers are among the most voracious consumers of energy in households. I am not against progress or machines, and I think the washing machine is one of the best inventions of the twentieth century, but I love to see laundry hung out to dry and have borrowed the chapbook title for my writing meditation. This is what I wrote:

Laundry Lines

See those waves of sleeves
on the roof, in the air:
how they shimmer like leaves
as they're hanging there
pinned to their string
like birds on a wire
—a so much better thing
than putting them in the dryer!
Let your machine tumble,

let it rinse out the soap.
Keep your ways humble,
your soul full of hope,
and your clothing mended
until it wears out.
That's what God intended.
It's what life is about.

Thursday, February 4, 2016

I've been acquainted with the mosquito biology community for decades. Until the 1980s there was virtually no up-to-date scientific literature on mosquitoes. Fotis was one of the very first modern biologists to commit himself to mosquito biology and genetics. He was a leader in the field, and he led the successful effort to sequence the varieties of mosquito genome.

Mosquitoes are annoying when they don't carry disease and sinister when they do. Mosquitoes that transmit malaria bring disease and death, to children especially, on a massive scale around the world and have done so for millennia, the malaria parasite having coevolved with humans and with the mosquito. In addition to malaria, mosquitoes also transmit dengue and other tropical diseases.

Disease rates can be reduced by draining swamps and removing pockets of stagnant water where mosquitoes breed, and also by using bed nets, since the *Anopheles* mosquito that carries malaria bites in the evening, when children are asleep under the net. Attempts to develop a vaccine against plasmodium, the disease-causing parasite that malarial mosquitoes carry, have so far had only limited success. One can take antimalarial drugs such as artemisinin or doxycycline, but it's not good to take them forever, and also, a mosquito population tends to develop resistance to any drug, and this evolution has been happening faster and faster with each new drug or drug cocktail. A still-hypothetical solution would be to "cure" the mosquito: that is, to genetically engineer a variant of the mosquito in such a way that it is healthy and yet can't carry the parasite, and to arrange for that variant to prevail in the mosquito population at large.

Now there is zika. Zika virus is not carried by *Anopheles* but by *Aedes aegyptii*, a species of mosquito that bites all day long, so bed nets are less help with it. Antimalarials are not relevant to zika. Total quarantine of infected people, or a mass moratorium on having babies, are not to be thought of, although some people may decide not to travel, or not to get pregnant just now if they live in a risk area. Abortion of affected fetuses, and incidence of microcephaly in some infants, are both going to happen.

What to do? It's very hard to eliminate large and small pools of stagnant water, although this is usually a good idea. Pesticides should not be overused to facilitate agriculture, but might possibly be deployed in a "smart" way against mosquitoes to interrupt an epidemic. Altering mosquitoes through genetic engineering has become ever more feasible, but there is presently no engineered mosquito that is immune to zika. However, it could already be possible through genetic engineering to eliminate a local mosquito population altogether. The trick is to alter the genes of male mosquitoes in such a way that their offspring can't reproduce. Release a massive swarm of such males into a population, they crowd out the non-altered males and mate with the females, and poof!

That's the idea. If it works, the main drawback I'm aware of is that mosquitoes are in the food chain. Is there enough other stuff for mosquito predators to eat? Can fish, and the world, get along with many fewer mosquitoes?

Friday, February 5, 2016

I drove to see Fotis in the normal way this morning, but the social worker at the Hjem, who enters the highway upstream from me, got to work an hour late. There was a general strike yesterday to protest changes to our social security system. Rather than cut pensions further, the government proposes to raise social security contributions. Just about everybody—lawyers, taxi drivers, pharmacists, shopkeepers, all government employees—around the country went out on strike, and the farmers blocked the roads with their tractors. In Athens there was a large demonstration, and a few Molotov cocktails were thrown. Alexía the social worker was late because, even though the farmers were no longer out in their tractors, road crews had blocked traffic so as to clean up the road where tires had been burned.

Capital controls are still on, and I asked our gardener Vangelis what effect he thinks they are having. He says that for the people he knows they don't matter at all, because we're allowed to take 420 euros, that is, about $500, in cash from our bank accounts each week and most people don't have nearly that much money to begin with.

Saturday, February 6, 2016

Today is a cold and stormy day, and our living room with its glass façade facing north toward the sea amplifies the buffeting of the wind. I sit sheltered at the kitchen table in the south end of the room, drinking tea.

I continue to muse about how to get started with a historical novel. My notion of doing one set in the distant past motivated me to refresh my Latin, which I'm glad I did, but now my musings have moved forward to the mid-twentieth century, which is, after all, by now a historical period, and the one that is home to me.

Sunday, February 7, 2016

I'm back from a long hike—six hours, and over ten miles across country—setting out from the beautiful monastery of Arkadi, built in the Venetian period in rural baroque style. With the decline of the Byzantine Empire, Crete fell to the Venetians for over 450 years and then to the Ottomans for over 200 years more, until 1898. There were frequent uprisings against the Ottomans, and in the great uprising of 1866 hundreds of Cretans—men, women, and children—who had barricaded themselves inside the walls of Arkadi were besieged by Turkish and Egyptian forces. As the Ottoman army broke through the gate the defenders set fire to their own powder reserves and blew themselves up.

An organization dedicated to getting to know one's country on foot might imaginably be imbued with nationalist feeling. But our hiking club doesn't have that character, any more than the English Ramblers Association has. The closest to it was a man in our group who comes from a village near Arkadi—as does Fotis' family—who said he was going into the church "to light a candle for the grandparents," which did seem to me to suit the occasion.

Monday, February 15, 2016

On Friday the Hjem rang me to say that Fotis was sick. The doctor on site said he had a low fever and low oxygen and recommended he go into hospital. He was in hospital for three days, during which time I was with him during the day, helping him eat and drink and keeping him company while he slept. Now he's back at the Hjem, his lung infection having responded to antibiotics.

The hospital staff seem constantly on the go and stressed. I asked the doctor attending Fotis whether she herself got any sleep last night and she said, "three hours." The nurses have almost no time to do any patient care, only strictly medical procedures such as drawing blood. At the end of the first day a doctor told me to stay overnight with Fotis, seated on a plastic chair next to his bed, but I said I couldn't and went home to sleep.

After that I dreamed that I had failed to take good care of Fotis and that as a result he had turned forever against me and refused to see me at all. In my dream I wept and wept about this but he was adamant. The next morning I told him, "I dreamed you're angry with me because I don't take good enough care of you, is that true?" and he smiled at me in a wan way.

Tuesday, February 16, 2016

Back at the Hjem this morning Fotis was in bed, comfortable, but dozing and not up to doing anything, so I didn't stay long. On my way home I stopped for a walk on the beach and my first swim of the year. The sea retains its warmth long into the fall but takes time to warm up again when spring comes. I stayed in for five minutes and that was enough.

While walking I thought about advice for living, and about what advice I might give to my sixteen-year-old self if I could. What I came up with was very close to what I in fact did do, even though no one had advised me to at the time: 1) find things you really love doing, that are challenging and worthwhile, and do them; 2) find people to love whom you trust and respect; 3) have adventures, and be safe; 4) don't smoke, and don't experiment with drugs.

As for my writing self, I recently came across a series in the *Guardian* where established writers offer their advice about the craft. The very best advice, I thought, came from Colm Toibin: Finish what you start.

Wednesday, February 17, 2016

Carnival, that is Mardi Gras, kicked off last week. I got in the mood by listening to a song from New Orleans, "Iko Iko," sung by Elijah Wald. Elijah grew up across the street from us in Cambridge. His parents, leading scientists and professors, were both political activists, and Elijah grew up to be a historian of American folk music as well as a performer of it. I've been enjoying his song-a-day blog on the web.

Thursday, February 18, 2016

The first little scrunched-up new leaves appeared the other day at the ends of a vine on our kitchen porch. Today Vangelis came to prune everything—vine, grapes, roses—and plant a magnolia, some rosemary, geraniums, and other things that have been waiting under a tree in plastic pots.

Saturday, February 20, 2016

I've finished a small painting, which is gratifying because for a long time I was baffled by it and didn't know what to do. I would go into my studio, look at it and go away again. Now it communicates to me a feeling of happiness and lively calm. There's no telling what others will feel, but I am pleased.

A good rule for painting seems to be that there must be enough contrast, and also enough harmony, and there must be balance. Contrast can be light/dark, warm/cold, rough/smooth, thick/thin, in terms of complementary colors—that is, those on opposite sides of the color wheel—or in terms of shape, or of abstractness vs. readability. All of these sorts of contrast enliven a picture. Harmony and calm, on the other hand, result from close light values (e.g., white and off-white, or light gray and medium gray), analogous colors, an admixture of white into pure hues, and simple, horizontal shapes. Of course, all of the above has to be arranged in a way that makes sense and communicates a memorable image.

Monday, February 22, 2016

On yesterday's five-hour hike we could look down from a mountaintop upon the seaside city of Rethymnon, surmounted by a huge fortress where the most prominent feature is the unadorned dome of a former Ottoman mosque: a modest, distant relative of the Dome of the Rock in Jerusalem.

Crete is now a peaceful, attractive tourist destination, but has been much fought over in the past. At lunch with friends earlier this week the talk turned to a project, proposed some ten years ago and then abandoned, of creating a container port on the south coast of the island. The proposal was Chinese, and was supported by some Cretan business interests but passionately opposed by many people who live in the area. The concept was that the Suez Canal would be widened to permit passage of giant container ships that would offload thousands of containers onto our rural, unspoiled coast, from there to be reloaded onto smaller vessels. Now, to our relief locally, the Chinese have focused instead on acquiring a majority stake in the port of Piraeus next to Athens. Chinese business interests in Crete at present seem limited to a chain of low-price retail clothing stores.

Saturday, February 27, 2016

A member of our yoga group spoke of the wonderment with which her two-year-old grandson, whom she was babysitting, greeted this week's full moon. "Der Mond! Der Mond!" he exclaimed, awestruck. I thought of giving her the book *Goodnight Moon*, which I had taken to the Hjem together with some other books last year. When I arrived there this morning I found Fotis, for the first time, in a wheelchair in his room. He could walk with me in the garden yesterday, but today he seemed not to understand how to, so the nursing staff had helped him into the chair. Probably he is entering the stage of no longer knowing how, and will remember on some days for a while and on others not. I fixed him a bowl of cut fruit as usual, and while he was eating it I reread *Goodnight Moon*. I noticed a number of details in the progression of time in the story, such as when the pair of cats begin to doze off and at what point the quiet old lady whispering Hush! is no longer there. And that is how I found myself practically in tears from reading a children's book.

Laundry Lines

See those waves of sleeves
on the roof, in the air,
how they shimmer like leaves
as they're drying there,
pinned to their string
like birds on a wire:
so tightly they cling,
with so strong a desire
to hang on while lifted
and dropped by the wind,
it's as if they'd shifted
shapes with our kind
as we try but don't know
how to hold on, or let go.

Wednesday, March 2, 2016

I'm in Athens and liking it very much. The news is of economic crisis, refugee crisis, tear gas, and graffiti, but the city center doesn't seem like that. I haven't been around much, but what I've seen so far strikes me as calm, stimulating, stylish, and of course much more metropolitan than Crete. I spent the afternoon in the new Hadzikiriakou-Ghika museum of the arts which is focused on mid-twentieth century Athens—a culturally rich milieu, and one I feel close to.

But I am here to deal with our house. I have had to ask our tenant Vassilis to leave, and he has reluctantly but amicably agreed to be out by the end of the month. He's not being evicted; he's voluntarily terminating his lease. The problem with him is not just that he hadn't paid for eighteen months and is unable to pay any rent; it's that he wrecked the premises and alienated the neighbors. He'd had a dog, Louiza, that I knew about. I didn't know, though, that Louiza had had puppies and the puppies had puppies and he kept them all at home. He had at least eight dogs in the house. They chewed on everything, damaged the floorboards, destroyed the furniture I'd sent from London, and drove the neighbors crazy with their bark and stink. The neighbors called the police repeatedly, but the police were ineffectual and no one knew how to reach me. A lesson is that if you own a rental property and don't visit it you are not doing your job, and I have learned this lesson now. The neighbors are very relieved and glad that I have come, they appreciate that Vassilis messed up my house and furniture as well as their peace and quiet, and they don't appear to hold this experience against me.

Vassilis says he views his dogs as family. He thinks everyone should love them and doesn't understand that they don't. Otherwise, as far as I know, he's a cultivated, intelligent, creative person, honest, responsible, and, until recently, well-liked. He says he wants to move to the country, where he can afford to live in some minimal sort of dwelling and have room for his dogs. He can stay with his parents while he sorts this out.

In the meantime a realtor I had contacted came by. She's American, from Amherst, Massachusetts, where her father was a professor, has lived here for decades and loves it. She was enthusiastic about the house, which is indeed a rare and attractive property in a charming neighborhood, and thinks that once I've made it shipshape again I can get a tenant for somewhat more rent than Vassilis used to pay. So that, it would seem, will be that.

Thursday, March 3, 2016

Today I did my morning jog on the original site of the ancient Olympic games. In 1896, the very first modern games were held just around the corner from our house, in a modern stadium that is a replica of the ancient one. The track underfoot is contemporary rubbery composite, but the entire surrounding structure is clad in marble, just as it was 2,000 years ago. It was exhilarating, although also somewhat boring, to run around and around the track by myself, with no one in the marble bleachers.

Friday, March 4, 2016

I met the poet Alicia Stallings for coffee. I'd contacted her, thinking we should meet because we both live in Greece and both have made rhymed translations of a classic author—she Lucretius, I Pushkin—besides writing poems of our own. She's received recognition far beyond the usual for her work, for example election to the American Academy of Arts and Sciences and a MacArthur grant, whereas I have hardly achieved any recognition at all, but that didn't seem to make much difference to our conversation about living here and about craft.

In the evening I had dinner with Ioanna Soufleri, an excellent Greek science journalist who has volunteered to be Fotis' biographer. We've become good friends in the course of her pursuit of this task. She's found a Greek publisher and an agent in England and is moving slowly forward with her book despite the great difficulties of being a working journalist in these precarious and stressful times.

Monday, March 7, 2016

Our daughter Helen has come for a week and we've spent two days visiting museums and walking around the steep hills in the center of Athens. When she learned about the condition of our house, she understood Vassilis' behavior at once as a variety of hoarding. Some people fill their houses secretly with junk, and some fill them with animals. Such people may be normal in other ways, as Vassilis seems to be, but in this regard they are suffering from a compulsion that they don't recognize as such. Helen says that, although this is a very intractable form of mental illness, some who have it can be gradually coached to discard their possessions or give them away.

Before coming to Athens I'd worried about the possibility that I might render Vassilis homeless by terminating his lease, but now I don't believe that will happen, since he has his parents as a fallback and also, he told me, a small but dependable stipend from an aunt.

Tuesday, March 8, 2016

Back in Crete, Helen and I have just been to a party for the residents at the Hjem, with three musicians playing in traditional

Veneto-Cretan style and line dancing for everyone who could get up. Fotis did get up and "dance," holding on to Helen and placing one foot after the other deliberately on the ground. Another resident, Aliki, a woman in her late eighties, said afterward, "that was the old Aliki—the real me. I felt the way I used to twenty years ago." The musicians themselves were very moved by the experience of performing for this group.

Thursday, March 10, 2016

I've read yet another memoir of Alzheimer's, this one by Jonathan Kozol about his father. He does a good job of bringing his father to life as a person, in the past of his high functioning as well as the present of his diminished capabilities, and also of portraying the changing relationship between the two of them over time. He doesn't focus on himself other than in his relationship to his parents, but there is a poignant moment when a caregiver tells him he should get married and have children himself, and his response to her is, "It's unlikely at this point that I will." Jonathan Kozol, a lifelong teacher and advocate for poor children, turns eighty this year.

Sunday, March 13, 2016

Today's six-hour hike in dense fog took us up to a mountain plateau and down again, past the foundation stones of a temple to Aphrodite that was, before the Christian era, a house of worship for 2,500 years. We stepped at one point over a conga line of "pine processionary caterpillars": tiger-striped creatures proceeding head-to-tail from high up in the pine trees, headed underground to await the end of summer when they will emerge as moths. They are a pest, as they eat the pine needles, and the trees were festooned with the silken sacs that are their nests.

Along the way I discovered how these weekly outings have been helping some of us in the rest of our lives. Vaso, a grandmother of three, had her own business in Athens which failed in the crisis. After a period of depression she found work in Crete where she didn't know anyone, and the outing club has helped her find her way socially. She likes to gather greens on our walks and bake them into small pies which she gives away on the next outing. Another hiker, a retiree, lost his wife to cancer and suffered from sleeplessness or nightmares, which have abated since he began hiking with the group.

A recent article in the *New York Times* focused on active older people as a prime demographic for outdoor recreation such as hiking and skiing. That makes sense: we have free time, want to maintain our health, and want to be out in the world as much as we can while we are still here.

Monday, March 14, 2016

Today is the beginning of Lent, and at the supermarket everyone was stocking up on traditional meatless Lenten delicacies, turning a fast into a feast. I, too, bought sesame-and-poppyseed-sprinkled bread, tarama, pickled beans, and green olives.

Friday, March 18, 2016

In Syria there is a ceasefire. But refugees continue to struggle toward Europe, and now the Balkan states have closed their borders, trapping thousands of refugees in rain and mud on the Greek side. An agreement that the EU has concluded with Turkey may possibly help reduce the level of chaos that those miserable people are exposed to.

Thursday, March 31, 2016

I've just read *Stuff,* an excellent book about the psychology and treatment of hoarding. People with this syndrome are often highly intelligent, creative, and charming, and would be well-functioning were it not for their hoarding. They usually have rich emotional and associative relationships with their possessions and always lack administrative ability with regard to them. They may or may not have insight into the harm their hoarding causes, but if so, they lose this insight when it is time to implement. If you clean up for them they will probably be traumatized and will be quick to recreate a hoarding situation around themselves again. They typically do this in secret, behind closed doors, which means that there are more such people among us than one would have guessed.

Some hoarders get better if they can be helped to focus on one object at a time, steel themselves to face the distress of parting with that object, and then actually let it go. This process can be exhausting for the hoarder and the helper, but it seems to be the only thing that works, and works whether one is a seriously ill hoarder or only just a little bit of one.

Friday, April 1, 2016

Vassilis has vacated the house in Athens. I've found a new tenant, and renovations there are about to begin. I'm particularly pleased that Vassilis and I remain on good terms. In our last phone conversation I asked him how he was feeling and he said he was presently too exhausted by his move to say, but that "changes can always bring something good, whether we want to make them or not."

Saturday, April 2, 2016

Our daughter Zoe has been visiting from Virginia and we've been seeing Fotis, socializing with each other, and enjoying the beach. She also has many friends in town and has been catching up with them.

We watched a film online: *Tea and Sympathy*, from 1956. In it, an eighteen-year-old, motherless young man, ostracized and called "sissy boy" by the other boys at his boarding school, falls in love with a thirty-or-so-year-old married woman, and she returns his love. The problem raised by the film is the extreme, narrow code of masculinity enforced at the school and, one understands, in the society at large. Tom is not gay, but he is artistic, reflective, sensitive, well-mannered, and kind. The code demands that he be incapable of insight, empathy, or solitude, dedicated exclusively to physical exertion, competition, and camaraderie, and emotionally unavailable to anyone not like that. Tom and Mrs. Reynolds, both excluded by this code from the world of men, find each other, resulting in a thoughtful and pathbreaking film, one of the best of that decade.

Sunday, April 3, 2016

I'm reading *Soumission* by Michel Houellebecq. Houellebecq is widely regarded as right-wing, he cultivates a dreadful public persona, and his fictional alter ego is an unhappy, self-absorbed, cynical materialist who cares only for food, alcohol, and impersonal sex. Thus he strategically disguises the fact, apparent in this book at least, that he is really a sophisticated, clever, funny, and accomplished writer with a commitment to Enlightenment values and a sharp eye for cruelty and oppression.

In the dystopian plot of *Soumission*, France in the year 2022 falls under the sway of a democratically elected conservative Islamic government. One should note that the cultures of Islam are not always and everywhere repressive toward women. But in the story, the unemployment problem in France is quickly solved by expelling women from the workforce, and the social welfare costs which ensue are ameliorated by cutting back on education for women. The nation-state is on its way to absorption, not in a secular European Union, but in a growing Islamic empire. The core philosophy of this new order is simple, and its essential feature is the exclusion, seclusion, and submission of women.

Houllebecq's book is not racist at all, and not disrespectful toward Islam. Its unpolitical French protagonist eventually complies with the new regime, adapts his thinking to it, and benefits from it. The book's message seems to me clear, though entirely implicit: that liberal secular society may or may not fulfill our deepest need for meaning, but that conservative, authoritarian, patriarchal alternatives to it are not a solution.

Wednesday, April 6, 2016

I've been watching the presidential primaries in the US and have noticed that distress over economic inequality and diminishing life chances is by far the main issue for a great many supporters of both parties.

Friday, April 8, 2016

My brother Jack is here this week, and we've been visiting Fotis every day. Jack is affectionate and attentive to Fotis, talking to him directly and easily and being natural and comfortable with him. This is high praise, for few of Fotis' visitors have been able to interact with him in this way. His relatives, colleagues, and friends come to see him but are very likely to start talking with me, or with each other, and to come across as awkward and uncomfortable if they do turn directly to him.

Monday, April 11, 2016

Jack and I took a walk beside the sea where two large, rusty, dilapidated ships have been moored for the past month or more. We learned that they've been impounded by the police, who caught them transporting a cargo of weapons, toward the combat zones in the Middle East, I assume.

Friday, April 15, 2016

I've just learned of the expected death, from cancer, of a very old and dear friend and neighbor of ours. Our children used to walk to school together, and I can't remember a time when we lived in Cambridge and she wasn't there. She was the person with the most open door, the one you could always drop in on for a cup of tea and an hour of lively conversation. She knew and cared about many people and many social issues, and had seemingly inexhaustible reserves of optimism and hope. Think globally, act locally was her style. The Cambridge Sister Cities program and the Cambridge Peace Commission with its affiliated activities were projects she nurtured for many years, alongside her poetry and music and other diverse undertakings. She helped me get started with my own poetry after a very long hiatus and shared difficult personal times with me. Such a sociable, sympathetic, and nurturing person, genuinely interested in everyone around her, is to be cherished, as Suzanne Schell Pearce has been by her very many and longtime friends.

Saturday, April 16, 2016

The work on our house in Athens is finished and the new tenant moved in yesterday. Laura, the real estate agent on the case, facilitated all this and has been a great help.

Sunday, April 17, 2016

I'm now in Cambridge, UK, on holiday with my brother and his wife, who are here on sabbatical (actually Jack, a scholar of medieval English literature, has retired from teaching, though he's still writing books; Carole, a professor of classics, is the one on sabbatical leave). Our holiday involves walking a lot and also visiting a few of the innumerable high points of the English landscape. We've just been to William Morris' house and garden, Kelmscott Manor, where so much innovative and collaborative work was done in so many of the useful and decorative arts. Morris was a businessman, a family man, a friend, a socialist, a linguist, a versatile, highly skilled craftsman, and indefatigable. His all-over way of designing a fabric, a house, and a life can still provide inspiration to those who would like to do something similar.

Monday, April 18, 2016

The weather in Britain is not so sunny as in Crete! But April brings sweet showers, as Chaucer wrote, and the sky changes constantly, reminding us that the whole place is at sea in the Atlantic.

The run-up to the June referendum—Britain in or out of the EU—has officially begun, and each side has now coalesced behind a single campaign organization. Obama is about to come and tell the British people politely but firmly that it's best to stay in, and that the "special relationship" will matter a lot less to the US if they don't. Chris Patten has argued persuasively for staying in Europe, and David Miliband in the *Guardian* has called the campaign to leave "Political arson . . . No nation in human peacetime history has ever voluntarily given up as much political power as we are being invited to throw away on 23 June." I agree with them and am crossing my fingers that Britain will stay.

Tuesday, April 19, 2016

Amazing good luck! I have close friends in London and Oxford, but since I knew that I'd have no time to visit them I didn't tell any of them that I'm here. Today, though, in the café at the Botanical Gardens in Cambridge, I happened to see my friend Judith, who lives in Oxford, chatting with a friend of hers at a table ten feet away. So Judith, her delightful friend, and Jack and I ended up having lunch together, a result that could not easily have been obtained by deliberately planning for it.

The immediate cause of this serendipitous meeting was the euphorbia. I had been admiring a specimen of this plant, which grows profusely in Crete, in another part of the garden, and had been touching the leaves, which were more tender than I'd thought they would be. At that point a grandmotherly person came up to warn me that euphorbia exudes a toxin which causes people's skin to break out in a blistering rash. If you break off a leaf and get the sap in your eyes, it's a medical emergency. A lecturer on plants, she went on to say, had told her group of amateur gardeners that he himself once touched euphorbia and then went to pee without first washing his hands, in that way causing painful trouble for his "willy." Alarmed by this information, I headed straight to the café to wash my hands, and that is how I found my friend.

Saturday, April 23, 2016

Jack and I have been walking on the Norfolk coast, a low land loved by birds where the tide goes in and out for miles. The occasional small village is unspoiled and prosperous, attracting artists and craftspeople as well as sojourning city dwellers. We walk and talk, and I'm struck by how similar the two of us seem to be.

Monday, April 25, 2016

I'm back in Crete after a plane trip that was more complicated than I'd expected. I was advised to take the Thameslink train straight from King's Cross in central London to Gatwick airport, and this would have been a good idea had the Thameslink station not been closed on Sunday for engineering work. After what felt like a very long detour by tube and train (for few things are more frustrating than being stuck in a slow vehicle when in a hurry to get somewhere), I did manage to arrive at Gatwick at the intended time. But alas! I had not double-checked the time of my flight, I'd misremembered it, and when I arrived the flight had already left.

This was not so bad. The customer help desk at Gatwick rebooked me for a less convenient flight out of Heathrow airport on the following day. I had to take the shuttle bus to Heathrow and stay there overnight, which I did at a very good, innovative facility: the Yotel, which rents cubicles by the hour. These are much like cabins on a ship: tiny, with just room for a single built-in bed, toilet, sink and shower, all high-quality, very clean and comfortable, and less expensive than a normal hotel room. With space at the airport at a premium, and I assume with some mechanism for excluding sex workers who might bring in their clients for short stays, these strike me as a great idea.

I enjoyed most of the time spent fixing my problem and getting home. On the plane to Greece I read a book about Ovid that Carole has written and that she gave to me, and on my stopover at Athens airport I bought another good book.

There was rough air during the journey, though, and at one point we were rattling around so much that I found myself gripping the arms of my seat, as though that would have saved me in a crash. Another thing that wouldn't have saved me was prayer, but all the same I began saying within myself, "Let this not be the end, I'm still needed and I still have something to give," which I soon amended to, "Let this not be the end, for all the people on this flight are still needed and we all still have something to give."

Saturday, April 30, 2016

I'm in the village of Tzermiadho, on the mountain plateau of Lassithi, where friends have invited me to spend the weekend. This is Easter week in Greece, and last night we followed the procession bearing the flower-bedecked, empty bier of Jesus around the village in the dark, stopping at every church to ring the bells and also at the rural health clinic to pay our respects to the medical staff there, a nice touch. The procession, which went on for about two hours, is somber but with an undertone of gladness and community feeling. However, I found myself feeling, as I often do, that too much of the culture of Eastern Christianity is just ritualistic, the church treating everyone basically like children, asking for prescribed behavior and not particularly inviting introspection or moral questioning. This is very likely a reason why many people's relation to it is occasional, conventional, and superficial. All the same, it would be very unsociable not to participate. Also, the very ancient symbolic representation of the year in its seasons is ever resonant, and these rituals help us experience it every year anew.

Sunday, May 8, 2016

I'm still only musing about writing a novel. But I may decide to translate Ovid's *Heroides*, his fictional verse letters by "heroines" such as Penelope, Dido, and Medea. An appealing aspect of this project is that in order to do the translation one must, like an actress studying a part, immerse oneself in the character in order to express her nature as deeply and effectively as possible.

Saturday, May 14, 2016

I've spent five days in Athens, meeting my new tenant, sorting out details with the house, walking in the city, and seeing old friends. The central city, despite its frequently shoddy construction, dereliction, graffiti, and grime, is at heart a splendid one, with its steep streets, its superb monuments and cultural institutions, its intimate neighborhoods, and the nearness of the sea.

Few visitors to the Acropolis pay much attention to the wide stone footpath leading around the site and up to the marble structures at the top. Whoever does look down at their feet will discover one of the finest examples of twentieth-century masonry, the work of the architect Dimitris Pikionis.

At the archeological site of Kerameikos, the cemetery of ancient Athens, one encounters an ancient sadness. The deceased person is often shown in marble bas-relief, seated, usually shaking hands with a surviving family member, often holding a small bird with folded wings. This image, which I noticed for the first time, put me in mind of a poem I wrote years ago for Helen, whose Greek name is Eleni, and her grandmother, also named Eleni.

Paradise

An injured redbreast lay in the shadow
of the flowering quince.
We'd raked the earth
that morning, it was bare and soft,
yet some danger must have lingered there,
something we couldn't see.
A child touched the thing gently—
it didn't fly away.
That child was you, Eleni.
You called to your grandmother Eleni.
   She came to find you
   and that mess of small, dirty,
   dun, beaked, quivering fluff.
In one cupped hand she lifted it
   to her lips
      and gave it to drink.
With quick, lapping stabs at her spit
   it began to live—
         next day it was gone.
Now you are yourself a mother
   and your grandmother a shade
      and the quince still bears its hard fruit.

In Greek we say *pétakse to poulí*: the bird has flown.

We live on here, who never wished to learn
   the tongue of other shades who lived here too,
   how they would say when setting free a captive bird

   azat buzat, beni cennet kapisinda gözet!

in plain folk Turkish:

watch over me when I come to the gate of paradise.

Sunday, May 15, 2016

Back in Crete, I find Fotis much the same as ever. He is growing weaker, and his eyes have less sparkle. He did respond, though, when I told him news of the friends I saw in Athens—Ioanna, Kostas and Eleni, Babis and Mari, Krystallia, Dimitris and Suzana—he still remembers them all. Dimitris and Suzana, the architects who designed our house, have just been awarded an honorary doctorate by the University of Thrace, and Fotis was particularly pleased to hear that.

Wednesday, May 18, 2016

I've begun work on my Ovid project, trying my hand at the first letter, which is from Penelope to the wandering Ulysses. It's a slow, steady, satisfying process, and I'm hopeful that I will want to continue.

Another project that I want to pursue is that of setting some poems to music. Several years ago I set two French poems of Rilke, using the piano, manuscript paper, and Sibelius, a computer program for writing music on a staff. I was happy with the result, and I'd like to try again with more of Rilke's French poems, as they are short, lyrical, and implicitly musical.

Saturday, May 21, 2016

Am I worried about the advance of Donald Trump? Yes! I am! My friend Vida writes from Cambridge, "They put his chances at thirty percent. If that were our chance of getting a serious illness, we would be worried."

Monday, May 23, 2016

Yesterday's nine-hour hike in brilliant cool weather, almost all steeply uphill and mostly cross-country over shady ground slippery with pine needles, culminated on a high granite outcrop overlooking the sea to the south and a beautiful green valley ahead. The village taverna at the end provided dinner with excellent local wine for our group of twenty hikers. Greece is in an economic depression, but such pleasures remain within the reach of many; the cost of dinner per person was five euros.

Thursday, May 26, 2016

I watched Elizabeth Warren make a speech, at the Center for Popular Democracy, which was eloquent, authentic, combative, and on point.

I also saw—in the *New York Times*—a story tentatively confirming that infection may trigger Alzheimer's disease. I've wondered about this in Fotis' case, since he had no other risk factors but did have a mysterious infection, for which he was briefly hospitalized, shortly before he began to develop symptoms. The idea is that as we get older, the blood-brain barrier becomes more permeable, and this permeability is particularly high in the region of the hippocampus where Alzheimer's typically starts. It seems that if a bacterial infection does succeed in crossing the barrier, the brain's immune system will act to surround each invasive bacterium with beta amyloid plaque. A healthy brain, supported by the gene ApoE-2, will then cleanse itself of the bacterium together with the plaque blanketing it, and all will be well. If the amyloid plaque is not removed, though, its presence will stimulate the production of strands of tau, which strangle nerve cells, and the process of Alzheimer's will have begun.

Friday, May 27, 2016

I continue to enjoy making my translation from Ovid, am giving it several hours a day, and am now on my second letter, from the Minoan Princess Phaedra to Hippolytus. Here she is declaring her love, in my translation:

> If only I had stayed at home in Knossos
> when I went to the harvest rites at Eleusis!
> I didn't dislike you before, but it was then
> that love drove its steel into my marrow.
> In white, with flowers twined in your hair
> and a discrete ruddiness in your fair lips,
> other women say you seem rigid, grim,
> but I, Phaedra, know that you are strong.
> I don't care for men who look like girls;
> I want a man to be reserved and manly.
> I love the rough, plain styling of your hair,
> the light film of dust on your fine features,
> the way you can rein in a stubborn stallion
> and make it wheel about in a tiny circle.
> My eyes follow keenly how your muscles
> ripple when you throw a quivering javelin
> or heft an iron-headed hardwood spear.
> Truly, I'm dazzled by everything you do.

This passage demonstrates Ovid's mastery of pictorial, vivid, fast-moving, dramatic narrative. It's no wonder that his work has been admired and read with pleasure for so many centuries.

I looked at another work of translation, of Goethe's *Faust* by Randall Jarrell, a poet whom my mother knew and whom I once met. In an afterword, Jarrell's widow Mary writes that when Randall was asked why he was doing it, he'd say "Why, for Goethe!" It was not done for fame, she goes on to say, or for a foundation grant; it was an assignment of the soul.

That is the best spirit, I think.

The Irish-American poet Michael Donaghy left his last poems, which were published posthumously, in a folder labeled "Safest." Nobody knows why he called it that. But I see that Mary Jarrell ends her remarks with a citation from Goethe that Randall had liked, and which is, "The safest way to avoid the world is through art; and the safest way to be linked to the world is through art."

Sunday, May 29, 2016

Doing things for their own sake—translating poetry, gardening, whatever—helps us feel safe, and feeling safe is of interest in the present moment, as one's adrenalin level rises in tandem with the rise of Trump. I trust his once-preventable rise will end this November in a crashing fall, possibly taking down with it the pathetic, immoral Republican Party apparatus that has capitulated to him. But as long as this issue is being contested it feels imperative to do something about it oneself. One wins elections by mobilizing one's own side, granted; but my own personal preference would be to have a serious, thoughtful conversation with some Trump supporters.

Thursday, June 2, 2016

Britain will vote this month on whether or not to remain in the EU, and the brilliant physicist Stephen Hawking has just made a brief statement in support of the campaign to Remain. In doing so he emphasized how much British science has benefited from the European-wide academic and scientific grants program created and administered by the European Research Council. This afternoon when I visited Fotis I told him this. Fotis was the founding president of the ERC, and remains honorary president. It's one of the things he's done that he is most proud of. I thought he would understand what I was telling him, and in fact when I did tell him he said, "Yes."

Monday, June 6, 2016

The classicist Mary Beard, writing in the *Times Literary Supplement*, also points to the ERC as a major factor in her wish to Remain. Most voters won't be thinking about that, though, or about other valuable European programs, alas.

Friday, June 10, 2016

I'm in the US for the month of June, staying with Helen's family in our house in Cambridge. A beautiful month in a beautiful place. Every garden is in bloom, and the Charles River, after decades of cleanup work, has been declared fit for swimming.

I was together last night with a group of people who did a great deal to support our cherished friend Suzanne Pearce, who has died. In talking over the experience, many said that they had wished to share it more fully with her by inviting her to talk about how it was for her to be facing death, but that she had not been open to that conversation.

Reflecting on this afterward, I tried to imagine myself in Suzy's situation. She evidently believed she might recover from her cancer and was willing to undergo grueling treatment while prolonging that belief, even when all those around her were sure that the end was near. It seems to me that, although she was not assessing her situation accurately, it would not be right to say that she was "in denial" by refusing to see what was happening.

In my thinking, there's an important difference between what was happening and what Suzy was doing. What was happening was that she was dying. What she was doing was surviving. Rather than say she was "in denial," I'd like to say that she was focused on what she was doing.

What people are doing is, from their point of view, what they think they are doing. Not what is happening to us, but what we understand ourselves to be doing, is the most important thing to us and about us, I think.

Saturday, June 11, 2016

Still reflecting about Suzy, I've been reading a book of her poems that her friends put together. This is from the last one in the book:

When I am a ghost
I will not sail in interstellar spaces.
I will orbit the Earth, touch down
on the rough and gentle ground
and rove among living things—
the geranium in the city window,
the backyard squirrels—

I will follow the fluff of milkweed
which pilots aloft
ever in the bond of gravitation.

In largeness of imagination, and in modesty and keen awareness of small everyday things, these lines represent the living Suzy
well, and express a very sensitive awareness of death also.

As for myself, what will I do when I'm a ghost? Since I was a child
I've loved the humble, expansive, inclusive poems of Walt Whitman
with his notion of the open road. I've been moved by a poet, whose
name I've forgotten, who wrote that he would be dust in the roadside
dust. Alongside that, I don't forget a line by a poet whose name I do
remember, Stuart Dischell, author of *Good Hope Road*:

Let us be pollen before we are dust.

Thursday, June 16, 2016

My month in the US provides an opportunity to do financial and
legal tidying up. It's occurred to me that, in the less-likely event
that I should die before Fotis does, I should review our will and
other legal documents to make sure that things will be in order.

Sunday, June 19, 2016

On Thursday the city of Richmond, Virginia, was struck by tor-
nadoes. This was only local news, and I didn't learn about it until talking by phone today with our daughter Zoe. Super-high
winds tore through her neighborhood, bringing down trees which
crushed cars, smashed the upper floors of several neighbors' houses, and sheared the side off of a large house down the street. Two
big trees fell onto her family's property, fortunately damaging the
yard only and not their house. No one was injured, since warning
sirens had sent everyone to shelter in basements.

Monday, June 27, 2016

We drove down from Cambridge to Philadelphia for the wedding of my brother's son Alan. The ceremony began with a tune on the bagpipe played by Alan, took place without any religious symbolism or reference to gender, but with vows promising commitment, love, and care, and ended as the presiding friend of the couple said, "I now pronounce you married." Alan and his wife Kelly, both with newly-minted PhD's in English, will begin teaching at Harvard in the fall.

The wedding celebrations and museums (the Philadelphia Museum of Art, the Barnes Collection) were great. But the dreadful news of the referendum on Brexit has darkened my mood and left me heartsick.

That referendum need not have been held at all; it came about through bad tactical decisions by David Cameron, which he made in a misguided effort to manage pressures on the right wing of his Conservative Party and from the UK Independence Party. The Liberal Democrats prevented it as long as they remained in coalition with the Conservatives, but they lost electoral support due to that very collaboration and so were deprived of the ability to keep it from happening. Labour, and the voice of the Labour leadership, has been ambivalent and losing influence very fast as well, and that contributed to this outcome too.

Beneath it all, apparently, is the fact that people who feel left behind, or who just feel threatened, amid all the rapid change and growing interconnectedness of our world, who aren't seeing the upside and don't want to take on the responsibility and challenge of managing it, are in revolt. The world is changing too fast for them, changing for the worse as they see it, and in some respects they are right. There are a lot of such people, and their dissatisfaction and resentments can be stoked even when no plausible solution is being offered to them.

What happened in Greece last year is happening, in a way, in England now. Britain is not in the eurozone, so there isn't that, but the way voters are responding to their frustrations is very similar. God help us if something of the kind happens in America and we find ourselves with a President Trump.

Saturday, July 16, 2016

The weather in Cambridge has been beautiful every day since I arrived, sunny and clear, and only lately somewhat too warm. I've needed to be here in order to do various tasks and I've loved the family time, in which I feel grounded. Besides many talks with friends, some highlights have been: a weekend visit to Virginia, a visit to our grandchildren's classrooms at local public schools, and weekly excursions to the town of Lincoln where our family have a farm share, paying a fee, helping out with tasks, and taking home our share of produce. A quiet, tranquil, peaceful existence, in short, which yet feels vibrant with small eventfulness.

Sunday, July 17, 2016

Helen rose early this morning to run a half-marathon, her third, in preparation for her first full marathon. How many people were doing this sort of thing fifty years ago? How many were keeping it up into middle and even older age? These days such activities are a source of health and happiness for quite a few of us, improving the quality of life even while making little or no direct contribution to GDP.

Monday, July 18, 2016

Today and yesterday I've spent hours dealing with software tech. I upgraded my old laptop to a new operating system, only to find that the old version of my Sibelius music composition software will not run on my new OS "El Capitan." I bought an upgrade of Sibelius, and have now spent several hours at my computer and in phone contact with a technical help person trying to get the Sibelius upgrade to install.

The important thing: I have remained (relatively) calm throughout. There was a time when technical difficulties like this would drive me crazy. Now I seem better equilibrated, and this is what I have learned.

Tuesday, July 19, 2016

An unsettling thing about Hillary Clinton is that she doesn't seem to inspire enthusiasm in people I know, even those who will vote for her. Maybe the upcoming Democratic convention, with Bernie Sanders now supporting her, will help. At present her campaign effort comes across to me as muffled, feeble, uninspired, reliant on old tropes.

Saturday, July 23, 2016

Crete seems bone-dry and desiccated after the luxuriously verdant landscapes of Cambridge. However, there is a cool breeze blowing and the sea is all around.

Fotis is still himself, and still recognizes and responds to me, but he's very quiet. He's intelligent and retains his sense of humor, but he expresses himself with small nods, not words, and doesn't project much feeling. He indicated that he'd like to get up to walk a little, but then couldn't stay up and sank back into his chair. In the end we just sat together holding hands, which I could tell was meaningful for him.

Sunday, July 24, 2016

Climate change on the way, a terrible, unacceptable Republican candidate for President in the US, disarray and random mayhem in Europe, massive repression in Turkey, war in Syria, a deep depression in Greece ... and I sit here translating Ovid, feeling like some bookish remnant of a tattered civilization.

Monday, July 25, 2016

My morning's email brings the news that someone I once knew has died of Parkinson's disease, thought to have been caused by his exposure to Agent Orange while a conscript in Vietnam. When I knew him—he married a friend of mine—he was a very attractive, thoughtful, and gifted young man, very much in love.

Tuesday, July 26, 2016

Cretan honey, and Cretan olive oil, are the best there is. At Formaggio, a gourmet grocery in Cambridge, Cretan thyme honey is marketed as the best, and the price is commensurate, that is, several times higher than it is here at the source. As for olive oil, growers in Crete sell it for three dollars a liter. Not much, but for local people who scrape along on small income streams from various sources, that is meaningful. European subsidies used to support farm incomes, but new Greek taxes, plus low commodity prices, now cut into them like scissors, as I am hearing from neighbors around here.

Wednesday, July 27, 2016

Stelios, the very capable electrician who installed the wiring in our house, came to reground it, and we shared a coffee break. He told me how electricity first came to his village when he was in elementary school, in 1956, and how he followed the workers around to learn what they did. A natural craftsman, he dropped out of high school to apprentice himself to a master electrician, earned a certificate from a technical college, and turned down a civil service job with the state electrical company in order to work for himself, doing what he wanted to do. He's never had an employee.

As I continue to worry about the US presidential election, I think about Stelios. I think he fits into the demographic which is known, in the US, as working-class white men. That is, the most important demographic that won't vote Democratic this time around.

Many of them are people who like to make things with their hands and fix things. They don't want a life of sitting behind a desk or in front of a computer screen, and they deserve to be doing something better than stacking boxes at Amazon. The way our economy, society, and politics have evolved means that they are being wasted and left behind, and they know this. Redistributive tax policies and supportive government programs might help them economically, but won't change a situation in which their kind of work, which should be a source of dignity and meaning, isn't sought after or valued.

I don't know what is the way forward for them, and, troublingly, the Democratic Party doesn't seem to know that either.

Many Democrats seem to regard them as politically misguided louts and bigots, and one trouble with that is that people tend to conform to expectations that others have of them and stereotypes that are imposed.

Thursday, July 28, 2016

Barack Obama's beautiful, heartfelt, poised, and utterly authentic speech at the Democratic convention kept me with a lump in my throat throughout. There, articulated by a person who lives by it, is a great public spirit. I can only add that every single other speaker at the convention that I've heard was also great. The Democratic Party is now holding the spirit of America.

One can feel satisfaction in this, and yet it isn't an optimal situation. Our winner-take-all elections are set up to be fought by two political parties, and we would be better off with more than one healthy party contesting them. The Republicans have disqualified themselves for that role, and I hope they fail miserably in this election (though I am not confident of this, which frightens me. Michael Moore, who is supporting Hillary, predicts that Trump will win, because he'll win the disaffected Rust Belt). What various configurations may evolve next is unforeseeable now. In an ideal world, people in politics would advocate for various priorities while sharing an ideal vision of a polity that is sustainable, democratic, free, prosperous, compassionate, and just. Is it naive or unrealistic to want that? It's the big picture.

Saturday, July 30, 2016

The mind in its associations can be so resourceful, so apt. For example, I've just misplaced the little plastic cup that fits on top of my blender. As I went about the kitchen looking for it I began humming "Where, Oh Where Has My Little Dog Gone," a tune I hadn't thought of for many decades.

Sunday, July 31, 2016

Crete is arid in the summer, but today's hike began at a waterfall pouring out of limestone into a deep and narrow gorge. We walked for hours in the rocky streambed, an oasis of sorts, immersed in water up to our knees. Coming out onto a bare mountain slope, we were quickly dried in a wind almost strong enough to knock us over. I needed to brace myself with my Nordic walking sticks against the wind, and got more sun exposure than I wanted because I couldn't keep my hat on my head. A steep descent brought us down to the south coast at Preveli, where we rejoined the stream as it reached the sea. Dense oleander, wild grape, and bamboo in the gorge were succeeded by palm trees at the mouth of the stream, where it widens to form a lake on the pebble beach.

Saturday, August 6, 2016

Reading books is good for our health. This is the take-home from a study, just reported in the *New York Times*, which controlled not only for age, race, health, depression, employment, and marital status, but also for being female, college-educated, and in a higher-income group, since this last represents the category of people who read the most. Book-reading, it turns out, adds nearly two years to one's life on average.

Does this mean, though, that we should be rushing from the gym to the farmers' market to the choral society to our book group, adding ever more components to our healthy lifestyle? Not at all, because it's also good to Go Slow, with Slow Food, Slow Parenting, and many other specialized Slow movements encouraging us to be aware of what we are doing.

The readers' comments on the book-reading article were all smart, and some made me laugh out loud. Several people pointed out that when you are reading you won't be doing things such as falling into an open manhole, jogging on a road with vehicle traffic, or breaking into houses that have an armed homeowner. Some said that at the rate they've been going, with this news they now expect to live past a hundred at least.

Sunday, August 7, 2016

Michalis, the house painter who maintains the insulation on our house, is a cultivated and interesting person. His work is seasonal, and earlier in his life, before he had a family, he used his winter downtime to travel in Latin America, India, and elsewhere. While at work he uses earphones to listen to classical music and jazz. A year and a half ago, as he was touching up our house, I chatted with him about studying Arabic and put him in touch with my Arabic teacher from Cairo. He'd hired workmen from North Africa who'd taught him a little— his accent is flawless—so he was intrigued and signed up for the evening beginners' class. We talked on the phone this morning and he told me he's just passed his lower level Arabic proficiency exam.

Monday, August 8, 2016

The only child of our oldest friends has died in his sleep, completely unexpectedly, of heart failure. I've just learned this and have only begun to grieve. He leaves a lovely wife and young daughter. They are devastated, bereft. The loss for them is irreparable.

Tuesday, August 9, 2016

In response to Zeke's death I spent this afternoon reading the diaries of Käthe Kollwitz, which I'd bought when we lived in Germany. Known for her compassionate, often militant, charcoal drawings and lithographs of working-class people, she also sculpted a memorial figure of a shrouded mother holding her dead son. In its place in the Neue Wache in Berlin, like Michelangelo's heartrending pietá in its niche in the Vatican, it seems to me one of the most moving works of art in Europe. A committed socialist who depicted women as workers and mothers, Kollwitz lost her beloved eighteen-year-old son Peter in World War I, and her beloved grandson, also named Peter, in World War II. "Du geliebter, geliebter Junge," she wrote of her son in her diary.

Wednesday, August 10, 2016

Today I finished reading *Townie*, the autobiographical book by Andre Dubus III, who is one of our very best writers. It was recommended to me by Helen, who said it was a good but hard read, and I believed it would be good because I had read his *House of Sand and Fog* and had also noticed the soul quality of stories by his father, Andre Dubus, who died in 1999. *Townie* is about growing up in white working-class Massachusetts, saturated in dead-end, self-punishing, angrily violent masculinity. Actually it's about becoming a writer, although that doesn't become fully clear until halfway through. Yet it isn't about that, finally, either, but about growing up to become a father and care for his own father.

About writing, he says, "I felt more like me than I ever had, as if the . . . real one had been underneath all along, and writing—even writing badly—had peeled away those layers and I knew then that if I wanted to stay this awake and alive, if I wanted to stay *me*, I would have to keep writing."

In the last chapter, after his father dies, Andre III and his brother build a pine coffin and Andre lies down in it, trying it out, and when the frost melts and they can dig the grave he gets in, six feet down, and lies down in it again. Then he gets up.

When I read that I couldn't help remembering my own father, and how we scattered his ashes by hand from a rented boat into the waters of the San Francisco Bay, and how my niece Margaret had thought of bringing flowers, so we threw the flowers in after him and they floated for a while.

Sunday, August 14, 2016

Zeke's funeral is taking place this morning. Helen and Zoe have flown up from Virginia, where Helen and her family were visiting, to be there. Far from them, I am focused on being there in spirit now.

Zeke lived intensely, passionately his forty-seven years on earth. He chose his own adventurous, challenging path, pursued all his relationships and interests with intense commitment, and stayed close to his family. In recent years I marveled at his tenderness and devotion to his wife and daughter. May his memory be a source of life, and his love a solace.

Friday, August 19, 2016

Fotis, eight years almost to the day since we first noticed any symptom of his condition, is now in a late stage of his trajectory. He can't get up from his wheelchair, and can't walk even with two people holding him up on either side. He hasn't said a word for weeks, and barely acknowledges anything said to him or anything happening around him. I feel he is still himself, still holds himself with inner dignity and worth. But it is hard to discern how much his life is worth to him now.

It's still worthwhile to me. It's still meaningful to me to visit him, talk and sing to him, and feed him the fruit I cut up for him. I like to do that, and he is not a burden on anyone. But these are not reasons to wish to continue when his vitality, or his health—for he is not ill, only incapacitated—comes to an end.

Driving home this afternoon, I listened to the adagio from Beethoven's sonata opus 27 #1: the slow repeated bass note like a pulse, scanned to the rhythm of the heart.

Sunday, August 21, 2016

Manolis Vergis, the tax accountant who helped us for many years, has died. He was a pleasant, charming man who spent much time babysitting his grandchildren in his home village, yet continued to work because his pension was small. I always enjoyed his company and appreciated his patient way of explaining to me anything I didn't understand. His humorous approach to his job relieved me of tedium and stress. He told me once that he'd never wanted to be an accountant—he felt he was just pushing paper around—but he was a modest person and he made the best of it. When I last saw him in April he was being treated for cancer and he understood that the outlook was not good. We both knew that we might not meet again, and we parted affectionately and with a smile. I see now, more clearly than before, that patience, kindness, and humor were his sort of courage.

Monday, August 22, 2016

This has been a month of reflection on the end of life. I've thought constantly of Zeke and his family. Now, looking through some old poems of mine, I've come across one I wrote after hearing that a friend had lost her companion to a long and finally fatal illness. I didn't send it to her at the time, feeling that it could be intrusive or as though I had appropriated an image of her life. But I will send it to her now. She is French and lives in France, but has a small traditional house on Alicoudi, a tiny, steep island in the Aeolian group, out to sea west of Naples.

The Sea at Alicoudi

From her terrace she watches the sea,
wavelets glittering, flashing in the sun.

She misses him. She's come here alone
to remember him. The hard stone table
holds up its basket of fresh-picked fruit
as a donkey learns patience by carrying.

She goes in to draw water from the tap
and comes out of the white house blinking
as though the day outside had gone dark.
She drinks the water, puts down her glass.

Sunday, August 28, 2016

It's good for us to do, every so often, something outside our usual repertoire. Last week I baked a cake, something that for many people would be a very ordinary thing to do, but which I had never done before. I told Helen about this and she suggested I write a poem about baking my cake, and now I have done so:

> Flour, eggs, sugar, oil, marmalade:
> mix all up, bake in oven—
> sunburst!

In writing this I had in mind an explication of haiku by Natalie Goldberg, a writer, writing teacher, and practicing Zen Buddhist. She says traditional haiku have three lines and seventeen syllables, but that isn't so important:

> If you read a lot of haiku, you see there is a leap that happens, a moment where the poet makes a large jump and the reader's mind must catch up. This creates a little sensation of space in the reader's mind, which is nothing less than a moment's experience of God, and when you feel it, there is usually an "Aah!" wanting to issue from your lips.

Monday, August 29, 2016

I've been listening to Bach's second violin partita as transcribed by Brahms for piano and played by Leon Fleisher with his left hand. Fleisher, a concert pianist, had to reorganize his musical life when his right hand became paralyzed and remained so for thirty years (he has now recovered its use). Bach composed the piece after the death of his first wife, and the testimony of loss and resilience in it and in this performance is beyond words.

Saturday, September 3, 2016

Today I stayed home and worked on music composition and painting. I want to set more of Rilke's French poems to music. The two I have already done are from his series *Les Quatrains Valaisans*, and I am now taking on his series *Les Fenêtres*, which is all about windows. My favorite painter, Matisse, made many paintings with windows as a feature, so this focus is congruent with my thinking about art generally.

I think that in making art, the most important thing of all is the process. Outcomes, finished works, are important. But the process, which is ongoing, includes outcomes along the way. It also produces, now and then, some things even more important than that: insight, a rearrangement of oneself in the world, even a small rearrangement in the lives of others who encounter one's work.

Sunday, September 4, 2016

My seatmate on the hiking club bus was an experienced hiker who prefers our most challenging routes and is going to lead a ten-hour trek next month. I asked her how she envisions her life once she retires from her professional life. She said, "Oh, I don't know, I haven't prepared at all, I don't have outside interests other than this . . . but I can't just hike all the time . . . reading books won't be enough . . . I don't want to think about it." Remembering my life-coaching training, I encouraged her to think about it some more. She said, "One thing is, I won't want to be home all day. I have to get out and do something . . . Maybe I could volunteer at the hiking club office." This is a real option; volunteers staff the office for two hours every evening. Then she said, "Actually there is a lot to do, to maintain the paths . . . educate people about the mountains . . ." She sat back, pleased to have answered, in the form of a tentative first draft at least, the question of what to do with her retirement years.

Saturday, September 17, 2016

Barbara and Jim, friends from England, are visiting me this week, and we've just completed a three-day excursion. We did a three-hour walk beside the sea on the Rhodopo peninsula, and on the next day walked for six hours through the famous and truly spectacular gorge of Samariá, with its towering limestone walls and very steep, narrow passage at the bottom. The gorge is overcrowded with daytrippers in summer but pleasant at this time of year, with an unceasing but thin stream of hikers. Barbara, who has hiked the Grand Canyon (down from the North rim, overnight at the bottom and up to the South rim), says the path is smoother there but otherwise comparable in terms of length and difficulty.

On our way back we stopped at a new and remarkable botanic garden. In the summer of 2003 there was a huge fire in that region of Crete. We were there, and I remember the flames rising above the seaside village of Sougia where we were staying. We took part in a volunteer bucket brigade that worked all afternoon to protect a house at the top of the village. Smoke filled the air, people stayed out on the beach overnight with wet towels wrapped around their faces, and I was fearful that the fire would reach the parked cars and set their gas tanks alight, which didn't happen. Vast slopes of olive and pine were reduced to ash, and the fire continued to smolder underground and occasionally break out again for a week or two.

After that, one family whose olives had burned decided to create a garden in their stead, and it is now very large and flourishing. On their steep hillside they've built winding paths and terraces which are now densely inhabited by over 150 species of shrub and tree from around the world, many of them raised from seed ac-

quired by mail order, all looking very healthy, all beautifully organized and labeled. We spent two hours walking through it and still
had to leave a large part out. The four Marinakis brothers, whose
initiative this is and who maintain it, have done something quite
beyond the ordinary for themselves, their visitors, and the island.

Sunday, September 18, 2016

I've just finished translating Ovid's fictional letter from Ariadne to
Theseus, after she's helped him kill the Minotaur and escape the
Cretan labyrinth and he in turn, after eloping with her, has abandoned her on a desert island. In this well-known myth the desert
island is usually said to be Naxos, as in Richard Strauss' (brilliant!)
opera *Ariadne auf Naxos*. But I've learned that Homer says the
island was Dia, which makes much more sense. Naxos is quite an
attractive place, whereas Dia, which I can see from my living room,
is a rugged, uninhabitable island opposite Knossos. I think the
people who made up this myth had never seen Crete.

Tuesday, September 20, 2016

Stephen Frears, who has made some delightful films about rich, unusual older women (*Mrs. Henderson Presents*, with Judi Dench; *The
Queen*, with Helen Mirren), has now made one about the splen-
didly off-key singer Florence Foster Jenkins, with Meryl Streep. I
would love to see it but haven't been able to yet, though I have seen a
charming documentary about Florence Foster Jenkins on YouTube.

From Barbara and Jim, I've learned of a literary counterpart to
Florence Foster Jenkins: the Scottish poet William McGonagall.
He has been "acclaimed as the worst poet in British history." His
poems, like her performances, are very popular and memorable.

Both artists possessed remarkable sincerity, verve, self-confidence, enthusiasm, and blissful unawareness of their inadequate mastery of their craft. Florence, as I've learned from the documentary, was infected with syphilis by her husband, and this may have been a reason for her inability to hear her singing as others did.

I've enjoyed my week with Barbara and Jim very much. They are a happily married couple with actively shared interests and very different personalities. Keenly intelligent, opinionated, managerial, detail-oriented Barbara tends to dominate; reflectively thoughtful, mellow, soft-voiced Jim speaks up for his own perspective on things in a kind, affectionate, and humorous way.

Wednesday, September 28, 2016

Michiko Kakutani, the reviewer at the *New York Times*, reviewing a new book about Hitler by Volker Ullrich, brings out the similarities between Donald Trump's rise and Hitler's. Astute, convincing, chilling.

Our daughter Zoe is here this week. We both find that Fotis, while apparently not uncomfortable or unhappy, does not seem to enjoy life much anymore. It seems to us that while not negative—he doesn't seem distressed—his experience of life has "lost its positivity," as Zoe says. His days are spent in bed or in his wheelchair, since he has very little energy and is unable to carry out any kind of physical task. His vision is good, but he doesn't seem to take in much visual information. He does understand things that are said to him, and though he's sometimes unresponsive, at other times he responds minimally yet in a way that is true to the way he's always been. A physical therapist now visits him three times a week for an hour of passive exercise, raising his arms and legs for him and stretching and moving his body generally.

Last week he developed a blister on his foot. The staff treated it at once and it has healed, but that is the sort of thing that leads to bedsores, a serious hazard for people who have lost mobility, as these can potentially become infected and ulcerated. Things like this will become more salient as we enter this stage of his trajectory.

Fotis and I have both prepared medical directives—"health proxies"—in the US. I've just reviewed the text of his, which is the same as mine. The key paragraph reads, "If I have a terminal and irreversible illness and there is no reasonable hope of remission of symptoms enabling a return to a conscious, functioning existence, I request that I be allowed to die. In those circumstances I do not intend to be kept alive by artificial nutrition or hydration. I ask that medication be administered to me to alleviate pain and discomfort even though this may hasten the moment of death."

This seems to me on the whole right, but I wonder whether we may not have been too strict in refusing hydration. That, it seems to me now, might alleviate discomfort while not materially extending life. My upcoming task is to talk proactively with people experienced in end-of-life care. We can use professional guidance with regard to questions of this kind.

Thursday, September 29, 2016

Zoe and I spent this morning downtown, where we came upon a film crew making a biopic about Nikos Kazantzakis. A large number of trucks with technical equipment were parked beside the harbor, where dirt had been strewn on the pavement to make it look like a premodern road. A large group of extras dressed in layers of period clothing made of real period cloth were standing around in the hot sun waiting to enact the same scene over and over again, rather like people in some circle of Dante's Inferno, though they seemed to be having a good time. Zoe says a particularly challenging job is that of the production assistant, who has to make sure that different takes don't contain inconsistent details.

Friday, September 30, 2016

We had lunch beside the sea and hiked to the summit of Youchtas and back in the afternoon. This has been a lovely week together. I will now be home alone from tomorrow through the end of November, when Helen will come.

Thursday, October 6, 2016

I've been working on my song cycle in my free hours this month, putting Ovid aside for the sake of the music. I can hardly say I'm in "flow," since there are many glitches with the software I'm still learning how to use, not to mention many points where my ideas are disorganized and have to be rethought. My accompaniments are sketchy. But it's fun, I'm learning a lot, it's working out, and I'm already on the fourth of Rilke's set of ten window poems.

Friday, October 7, 2016

The order of procedure in writing a song, usually, is to begin with the words. Then look for some notes, a rhythm, and a key signature to reflect the words. Write out the melody, adjust it, then add the accompaniment. (This is not hard and fast; when setting the third poem, I sketched the first notes of the accompaniment first of all.) I've been proceeding in this way to set "Fenêtre IV," and began writing the accompaniment today. I'd established the key signature as F minor and decided to use arpeggiated triplets in the accompaniment, supported by the occasional single note in the bass. But my arpeggios were much too busy and noisy, so I doubled the length of all the notes in the piece to calm it down and also marked the accompaniment *pp, pianissimo.*

Suddenly and unexpectedly, just at that point, I discovered myself to be writing a version of the Moonlight Sonata! Beethoven's famous first movement of that piece in C sharp minor has an accompaniment marked *pp* arpeggiated in triplets, and employs—just as I am doing—well-spaced single notes (as octaves) in the bass.

Was this unconscious plagiarism on my part? I don't think so. My piece doesn't really resemble Beethoven's at all. I was simply doing some problem-solving, just as Beethoven was when he wrote his ineffable, unsurpassable music . . . and we both made use of a couple of the same tools.

Actually, though, I don't at all think Beethoven was problem-solving in the manner that I am. He is known to have labored over every composition, tirelessly revising, and yet I expect that the first movement of Opus 27 #2, the "Moonlight Sonata," came to him whole in his imagination.

Saturday, October 8, 2016

The autobiography of Mikis Theodorakis—two volumes, over a thousand pages—has long stood unread on my bookshelf, and now I have taken it down. He writes very well, with much fresh and vivid detail. His thrilling and inspiring music was enormously popular here in the 1960s and '70s and was forbidden by the military junta that ruled Greece from 1967 to 1974. Enormously gifted and productive, he's worked in every classical genre from string quartet to symphony to opera, and his numberless songs have been recorded by the best possible performers and sung by everyone.

He drew on modern Greek poetry for the lyrics of his songs and also called on his brother, who is not well known but who wrote some of the best. In the book he describes being in a group of people and inviting each of them to make up a line for a song. Together they decided which lines to keep, and he took the resulting text and wrote music for it the next day. There is a facsimile of an early sketch of it in the book, and I see that he's written out the words in the treble clef, filled in a few notes, and written out the rhythmic patterns in full.

That song-writing episode took place in 1947, in a camp on the island of Ikaria where he was confined as a political prisoner. He had taken part in the resistance to the German occupation and following that in the civil war, and in time became a standard-bearer for the left, sometimes in prison or exile, sometimes in, sometimes out of the Communist Party. He was a heroic, charismatic, nonconforming presence for a long time.

Sunday, October 9, 2016

I went with the hiking club to Mt. Ida, the highest peak in Crete (8,000 feet above sea level). We drove for two hours to our starting point, then gained 3,000 feet of altitude on foot on the steep rocky trail to the summit. The sun shone, the slopes were brown and bare, and the splendid view took in calm blue seas to the north and south and rugged mountain chains to the east and west. The walk uphill took three and a half hours, the walk down two and a half.

On the way up I met a lone hiker, a tall, fit man seventy or so years old, I guess, an Austrian physicist on holiday. I asked him how he felt about this year's Nobel Prize for physics and he said he was happy with it, but would have preferred that the prize go for gravitational waves, as he expects it may do next year. We soon parted company, but I saw him again in the parking lot as we were waiting for stragglers from our group to arrive. He and I exchanged a few words and he got into his car, where I saw him sitting for a long time in the driver's seat without driving off. After a while he got out, shyly approached me, and said that he couldn't start his rental car. I announced this to our group, and right away one of our members fixed the problem for him.

What if we hadn't happened to be there? He would have been stranded, alone, in the gathering cold, many miles up from the nearest village, with night coming on.

Tuesday, October 11, 2016

The Nobel Prize for Peace has just been awarded for the pacification agreement in Colombia that, unfortunately, was voted down in a referendum. Among the runners-up for the prize were the White Hats, a group of Syrian volunteers who, at great danger to themselves, have been rescuing people from the rubble of bombings in Aleppo and elsewhere, without, however, being able to affect the course of the war.

It's evident that efforts, be it through political negotiation or direct humanitarian aid, to reverse processes of violence and war are arduous and very rarely successful in full. Once all-out warfare has begun, the most common road to "peace" has ever been either a separation or a decisive win by one side over the other. Prevention—while often not very visible or "newsworthy"—will always be vastly preferable to intervention after the fact.

Thursday, October 20, 2016

I've completed my cycle of songs to texts by Rilke and turned my hand next to a lyric by Heinrich Heine, "Leise Zieht Durch Mein Gemüt." Having just finished writing that, I've discovered that it's been set before, by Mendelssohn. His version is simpler, more lyrical, and more beautiful than mine, but I like mine all the same. The Mendelssohn one can be heard online, as sung by the fabulous Marlene Dietrich in the film *Blonde Venus* of 1932.

Friday, October 21, 2016

I'm reading *The Stranger's Child*, a novel from 2011 by Alan Hollinghurst. I'd read *The Line of Beauty*, for which Hollinghurst won the Booker Prize, ten years ago and admired it. A few years ago I began reading this book but didn't stick with it; the narrative tension was very slack. I'm sticking with it now, though, with appreciation for its kind of fiction, all scene, in which little seems to happen but much is experienced.

Possession, by A.S. Byatt, deals with the life and work of a fictional Victorian poet, as filtered through the lives and relationships of literary scholars living a century later. *The Stranger's Child* deals with the life and work of a fictional Edwardian poet, as reflected ever more faintly in the lives of other people living in each of the eight decades following his death. I've therefore thought of comparing the two books, and find *The Stranger's Child*, to my mind, to be better. Why?

Byatt's book, clever as it is, has been written from the intellect, it seems to me, while Hollinghurst's, just as intelligent and poised, is written out of internalized, imagined experience.

In my own experience of writing fiction, the easiest part has been to write the words, the sentences. Finding the architecture of the whole, the composition, has been more difficult for me. But the hardest part of all by far, the real work, has been that of imagining scenes that bring one's characters to life in a world. Hollinghurst, in his meticulously observed, tragicomic novels of English society, does that very well.

Saturday, October 22, 2016

I went to an organizational meeting of the Visual Arts Association of Heraklion, which has been dormant but may be revived. Some exhibitions and other activities may be organized, as in the past, and some European funds may even be available. While Greece remains economically depressed, low-budget cultural activities can contribute a lot to the social fabric and give people something constructive to do.

Sunday, October 23, 2016

Crete consists mainly of mountains, and with a modest thrill I note that our mountains are much higher than any in Great Britain or the United States east of the Rockies. I was out again today with the hiking club, in high pine forest in beautiful weather. I'd forgetfully left my Nordic walking sticks at home, and a fellow hiker kindly found me a dead branch which substituted for them very well on the steep downslope. I learned over coffee at the end of the excursion that he is a taxi driver. In 1985 he was able to purchase half a taxi. About twenty years later he managed to buy another half, but not of the same taxi, since his partner didn't want to sell. Now he'd like to consolidate his investment and become the owner of both halves of one vehicle, but he can't because his two partners don't get along with each other. (Maybe he's better off this way, though, I prudentially think, not having all his capital at risk in a single car.)

Friday, October 28, 2016

Today is a rainy day, a good thing since we've had almost no rain since this time last year.

Sunday, October 30, 2016

Resting in a village, the terminus of a hike through a wooded gorge, I happened to see the side of a pickup truck reflected in a window. The slight estrangement effect of the mirroring prompted me to notice the special visual quality of the logo: if you take away the A, it reads TOYOT, which is not only a palindrome but also visually perfectly symmetrical. What other words are like this? I thought of AVA (Ava is the first name of someone I know, and also the name of a dishwashing liquid produced here), then of one of our very most basic words, MOM or MUM (but not DAD or POP), and, last but not least, of WOW.

Saturday, November 5, 2016

I've composed a song setting for Goethe's short poem "Anakreons Grab." The text, in my approximate translation, reads

Anacreon's Grave

Here where roses bloom, where grapevines climb in the laurel, where dove calls to dove, where the cricket delights—

what grave is this, that the gods have dug
and adorned with life? It is Anacreon's rest.
The happy poet loved spring, summer and autumn;
now at last he shelters from winter under this hill.

I faced a technical problem in setting it, which is that Goethe's original hexameters seem to me to fall best into 3/4 time, but because the theme is of death and repose in the midst of life it would feel very wrong to express it in waltz rhythm or with an oom-pah sound. I hope I have finessed this difficulty.

"Anakreons Grab" has been beautifully set by Hugo Wolf. My own setting is close to folksong, and I like it for what it is even while being aware that the other version is infinitely better, more complex and more refined.

Wednesday, November 9, 2016

Hell, hell, hell and damnation. The American people, having had more than ample opportunity to know and understand the candidates and educate themselves on the issues, have voted. I still love our country and people. But we have elected an unqualified, ignorant, irresponsible demagogue, a racist and misogynist, a proven liar and cheat, an insecure, impulsive, unprincipled narcissist, to the presidency. Everyone in the world is less safe than they were yesterday. I feel sick.

I believe Hillary Clinton would have been an excellent president, as good as Obama. She's a super policy analyst, she's an incrementalist and a conciliator, she's dedicated and indefatigable, and she could and would attract very honest and capable people to her administration. She's not an ideologue but does have long-held core values, and these seem to me forward-looking, thoroughly grounded in justice and human rights, and compassionate.

I think that, if allowed to govern, she would have worked to make everyone in our country more prosperous, including the white working class that rejected her. As for all the mud and implausible detraction that has forever been slung at her personally, I find her thoroughly honest but reserved. She's not the kind of extrovert that is exhibitionistic and all about herself, she's prudent and she wouldn't say anything she doesn't mean.

. . . Later in the day, I've detected just one potential silver lining in this outcome. It is a weakness of mine to always look for silver linings, and what I am thinking of is that we really do need to rebuild our bridges, tunnels, train lines, and so forth. Obama spoke of wanting to do this, and so has Hillary, but Congress wouldn't let Obama do anything, no matter what, and the same gridlock would have continued in a Clinton presidency. The idea of Trump in power fills me with horror, and I believe his presidency will be massively destructive and dangerous for the US and the world. But he will be in a position, if he so chooses, to stimulate physical infrastructure renovation, and that is a thing that his constituency will want and will benefit from, as (depending on how it was done) might we all. If he's a fascist, let him remember that this is something that fascists do. Forget the "wall," which is only a slogan and potential boondoggle that, hopefully, will be forgotten, and hope that he will see this point. Because we are stuck with him for now.

Will Trump increase inequality in America? It looks like it, big time. Will he discourage immigrants and make America unwelcoming to nonwhite people? Yes. Will he do serious damage to women and women's rights? I expect so, not only because of personal traits that bring out bad attitudes in his supporters, but mainly because he will change the Supreme Court. I don't think gay or transgender people are a particular target of his, but his milieu is unfriendly to them too. Will his presidency be harmful to the comity of our political life? Of course. Will he try to violate or abrogate legal democratic processes in America? He seems willing to do that. Will he facilitate the industrial pollution and destruction of the environment, our planet? Yes. Will he be irresponsible with our foreign and military posture, including nuclear weapons? Very likely.

Thursday, November 10, 2016

It is, sadly, true that the Democratic Party has been letting go of its old core connection to the working class. Bernie Sanders tried to do something about this and did succeed in pushing the campaign a little bit. But Democratic identity politics, which are a form of interest-group politics like any other, while rightly helping many deserving groups to come into the light, have tended to obscure class issues and have done nothing for the working class or the many downwardly mobile members of the middle class.

We are still grieving, but now that the election has taken place we will have to begin to turn to the question of what to do going forward.

Saturday, November 12, 2016

I'm now reading Arlie Hochschild's *Strangers in Their Own Land: Anger and Mourning on the American Right.* She spent five years in rural Louisiana trying to get to know local people empathically, from inside, and understand why they supported the Tea Party. She provides portraits of intelligent, morally aware, caring people who know very well that their beloved home places are being despoiled and their health endangered by the oil and gas companies, yet who feel angry and rejecting, not so much of the management practices of the industry but of the Federal government and the EPA. Why, why, oh why do they feel this way? She tries very, very hard to understand why people, who do indeed perceive the problems that she too sees in their lives, turn to solutions that are the opposite of what she believes to be best.

I haven't read Thomas Frank's *What's the Matter with Kansas*, but I understand it to be a book about false consciousness, about being fooled into voting against one's interests. This book is not about that. It's not about what people think but about how people feel, in context, and what they value. Loyalty is valued by her informants, and also endurance and hard work. The anger they feel is directed mainly at outsiders: the distant Federal government and its ineffective local representatives (it seems the EPA has been coopted in Louisiana), as well as the remote beneficiaries of affirmative action and other policies who are seen to be "cutting in line" ahead of long-suffering local people. The mourning that people feel is for themselves, their way of life and their attachment to place. Halfway through the book, I'm less affected by the anger she discovers, which seems muted and not vindictive, than by the mourning, the discouragement. It makes people acquiescent in what is happening to them. Their anger is projected outward, far away, while their grief renders them passive near at hand.

There is more in this book, much more, and I recommend it very strongly right now. We should try hard to understand one another.

Monday, November 21, 2016

This weekend I was in Athens for the award of the first Fotis Kafatos Prize. I spoke briefly, telling the audience of young scientists that, as Fotis liked to say, they should go on to be better than we were. Several speakers commemorated Fotis' achievement in bringing the concepts and practice of modern biology to Greece as a young and refreshing professor at the University of Athens. We were reminded that he had to fight the academic establishment in order to do this. The old system featured one socially well-connected, aloof, authoritarian chair with sole responsibility for his domain, rather than the collaborative departmental model that Fotis brought in. The curriculum also was never the same after Fotis reorganized it and wrote a new, modern textbook. We were reminded, too, that the biology department in Athens went backward a bit after Fotis left to create a new research institute at a new university in Crete, since none of his former students in Athens were yet senior enough to carry on and lead it forward.

I also saw several friends, visited several museums, walked around the city, and spent several hours at the brand-new cultural complex, endowed by the Stavros Niarchos Foundation and designed by Renzo Piano, where Obama had spoken a few days before. It is spectacular and already popular with the public. From the gallery terrace at the top, overlooking a very long, narrow pool (where children could sail and kayak) on one side and an extensive park (where people could compete in a race running backward) on the other, there is a 360-degree view of the white city and the sea. I felt it to be a building designed—in the words of the poet Seferis—"according to the measures of the heart."

Obama's speech in Athens was excellent. At a dinner party of Athenian Greeks where I was on Saturday, people were talking of it. They had all heard it, and one person said it should be written out and given to children as a text in schools.

Wednesday, November 23, 2016

I've joined a group of half a dozen fledgling composers who meet weekly in an informal community center/café. Our young teacher, Isidoros Papadakis, has written various kinds of music, including

film scores and several operas. Right now he's introducing us to
1960s Minimalism, and in that context I spent a quarter of an
hour hitting the same four notes of the pentatonic scale in the
same order on a marimba while other musicians did other things.
I found this task to be pleasantly relaxing and also to require some
concentration, since whenever my mind wandered I was in danger
of losing the beat.

Monday, November 28, 2016

Our daughter Helen is here this week, together with her ten-year-
old daughter Anna. We visit Fotis every day, and he perks up when
Helen is there. Today he spoke to her, noticed when she pointed
out the rosemary in the garden, and gave her a kiss.

I love talking with Helen. She is a very attentive, patient lis-
tener, and she always has something refreshing to say.

A few weeks ago I set "New Hampshire Shade," a poem by
Jane Duran, to music, having chosen it partly for its very natural,
informal rhythms, its relaxed, free syntax held within tercets. It
speaks out of nostalgic longing and regret for a scene of childhood.
I liked the melodic line and the simple harmonies I found for it,
but felt that the shape of the accompaniment I'd written was not a
good fit. Consequently I turned to another reminiscence of childhood, "Knoxville 1915," with text by James Agee from the novel *A
Death in the Family*, set to music by Samuel Barber, to see what I
could learn from it about managing things musically. This did help
me to work out a better voice for the piano in my piece.

Agee's text includes the beautiful passage,

> On the rough wet grass of the backyard my father
> and mother have spread quilts. We all lie there, my
> mother, my father, my uncle, my aunt, and I too

am lying there. They are not talking much, and the
talk is quiet, of nothing in particular, of nothing at
all. The stars are wide and alive . . . and they seem
very near . . . and who shall ever tell the sorrow of
being on this earth, lying, on quilts, on the grass, in
a summer evening, among the sounds of the night.

Studying this, I realized that my mother, an artist born a few
years before Agee, is remembered by me in a poem in a similar
way. My poem ends this way—and maybe I will set that passage
to music someday.

> The distance from here to 1931!
> That summer, posing a young woman
> with her half-read book under a maple,
> you scumbled a lump of cream and green
> onto a canvas where it took her shape.
> Pensive, her elbow denting the tablecloth,
> she looks conversationally out at me
> from the painting on the far wall of my room.
> When she sat down, I wasn't born.
> There were other smells, other illnesses;
> the dollar had a different weight.
> In the humid shade of summer
> in that small yard, the light
> touched colors I've never seen.
>
> In yet another, earlier back yard
> you lay looking up—a child
> wrapped in a coarse wool blanket,
> allowed to sleep in the hammock,
> visiting your aunt and uncle
> a few years before World War One.

Last week, when you wrote me of it,
I felt no time had passed:
there were the leaves, the constellations,
a flower-bending breeze across the garden,
the unrendable night rocking you.

Friday, December 2, 2016

Which is whiter, whitecaps or fresh-fallen snow? A few days ago we were swimming in the sea, but yesterday brought cold wind and rain, and this morning there is deep snow on the mountains. We went to the beach nonetheless to run into the surf, collect sea glass, and have a fish lunch.

Monday, December 5, 2016

A report on two small bumps on my skin that were excised finds that both were basal cell carcinomas and both have been removed completely. I think of myself, having been fair-skinned, freckle-faced, and often sunburned as a child, as particularly vulnerable to this sort of thing and am vigilant. My generation grew up in an era without effective sunscreen, or awareness of sunburn as a serious health hazard.

More and more, I appreciate the importance of public health education, and of persistent improving of our cultural and physical environment in order to sustain health.

Tuesday, December 6, 2016

We visited Fotis every day this week. Helen spent all her time very close to him and created a beautiful rapport based on his slightest response, while ten-year-old Anna and I sat upstairs together reading.

This is perhaps a good moment for me to recapitulate a few observations about Alzheimer's as we've experienced it. Early on, there is loss of spatial orientation: that was the first thing that happened to Fotis, as he began to get lost indoors as well as out, and his handwriting deteriorated and began sloping down the page. Conceptual categories lose specificity: he would conflate similar things with each other, for example mistaking a rather different house down the street for our house. One loses executive function, including the ability to choose between alternatives, or to manage the sequence of steps in a process such as getting dressed. He could speak normally, but when he'd try to write down a thought he could only begin over and over, repeating the same words.

There is compensation for such losses. The situation can bring people, families, closer together. Giving up some things, some responsibilities, can be a relief. Living more in the present can bring out the beauty of the world as perceived. A person in the middle stage—someone who can't drive, or walk around outside alone, or live at home alone—can still travel, do many things with help, and have a full and satisfying life.

In this late stage, it seems one's appreciation of life is dimmed. There seems to be less going on, less to respond to. Fotis seems, most of the time, to be half-asleep. He will smile and respond warmly to a visitor, but not always and just for a very short time. He shows his appreciation of music by moving a finger. I talked to him the other day about his earliest research, on the life cycle of the silk moth, and he did seem to perk up and pay attention for a while.

Earlier on it seemed to me that while his cognitive life was impaired, his emotional life was intact. Now, though, it would appear that there is no aspect of his being that is not diminished. All the same, he has no delusions or discomfort, apparently, he's not anxious or unhappy, and his responses to everything that he responds to are always appropriate and consistent with the way he always was.

Friday, December 9, 2016

I had thought I'd spend my time this fall and winter painting and working on Ovid, but I haven't been in my studio since September and have put Ovid aside after translating five and a half letters. Rather than pursue those things, I've become immersed in writing music, which feels like the most exciting and rewarding thing I'm able to do right now.

Painting, writing, and composing are equivalent activities in many ways, and equally valuable. It's my goal to write music as well as I do the other things. Hopefully I will be able to create some pieces that people will like to listen to.

Monday, December 12, 2016

Our hike yesterday, with snowy peaks opposite us and blue sea below, began and ended in the steep hillside village of Mélambes, which has 500 year-round inhabitants, down from 1,000 fifty years ago but still enough to sustain an elementary school and community center. After the hike there was dinner in the community center with live music—two old men from the village—and dancing. Traditional Cretan dances remain popular, part of any festive occasion, and many of us threw ourselves into the dance.

A favorite line dance—the Pentozális, a name which one can imagine means "make you dizzy five times over"—begins very slowly and simply, goes on for a few minutes, then suddenly speeds up as quick intermediate steps are added and the lead dancer launches into leaps, turns and heel slaps, going on to the skirling tunes of the Cretan lyre and fast thrumming of the oud until everyone is exhausted.

Couple dances are very rare, but there is one—an ancient one, the Sousta—in which the couple stand tall and dance opposite each other, with hands either folded behind their backs or held out to their sides and fluttering like wings: it is totally charming, evoking the mating dance of two birds.

Among us this time was a young man with very poor vision and problems with his gait. He managed to negotiate the steep, uneven, rocky terrain with the help of a walking stick in his right hand and a short cloth, held at its other end by a companion, in his left. (Come to think of it, this short cloth was much like the one a lead dancer shares with the one behind, holding tight and supporting himself on it through the turns and leaps of the dance.) I talked with him afterward and learned that he is completing a distance degree in special education in order to work in the public schools. Bravo for him, and for the support and resources behind him.

Sunday, December 18, 2016

I took the overnight ferry to Athens to attend an all-day event for Dimitris and Suzana Antonakakis in celebration of the fiftieth anniversary of their joint architectural practice. They designed our house and supervised the building of it just as closely as if they hadn't also had projects underway for a new university campus, several large hotels, a workers' housing complex, and a stadium.

When I think of Suzana and Dimitri I see a picture of uncompromising integrity, dependability, and taste, constant hard work, and lightness, playfulness, and tenderness in their relationships with each other and everyone else. For fifty years they've lived and

worked in the same apartment building in central Athens, raising
their two children there and housing their architectural practice
with its ten or so younger collaborators and students on the lowest level, halfway below ground level. They created the building
as a joint project with three other couples: one contributed the
land, one provided financing, one handled legal and administrative
matters, and Dimitris and Suzana designed the structure. They all
then lived there like an extended family, with no locked doors and
children circulating freely from floor to floor.

Each of their houses is different from the others, but there are
common themes. They take the site, and orientation on the site,
very seriously, and pay particular attention to the sunlight and pre-
vailing wind. They build in reinforced concrete complemented by
local materials, and maintain strong, durable working relationships
with craftspeople such as carpenters and metalworkers. Their way
of envisioning a building is multidimensional, treating inside and
outside spaces on an equal basis; they don't emphasize any façade
or attempt to make a grand impression of any kind, but rather seek
functionality and harmony throughout the whole. When designing, they think in terms of a grid within which parts can be moved
around freely during the planning stage, and of pathways along
which elements in the finished structure will flow. Some of their
houses are built on steep sites and have as many as six floors with
the main entrance somewhere in the middle, the vertical element
being as important as the horizontal to the design. They feel color
to be a structural aspect of their work, and when we repainted our
house this year I consulted closely with Suzana about the color.

The look of their buildings recalls the Bauhaus much more
than it does vernacular architecture, but elements of both are present. Ours consists of four separate structures fitted in among olive
trees (a small house for each of our daughters, an office for Fotis
and studio above it for me, and the main house with living room
and kitchen downstairs and two bedrooms with bath above). The

stairs and paths connecting each part of the whole, roofed and unroofed, upstairs and down, evoke the passageways in a Cycladic village, the freestanding structural columns recall ancient columns, and the accessible flat roofs represent a constant feature of Cretan houses throughout history.

Wednesday, December 28, 2016

It's the season of Christmas letters. A friend in Cambridge writes, "I continue to volunteer as a writing coach and 'publisher' with kindergarteners at the Martin Luther King School. Among the standout front-list titles: *My Three Geckos, My Nice Day, The Princess's Party, Ethiopia, Mimi The Bunny, The Ninja Fights A Robot,* and *Sleepover With Fiona.*" That's wonderful, but on another, much sadder, note she also reports that the MLK school is always tightly locked and secured against potential active shooters.

Friday, December 30, 2016

The close of the year is traditionally a moment for reflection, inner dialogue with oneself, and the resolution to be a better person. I find myself thinking ever more often of my mother and father. I live with them more and more, but not with them as they were specifically at any one point in time. It's my love for them, and my wish to emulate them—my father's unselfish regard for others, and my mother's never-ceasing desire to learn and improve as an artist (as she constantly did)—that stays with me.

2 0 I 7

Sunday, January 8, 2017

I spent over an hour this morning knocking heavy, clinging, icy snow from our trees, and was in time to bring relief to all of them, with the exception of one large olive branch that broke under its unfamiliar burden.

Before the branch fell I'd been sitting in my kitchen comfortably observing the whiteness outside while reading the *New York Times*. I'd been drawn in to an article on attachment theory and was taking the online test, which showed me to be living in the "secure" quadrant of the population with regard to attachment-related issues. This represents a lifetime achievement, even considering that I didn't have a particularly bad start.

There are two dimensions to the test: attachment-related anxiety, especially fear of rejection, where I scored a low 2.0, the highest (worst) possible number being 7; and attachment-related avoidance, that is, discomfort about depending on others or opening up to others, where I score in the middle of the range.

My great score of 2.0 doesn't mean I'm not anxious at all; I am, about other things, but not much about being let down by others. It reflects very good life experience, with my friends who have been on the whole very reliable, and with Fotis who has been—as I grasped from the very start—totally dependable and trustworthy. I thank him from my heart for that.

I think my "avoidance" score is accurate, so I'm making it my

New Year's resolution this year to improve that somewhat. I hope I remember to keep this in mind.

The test is the Attachment Styles and Close Relationships Survey. Other than the "secure" quadrant, one might fall into the "preoccupied" one (anxious, not avoidant), the "dismissing" (not anxious, avoidant), or the "fearfully avoidant." I expect most of us can place people we know, and indeed ourselves, in one quadrant or the other on the basis of behaviors that we observe.

Tuesday, January 10, 2017

The snow and ice around our house have melted. Meanwhile, transportation in Istanbul is paralyzed by snow. Refugee camps in Northern Greece and the islands, which still harbor around 60,000 people, are drenched in icy rain and snow.

Thursday, January 12, 2017

Next week the United States will inaugurate a new President. I watched Barack Obama's farewell address, feeling yet again the greatest admiration for a man who has brought so much grace, so much principled and thoughtful judgment, and so much inspiration toward betterment to a country that failed to make the most of it.

Friday, January 13, 2017

Oh, today is Friday the 13th. But I'm not going to dwell on that. As Franklin D. Roosevelt said at the outset of his presidency, and Barack Obama also said very pointedly at the close of his, fear is not what will lead us forward.

Instead I'll review my progress in making art. Basically, I have a lot of work to do right now. I continue to study music and have made a minimal, clumsy, lumbering orchestration of one short piece I wrote. The way forward in this endeavor is infinite.

I've returned to my studio but am still stymied by a large canvas I began working on months ago. I do keep having ideas and trying them out, but I lack a good concept for the whole. I've just read an interview with the neoexpressionist Frank Auerbach (probably the best living English painter, unless David Hockney is), who said that he never just works on one part, but paints every canvas over again, all over, every time he works on it. Can I be more like that?

I have only about a hundred lines still to go in translating Sophocles' play *Oedipus at Colonus* from classical Greek. I began that years ago, having already done his *Antigone* and Euripides' *Hippolytus*. Then I took a break and didn't return to it. But yesterday I looked at Robert Fagles' versions of Sophocles, compared them to mine, and preferred my own work. This has motivated me to finish that job.

The past month has been quiet, with inclement weather and few social engagements. So I've also reviewed my Arabic. I'm very fortunate to have so much to do, at my own pace, on my own time.

Tuesday, January 17, 2017

I did return to my large canvas and make a large, impulsive gesture in red paint that disrupts and rearranges everything—and now I think I know which way to go with it.

It always takes me a long time to invent a syntax and subject for a new painting. I never know very well what I'm doing, but I'm willing to pay that price in time and frustration, since the reward is a different and unanticipated result every time.

SARAH KAFATOU

Saturday, January 21, 2017

Our daughter Zoe is in DC at the Women's March On Washington, and I've been following it live online. Photos are appearing of Women's Marches around the country and in many cities of the world. People are holding up homemade signs: Make America Kind Again. Make America Think Again.

Sunday, January 22, 2017

Our hike today, the first of the new year, involved a lot of clambering around in slippery mud. In the end we arrived at a well-kept, but deserted, stone-built monastery and a breathtaking view from there of a mountain peak covered in impeccable, shining white snow. "Like the view of Mont Blanc on a box of Swiss chocolates," said one person.

Home again and catching up on the news, I watched a video of Donald Trump's horrible talk at the CIA. He insisted, three or four times, that when the US invaded Iraq we should have "taken their oil," and muttered that we still might do so. (Hillary Clinton responded to this idea of his during the campaign, saying, "The United States does not pillage.") Then he began to talk, for the remaining nearly half of his time, about how journalists are the most terrible and dishonest people in the world. He was obviously in acute emotional distress over his perception that the press had undercounted the crowd at his inauguration (it hadn't), causing him to forget completely where he was and why.

I recall Obama, in his first inaugural address, quoting the Bible: "It is time to put away childish things." Alas!

To make a really dark speculation: Trump is very possibly doing all the things he does, not because of what they would normally signify, but strategically, in order to provoke a reaction. To arouse, and to distract. To so undermine deliberative democracy that it really stops working, and so antagonize half the people in the country that we get on our feet and give him an excuse to impose martial law. It happens, elsewhere in the world.

Friday, January 27, 2017

America is on my mind. We are facing an acute crisis, not so much because of one particular thing as because of the entire shape and drift of things since the election. Since one of the few things I feel I can do in response to it is to read, both the news and books, I've been doing that.

Matthew Desmond's book *Evicted* is a window into the state of affairs at the bottom of the private rental market in cities across the US. It's both a nuts-and-bolts analysis of the situation and a finely observed ensemble of human stories illuminating it. It's troubling and heartbreaking, and I couldn't put it down.

Following that, I've begun reading Philip Roth's novel *The Plot Against America*, about the America Firster Charles Lindbergh winning the Republican nomination and the Presidency in 1940. I missed it when it first came out, which is just as well because it is twice as chilling and compelling now.

Much more cheering is Kevin Starr's multivolume history of California. I have the book on the 1950s, the decade when our family lived in Palo Alto. It covers with great enjoyment and enormously rich detail many diverse sides of life in a good time and place. Kevin Starr and I were graduate students together in English and American literature at Harvard; I remember him only slightly and knew nothing at the time about his background, including the fact that he spent much of his childhood in an orphanage, as was recorded in his obituary which appeared this month.

Monday, January 30, 2017

In competition as it were with Debussy, I've set to music a poem by Baudelaire, "Harmonie du soir," for which he created a song setting, and a line of which he used for the title of a beautiful prelude for piano, "Les sons et les parfums tournent dans l'air du soir." It's a good idea to take on a subject that a master has addressed and so learn from the comparison between my work and his.

Tuesday, January 31, 2017

I've been reading the journal of Hélène Berr. A young woman in Paris in 1942, a violinist and student at the Sorbonne, she left an affecting record of her inner and outer life as it unfolded from day to day: "Today we played the Trout quintet . . . Today I sewed on the yellow star."

Saturday, February 4, 2017

I woke up this morning with a tune in my head, and it was the Scottish ballad of Lord Randal, who died poisoned by his true love. As I made oatmeal for breakfast I hummed the line about the murder potion: "It was eels boiled in brew, mother make my bed soon." Now what brought that to mind?

At first I couldn't guess, but then I remembered having watched the Nobel Prize ceremony for Bob Dylan, when he didn't show up and Patti Smith sang "It's a Hard Rain That's Gonna Fall." Dylan based his song on the ballad (and, I guess, the Book of Revelations). Transformed by his words and music and her performance, the result is monumental, very topical and hair-raising. Patti Smith and I are not soulmates politically—she campaigned for Ralph Nader for President and has taken a few other stands that I wouldn't—but that she has soul, no question.

What d'ye leave to your true love, Lord Randal, my son?
What d'ye leave to your true love, my handsome young man?
I leave her hell and fire; mother, mak my bed soon,
For I'm sick at the heart, and I fain wad lie down.

Monday, February 6, 2017

I've received very gratifying affirmation of my own efforts at musical composition. My neighbor Ruth came over this morning, bringing her two-year-old daughter. Little Sophia was cranky at first, but when I played my music for her she began dancing around, and when it stopped she shouted, "More!"

Wednesday, February 8, 2017

Colleagues of Fotis sent me a lovely photo of him, taken about five years ago. I tried to show it to him but he didn't respond. When I point things out to him—flowers in the garden, for example—he usually doesn't understand where to look and so doesn't seem to see them. I think he may have lost the ability to interpret a two-dimensional image. He always recognizes me, though, when I visit him. I plan to frame the photo, keep it in his room, and show it to him another time.

Friday, February 10, 2017

I showed Fotis the photo again and he did recognize it this time and smiled approvingly.

Wednesday, February 15, 2017

The weather here has been cold and overcast for over a month, with wind and rain—a rare exception being one sunny day last week when I went running barefoot on my usual sandy beach and afterward swam in the sea.

So I've been reading books. One is a short one by the English memoirist Diana Athill. An editor by profession, she's provided us with very frank, lively, and affirmative accounts of her life in several books (one of them, cleverly and appropriately, titled *Stet*). In her mid-nineties she moved into a small, nonprofit, old age home in North London. At ninety-seven she took part in a residents' project to plant rosebushes on the grounds, and writes of it, "One good thing about being physically incapable of doing almost anything is that if you manage to do even a little something, you feel great." She goes on to say of her life in the home, "Plenty of entertainment is offered—concerts, talks, exercise classes, poetry and discussion groups and films, none of which is obligatory . . . All that is valuable, and so is the luxury of being free of domestic worries and knowing that kind care is available if one needs it; but nothing is more valuable than being free to do whatever you are capable of doing." This I think is true of us at every age.

I also read *Jigsaw*, by Sybille Bedford, another English writer. The best, most perfect novel of a girl's adolescence is, I will always believe, Françoise Sagan's *Bonjour Tristesse*. This book, less composed and shaped than that one, more a memoir than a novel, focuses, even more than that one did, on the imperfect adults who provide a context for the life of the almost autobiographical narrator. Her childhood and adolescence made her into an insightful, incisive observer of other people. Having liked *Jigsaw* I've begun reading *A Legacy*, said to be Sybille Bedford's best book, but am finding it less good so far.

Friday, February 17, 2017

Our friends Stelios and Lenya came for tea. Stelios, once a prominent lawyer, has in retirement become a novelist. His first book, recalling his student days in Athens, came out about three years ago, and his second, based on a family tragedy, will appear this spring. He said he wasn't sure yet about the title: maybe "Dreams of Decline." I said, Why don't you call it "The Bankruptcy" (that's what it's about)? He saw the merits of that, and maybe it's what he will choose. Poor Stelios! He's an artist at heart. If his father's grain mill had not gone bankrupt he might not have had to become a lawyer at all.

Sunday, February 19, 2017

On today's hike (seven hours, eleven miles, 2,000 feet ascent) I met a Scottish couple who're here for a summer course at the University of Crete. She is a wildlife conservationist and he's learning to do marine farming. It's nice that people not from Crete discover our group; I've also met a sculptor from England and a poet from Taos on recent walks.

Monday, February 20, 2017

I grow a bit more integrated into local institutions. Recently I gave a talk about Alzheimer's, assuring my listeners that this disease, though it involves loss, is not necessarily stressful provided that one has enough help. Now I've been asked to provide translations of texts for the Historical Museum, and also to join its board, which will meet in early March. Plus, I'm eligible (one must have taken part in twenty excursions over the past two years, and I've done twice that many) to be a voting member of the hiking club, and I will attend its annual meeting tonight.

The hiking club is a bargain. A person who goes on half the Sunday excursions in a year will have enjoyed the equivalent of a month's active vacation, with minimal inconvenience and at a cost—for bus transportation to and from the trailheads—of 300 euros total. A super deal in economically depressed Greece, where I often see people (sadly, many here are smokers) rolling their own cigarettes, because that's cheaper than buying the packaged kind.

Friday, February 24, 2017

Speaking of being "integrated into local institutions," I need to renew my Greek passport. It can be fun to watch a situation comedy, but less fun to find oneself in one, and I anticipated getting a headache in this situation; bureaucratic procedures have improved a lot in recent decades but they still have a long way to go. Today I went to my appointment and found that my particular difficulty is having been born in New York. That's not a problem in itself, but under new guidelines one's place of birth must be specified exactly, and "New York" is not an exact specification because it can refer to a city or a state. OK, so let's put "New York, NY." No, impossible. The authorities—who were nice enough, one of them offered me a coffee and said that she hopes to visit New York herself one day—kept me for two hours while they dealt with this problem, making several phone calls to Athens in pursuit of a solution. The result: my passport will say that I was born in "Manhattan, USA." I pointed out that there is no city of Manhattan where I was born, but there is a Manhattan in Kansas (I know someone who lives there!). Never mind, Manhattan is acceptable and I will get my document and be able to travel on it.

Greek authorities always transliterate foreign words into the Greek alphabet according to their own system, and then if the word needs to be restored to its original form, let's say put back into our Latin alphabet, they do that their way too. My father, whose given names were Walter Wheeler, has been put through this process and will appear on my passport as "Oualter Chouiler."

Saturday, February 25, 2017

I've written a trio for flute, clarinet, and cello which takes two minutes to play. Thinking about how to write something longer, I decided to choose some sort of story whose various incidents can add up to six or seven minutes of music. What story? I plan to use the hike we'll do tomorrow, up to the summit of a nearby mountain and back down again. There is a fine precedent for this: Richard Strauss' *Alpine Symphony*, describing a hike he took in the Alps. His piece took him years to write, lasts almost an hour, and calls for 125 instrumentalists; mine will be vastly more modest than that.

Tuesday, February 28, 2017

Every so often I come across the term "design thinking." As I understand it, this refers to the process of discovering new things: problems not yet identified, outcomes not yet envisioned. Rather than goal orientation, this is a kind of wayfinding, a kind of Tao. Trying things out, being active, observing, consulting, and letting one thing lead to another, without knowing in advance what you want the end result to be. Not narrowing your focus toward a specific end, but keeping the whole picture in view as you adjust it and it changes.

That is what I like to do when I'm making a painting. I start with scribbles and see what happens. Once I tried starting from an existing image, in the hope that it would make the process easier. It didn't, but I did have fun as I copied a picture by Picasso and turned it, slowly, into something of mine. The red stripes of rungs of my lifeguard's ladder, and maybe the color of the sand, are almost all that remain from before.

Monday, March 6, 2017

I'm feeling that my life at present is well-integrated and in place, which is a good feeling.

Thursday, March 9, 2017

The piece I'm writing now attempts to represent a hike in the Cretan mountains, but the rhythm I have for it sounds to me too much like stamp-stamp-stamp. What to do? One can look up a piece of classical music online, and listen to various performances of it while either watching the players or reading a written score. I've been doing that, listening to learn the secret of flow. The rhythms I'm hearing don't go stamp-stamp; they carry one along and along. How do they do that? Syncopation always helps, as does sustaining notes across the bar line.

Friday, March 10, 2017

This morning I had a studio visit from the owner of the main private art gallery in Heraklion, together with the local painter whose work I like the best. I know them both, I happened to meet them at the gallery where I'd gone to see the current show, and they volunteered to visit me. I solicited advice from them as to how to go beyond where I am now with my work, but no advice was forthcoming.

They both seemed to like best my most monochrome paintings, which did give me some food for thought. I myself prefer fine black-and-white photography to fine color photography. Lights and darks are more fundamental to a visual impression than color is. If you look at a painting by a really good colorist (Matisse!) in black-and-white reproduction, the lights and darks will always be convincing. I like to keep in mind the following rule (easy to say, hard to do): first attend to light and dark value, then the degree of warm or cold, and only then the particular hue. Something similar holds for music: first in order of importance comes rhythm, then harmony, and last though not least the melodic line.

So I suppose the implicit advice I got from them was—to continue to be a colorist, but—to pay closer attention to the tonal values in my work. We had a good social time. I get along well with the gallerist and with Vassilis, the painter. He graduated from the Athens School of Fine Arts, got married, moved to Crete and worked for decades for the phone company. Retired now, he teaches art from his studio and continues to educate himself: he's learned to do mosaic and is studying photography. A strong, self-respecting, modest man.

SARAH KAFATOU

Saturday, March 11, 2017

More rain, and I've read two more books about the condition of America. In *We Do Our Part*, Charles Peters, ninety years old, a lifelong Democrat and the founding editor of the *Washington Monthly*, longs for a revived national ethic of public service for the common good. We should all want to work in an ongoing way to improve our society and our government. Too many of us are failing to do our part, as the New Deal slogan asked of us. He tells a story of how, decade by decade, we have fallen away (money—that is, growing inequality—is a huge reason).

In *Coming Apart*, Charles Murray, on the right-hand side of the spectrum politically (but a Trump opponent), has the very same concern. He finds that a meritocracy of increasingly wealthy strivers has been isolating itself culturally, politically, economically, geographically, and especially psychologically from the more numerous part of the population that is not doing so well. He too cares for the common good, deplores this falling away and fears that the texture of our democracy and our common life may be shredded irreparably because of it. Being a conservative pundit affiliated with the American Enterprise Institute, he does not blame the increasing wealth of the one percent for this shredding (he seems to think that wealth simply accrues naturally to the most talented percentiles) but rather places blame on our social safety net for undermining personal initiative and responsibility among its recipients, who would otherwise have to do or die and so would learn the hard way the satisfactions of taking responsibility for themselves.

I don't agree with that at all, but I also very much don't like the fact that Charles Murray has been targeted by campus protesters, and most recently at Middlebury College by violent protesters, who don't want his voice to be heard. His earlier book *The Bell Curve*, which was much criticized, which he hasn't repudiated and which I haven't read, apparently used IQ data to draw racist conclusions. But *Coming Apart* is not racist in the least; it's concerned exclusively with the class gap that has widened among white Americans. The class gap has actually widened among all Americans, for a number of reasons, I think, and is a very serious matter that we should be paying attention to and addressing.

Monday, March 13, 2017

With regard to the matter of people in an elite bubble isolating themselves, I must comment that this is not at all true for many of the people I know. My home in the US is a "superzip" such as Charles Murray describes. But it is thoroughly honeycombed with individuals, social and political service associations and institutions that are not at all inward-looking, but are focused on local, national, and international problems in need of solutions. Indeed, that is the reason why many of those people are there.

Wednesday, March 15, 2017

Those liable to disparage the political and social attitudes of working-class people can readjust their perspective by reading *Guardian* columnist Owen Smith's book, *Chavs*. "Chav" is a derogatory expression in Britain, and Smith demonstrates that to use it to characterize the working poor is prejudicial and wrong. A key point: when a member of an ordinary middle-class community behaves disappointingly, we don't see that as a reflection on the middle class per se; but if a person whose behavior we disapprove of belongs to a disparaged group—be it black, Muslim, poor white, or something else—bankers, even—then we are liable to generalize our disapproval to that group as a whole.

In Britain, Old Labour was proudly working-class, and a great many people still proudly regard themselves as working-class. Tony Blair said, apropos of that, on behalf of New Labour: "Old Labour didn't *get* aspiration." I think he had a point, but that point was carried much too far when it began to be thought that the aspirational people had gotten out of the working class, leaving only the dregs of their communities behind. In fact, there are mainly decent, hard-working people in every demographic.

Tuesday, March 21, 2017

Our daughter Zoe is here this week, luckily the first week of bright sunny weather we've had since December. We've been visiting Fotis, who is not able to respond much but is obviously happy to see her.

We went on the Sunday hike, ascending steeply for three hours through pine forest and scrub oak to a high plateau that was green and smooth as a soccer field—six hours altogether, nine miles, 2,300 feet up, 2,300 down—and she loved it. She'll bring her whole family plus another family of friends here in the summer, and we've planned a hike for them.

Wednesday, March 22, 2017

There is serious illness among too many people close to us. Several friends in England are dealing with major health problems despite having been extraordinarily fit and active people. Vangelis, our neighbor and helper in the garden, an excellent person and a great support to us, has been suffering from a mysterious illness which turns out to be non-Hodgkins lymphoma. Another friend has myeloma, still in an early stage. She is managing very carefully and competently, and has also succeeded in not focusing only on that; she has just begun taking piano lessons.

Friday, March 24, 2017

Zoe left this morning. We've spent time walking on the beach and seeing people, she's helped me rearrange my basement, and we've put thought and energy into supporting her daughter Sophia in an important life decision. Sophia, who will begin high school in Virginia in the fall, was admitted both to the Appomattox regional public magnet school for the arts and to a very attractive all-around private school that offered her a full merit scholarship. These were both good options for Sophia, but they were very different, and it can be difficult for a person to decide between good alternatives. She succeeded in making her decision clearly and autonomously, with as much information as possible and without any constraint other than the decision deadline. She chose the public arts option and will concentrate in theater.

Zoe has been helping her parents-in-law prepare a move into assisted living, and she and I discussed the matter of assisted living for me. I bought long-term care insurance for myself when Fotis fell ill. I also thought of some conversions that could be done in our house in Cambridge if needed, and at that point I stopped thinking about it. I feel youthful and fit, and since I don't have any illness I've imagined that I'll just continue with some version of my present lifestyle for the next ten years or so and then reassess. But, of course, one never knows. Zoe recommends that when next in the US I check out some facilities and put myself on a waiting list, since the best ones often do have a waiting list, sometimes one that is several years long. Once one reaches the head of the queue one has the option, but is not obliged, to move in, and one can keep one's option open for a while. On that basis, it does seem sensible to put down a deposit and join a queue somewhere, since, as I've just said, one never knows.

Sunday, March 26, 2016

Our hike today was memorable for mountain meadows sprinkled with wildflowers, most brilliantly anemones and poppies, now at their peak.

I'm close to finishing my rendition of our ascent of Mount Stroumboulos, condensing the day's experience into five minutes of music. Shades of Debussy, who in "La cathédrale engloutie" managed to raise from the sea and resubmerge an entire Gothic cathedral in a similar length of time!

Monday, March 27, 2017

Having written and thought about class and class politics this month, I will try to formulate some conclusion. Class can be defined in various ways, but I would define it in terms of what work one does. I greatly admire people who find it in themselves to be outstanding and innovative in some way and make a contribution; I also greatly appreciate people who are simply doing their job, whatever that may be. I think that these two categories of people overlap quite a lot.

Beyond that simple observation, I can only say that the reduction of injustice in society must be one of the most complex, and compelling, objectives we have.

A few years ago I wrote a poem, "The Cannery," looking back to a summer job I did to earn money for college. At first sight it might seem to be about immigration or ethnicity, but it's not; it's about the perennial salt of the earth.

> *O sole mio* she sang, for a bar or two
> on the swing shift—4:00 to midnight—
> in the dark shed of the S&W cannery
> just off a California highway,

the machinery drowning out her voice
where we stood at the rubber conveyer
picking cherries, fifty or sixty a minute.
Sulfur dioxide had dyed the fruit
a whitish yellow, so our hands turned yellow
and peeled down to a yellow beneath the skin.
O sole mio of Napoli, of wide blue water
of the shining bay of Naples, of women
standing at the belt eight hours a day
to earn a dollar fifty an hour in California.
Not all of us were Italian, some were Mexican
or Chinese, but it was the Italians who sang,
with swollen ankles, with yellow peeling hands
from those moonlike maraschino cherries
o sole mio, and every time I see the sun
I should think of them.

Sunday, April 9, 2017

The winter rains are ending. We have been busy pruning, planting, and loosening up the soil in the garden, and I've scrubbed the dark, slippery moss from the flagstones. The olive grove, where waist-high weeds have sprung up riotously, is still too wet for a hired tractor to come in and do the annual ploughing-up.

Today's hike, in bright cool weather, took us to the inland site of the ancient city of Eleftherna, which flourished from the ninth century BC into the Christian era. In the Hellenistic period a father-and-son craft workshop, established there and transported to Rhodes, produced the stunning sculpture of the Victory of Samothrace which is now in the Louvre. Our hike concluded in the village of Alfá, where many of the inhabitants are named Kafatos. The original Kafatos family were Byzantine nobility, transplanted from Constantinople to that region of Crete in the tenth century AD, following the reconquest of the island from Andalusian Arabs. Did they go freely, I wonder, or were they told to go? Perhaps they went gladly, since they were awarded a large territory and succeeded in holding on to it, more or less, until the acquisition of Crete by the Venetians in the thirteenth century.

I talked with a fellow hiker who reads a lot and likes to pose philosophical questions. She asked me whether or not I believe in God, and I answered that for me, religion has nothing to do with any belief as to what is or is not the case. She responded that for her, the universe is so splendid that there simply must exist some marvelous being who created it. If that's so, I wondered, then who created that wonderful creator? Rather than answer this, she changed the subject.

Monday, April 10, 2017

When I arrived to visit Fotis I found that the staff had just tried to reach me by phone, because he fell while being bathed this morning. I found him asleep in bed, with a compress on his forehead where the skin had been broken in the fall. He lay on his side, in a crooked posture, and didn't look well at all. A doctor will come in the afternoon to check on him.

Tuesday, April 11, 2017

Fotis is himself again today, sitting up in his chair and responding to things I tell him, despite a black eye and a small plaster on his forehead. He seems OK.

Friday, April 14, 2017

I spent the day with my friend Klairi. She lives in a landscape of olive groves and vineyards on the west side of the city, an area she calls "our Toscana." The stone-built hilltop villages and well-kept fields remind her, she says, of the allegorical painting in Siena, "Les effets du bon et du mauvais gouvernement," the countryside in her particular part of Crete being symbolic of bon gouvernement. After lunch we spent an hour picking artichokes in her fields. She has a large grove of olive trees, several rows of fruit trees of various kinds, and eight very long alleys of artichokes which must be harvested daily, new ones coming to ripeness every day among the thorns. We picked a crate of them, which were then collected by a man in a truck who will sell them in the farmers' market tomorrow. When not editing, writing, and translating (Klairi is director of publications at the Historical Museum, and has translated all three volumes of Fernand Braudel's *Histoire de la méditerranée*, as well as a significant amount of Proust's *Recherche du temps perdu*, into Greek), she has her farm work to do.

Saturday, April 15, 2017

After visiting Fotis, who seems recovered from his fall, I dropped in on my friend Natalie Ventura. Originally from New York, she is one of the very few people in Crete with whom I speak English. She and her husband are two of the three Jewish people living in Heraklion, there being perhaps twenty Jews living in Crete altogether. That is not a large number, but some three hours from here, in the city of Chania, is a very lively synagogue-cum-cultural-center, actively supported in large part by non-Jews. Natalie and Joseph serve on the board and have just been there for the Passover seder, a very warm and meaningful occasion, she said, with eighty people participating.

Local and international support has been all the stronger since the synagogue was vandalized and almost destroyed in 2010 (the perpetrators were two Englishmen and a Greek).

Wednesday, April 19, 2017

Today I'm on the island of Kalymnos, in the Eastern Mediterranean very near Turkey, on a four-day excursion with the hiking club. In the course of today's walk on a mountain path—paved with unhewn stones and known as the Italian Path, having been built by the Italian, eventually Fascist, government which ruled the Dodecanese group of islands from 1912 until 1945—and the coast road, I've had my first swim of the year, for about fifteen minutes in clear, cool water in a narrow, rock-rimmed harbor with a few boats at anchor. Later I learned that the harbor, called Vathí—meaning Deep—has been in use as a port since the Neolithic era. I'd started walking with the group, but though I'm fine walking uphill I'm slow on the downslopes, being careful not to slip and fall, and for that reason we decided that I shouldn't continue with the others after a certain point but instead should walk down a road to the harbor where there was bus service. Rather than take the bus, I then walked the few miles back to town on the corniche. It was right, as it turned out, for me to drop out, for the others had a very rough time and, though we had set out early in the morning, didn't get back until nightfall.

In rocky Kalymnos, where few crops grow, people have survived by diving for sponges in waters as far away as Crete and Libya, going out to sea in the spring and returning in the fall with a harvest to be sold in places as far away as England and Russia. This evening I stopped for dinner at a hole-in-the-wall taverna on the waterfront where the grilled mackerel was the best I've ever had. I talked with the cook's father, who had been a sponge fisherman from 1969 to 2012.

He would dive in a wetsuit with an oxygen tank strapped to his back. The deepest depth at which he has worked? Fifty-five meters.

Saturday, April 22, 2017

I enjoy meeting new people on these excursions. Kiki, a tall, red-headed woman able to stride briskly up any mountain, is the Greek translator of Paul Ricoeur and Maurice Merleau-Ponty. Calliope, a civil engineer who works for the Heraklion water department, is less fit but enthusiastic and great fun. She's involved in amateur theatrics. In a comedy by Aristophanes, where the hero has to sleep with an unattractive woman in order to win an attractive one, she told me, laughing, "I was the ugly one!"

Sunday, April 23, 2017

Our group has returned to Crete but I'm staying on for a while in Kos, an island half an hour by boat from Kalymnos and also from the Turkish city of Bodrum. Kos was the birthplace of Hippocrates, father of scientific medicine, and has a very impressive temple to Aesclepius, the mythical god of healing. The temple, built on a slope, has several very wide tiers of stairs leading up to the central shrine. They bring to mind the long slope up to the church of the healing Mother of God on Tinos, the Greek Lourdes, which people on pilgrimage ascend on their knees; also the steps of Widener Library.

Not only has Kos been a center of healing, but Kalymnos in the twentieth century had its own, locally funded, public health insurance system which covered everyone. This was particularly important for the divers, who could be attacked by sharks and who were often blinded or rendered paraplegic by the bends.

Monday, April 24, 2017

Kos town is tranquil and quiet. Many refugees fleeing war zones came here by boat in recent years, and some drowned. I believe the people here helped them at their own expense for a long time. Now there is no sign of any refugee anywhere in Kos town. Instead there is a long-term camp in a remote part of the island. The local people living near the camp demonstrated against it when it was being built, and once it was up the inmates demonstrated against it too, but it represents the status quo for now. I don't know how many people are there.

Tuesday, April 25, 2017

I spent the day in Bodrum, the present version of ancient Helicarnassos, birthplace of Herodotus and also of the forebears of many people in Heraklion, where there is a large neighborhood called Nea Helicarnassos.

A referendum has just taken place, but there is no sign of it in Bodrum. I've read that the cities—and that would include this one, which is a prosperous holiday town—voted No to Erdoğan's assuming more power. The only posters I saw in this town were of Atatürk, not Erdoğan. I saw many women dressed and behaving in a Western way, as well as a few older women wearing the traditional headscarf, sweater, and Turkish trousers.

I visited the ruins of the tomb of Mausolus, which gave us the word "mausoleum," now a lovely garden, but once one of the Seven Wonders of the ancient world. Then I walked along the waterfront, passing a monument to a woman doctor, Türkan Saylan, who eliminated leprosy in Turkey. Enjoying the sea breeze and occasional glimpses of the splendid shining bay behind the cafés and shops which have turned much of the seafront into an enormous souk, I was headed for the Zeki Müren Museum, created by the Turkish Ministry of Culture in what was the house of one of the greatest musicians of modern Turkey. Zeki Müren adopted an ever more feminized persona, to the point where from his looks—but not his voice—you would mistake him for a woman. He wore fabulously glittery, sinuous costumes—going way beyond Liberace in this regard—and captured the hearts of the Turkish people with his profoundly emotional, expressive, beautifully crafted songs. His music, coming out of Middle Eastern classical tradition, seems to me more intimate, and moves me more, than that of the Egyptian diva Umm Kalthoum.

Wednesday, April 26, 2017

Today I visited the Kos archeological museum. How in the world did ancient Greek people ever clean those elegant, very narrow-neck vases that they had? After admiring the sculptures and asking myself this question I sat in a café and made a drawing of the Defterdar Mosque, since one of my purposes in being here is to draw.

I also finished reading *Behind the Beautiful Forevers*, by Katherine Boo, a superbly researched and narrated account of survival and failure to survive in a Mumbai slum. ("Beautiful forever" was the slogan written on billboards advertising floor tile that kept travelers to and from Mumbai International Airport from seeing the slum directly behind them). Like Matthew Desmond's *Evicted*, what this book describes, with exquisite empathy and insight, is the dystopia of an almost totally transactional world.

A few days ago Sheryl Sandberg published an account of what she has learned since her husband's death about how to help children become resilient in the face of adversity. One point was that children should be helped to realize that they matter: that other people notice them, care about them, and rely on them.

Many of the people whom Katherine Boo introduces us to are

children, and unfortunately it is rarely evident that others notice or care about them in a constructive way. I was struck by her account of the thoughts that one young scavenger, Abdul, reported to her: that he didn't matter to anybody, "but something he'd come to realize on the roof, leaning out, thinking about what would happen if he leaned too far, was that a boy's life could still matter to himself." In fact Abdul's family is intact, his father is an upstanding, principled person and his mother does an enormous amount for him and their family, but what he is made to feel by the larger, public world is that he is expendable.

Sunday, May 7, 2017

France votes today in an election crucial for the future of the European Union and the civic fabric of France.

Monday, May 8, 2017

Puerto Rico has declared bankruptcy, thus entering into a situation comparable to that of Greece. Its government became overindebted for similar reasons. Its people, as in Greece, now find that personal incomes and public expenditure have sharply declined and taxes gone sharply up, and like the Greeks, those people are legally entitled to leave home for the continental mainland. Many are doing so, as in the past when so many went to New York. How will they find ways to sustain the unique culture of their island? And who will create any investment there—or in Greece—and why, and in what?

Tuesday, May 9, 2017

I'm in Cambridge, Massachusetts, for a month. Immediately, and happily, I feel as though I'd never left.

Thursday, May 11, 2017

My nephew Alan and his wife Kelly came to dinner. We spent some time on the stimulating dinner-table subject of how people make choices. Afterward I had a thought about tragedy, what tragedy is, understood in terms of the choices we make. I don't mean classical Greek tragedy, which is mainly about fate. Oedipus didn't mean to kill his father and marry his mother; indeed, he didn't even find out until much later that he had done so. It wasn't his choice to do what he did, but he had to live out the consequences nonetheless.

In our morality today we wouldn't blame Oedipus for what he, through no fault of his own, had done. So what might be the meaning of tragedy for us? I think it has to do with the burden of commitment. Suppose someone today were offered a momentous choice between A and B, let's say to marry one person or the other, and chose B. Suppose then that B turned out to be different from what one had thought, let's say for example that B was actually not trustworthy, or maybe just not compatible. Then I think one might well regret having chosen as one did, and might possibly end the relationship. That would be unfortunate, but I don't think we'd call it tragic.

Suppose, though, that B fulfilled every expectation, but that B then died. I think most people, in that case, will not feel, Oh, I should have married A instead. Most people will stay loyal to a commitment they have made and feel, I would make the same choice all over again even though I'd have to suffer for it. They relinquish what had been the alternative, they accept the consequences of their commitment, they take on the possibility of suffering and loss, and I think that this is what brings them into the world of tragedy as we understand it. They may be resilient, they may go on to live a full life, but it will be a life lived in that world.

Saturday, May 20, 2017

With our daughter Helen, a clinical psychologist, I had a conversation about what it means to be transgender. She was helping me to think about the subject, which she understands better than I do. Many people, it seems, feel firmly identified with the gender they apparently belong to, but there are some people who feel very strongly, in fact are certain, that they've been misidentified and really belong to the opposite one. I commented that personally, I'm content with my gender and would never go out of my way to change it, but that if I were to be told that I was going to be changed magically, all at once, and there was nothing I could do about it, I would probably just agree to that and go on getting on with my life. Helen suggested that in that case, I could say that I'm "gender fluid." I thought it more accurate to say I'm "gender indifferent." "You're adaptable," she concluded. I thought that was about right.

Sunday, May 21, 2017

I went this morning to the Society of Friends meeting for worship in Cambridge, a Quaker spiritual and service community to which I always return when here. It's a good thing to share in the quiet attentiveness cultivated there, to turn down the noise of daily life and find my way to a more open, more attuned, more serene way of being.

Sunday, May 28, 2017

I'm here for Memorial Day weekend with Zoe and her family in Virginia, spending part of the time at Zoe's husband Ben's parents' house in the small community of Deltaville on Jackson Creek, where the Piankatank and Rappahannock Rivers flow into the Chesapeake Bay. Deltaville was once a major center of boat-building, a craft still celebrated and sometimes practiced there. The working boats fished for crab and oysters and sold their catch as far north as Baltimore.

At the local Maritime Museum I learned some things about oysters. They have a lifespan of twenty years and change gender in the course of it, perhaps even changing back and forth several times. They were once a very common, abundant food (I already knew this, from reading *Moby Dick*), and their shells were used by the local Powhatan tribe as tools, for example when scraping out the insides of tree trunks to make dugout canoes.

Monday, May 29, 2017

Sadly I learn of the death of Jack Power, a member of my high school class. A practitioner of family and emergency medicine, he worked on Hopi lands, and in Alaska, Puerto Rico, and Sonoma County, where he and his Puerto Rican wife raised their family. He went as a medical volunteer to New Orleans after Hurricane Katrina and to Haiti after the earthquake. A modest, empathic, thoughtful, vigorous man, a fine amateur pianist, one of our best-liked and most admired classmates.

Sunday, June 4, 2017

At the Sunday morning Friends Meeting, where there is no formal leadership and no agenda other than to sit together for an hour, we each search for some way of being, insight, or "leading" that is profound for us personally and at the same time, hopefully, meaningful to others. Today I began by wondering why I do the things I choose to do. Then, as very often happens, a few people stood to speak of difficult and troubling things happening in their lives or in the world.

My reasons for living include health, happiness, joy, and the satisfaction of understanding and expressing something. I love my family, friends, and others beyond them, but helpfulness to others is not paramount for me, though I do try to do my part. One thing helpfulness means to me is to be responsive, rather than reactive, to troubles and problems that arise. Which is what Quaker tradition, evolved in the absence of dogma, teaches us to do.

In the afternoon there was a block party on our street, and from there I went to a fundraiser for Elizabeth Warren, who will be seeking reelection to the Senate from Massachusetts. Her core issue is economic justice, to which she is deeply, passionately committed. As an advocate for ordinary working people she is an outstanding, and much needed, presence in government. I think it's helpful to all of us to try to help her.

Tuesday, June 6, 2017

My tax accountant here has a client, an artist, who pays his bill with large watercolor landscapes. I gazed at one of these while waiting for some papers to be photocopied. What struck me was the thought process it seemed to reveal: a scene with stately trees casting shadows on a lawn seemed to exist on two planes. The artist had taken note of the main features of the scene while translating them into something else, namely pools of color distributed on the page. The approach was not at all one of "coloring in." On the contrary, the features of the scene did not determine the design of the work; they were there as a framework for color shapes on paper.

The ability to see a thing two ways, as itself and as its translation into something else, is fundamental for artistic work. That is one of the ways in which artistic activity stimulates our ability to think.

Saturday, June 10, 2017

Helen, ten-year-old Anna, and I went as spectator-supporters to the Pride Parade in Boston, being perhaps the only three-generation contingent present. I attended the San Francisco Pride Parade with my mother many years ago, so altogether that makes four generations of our family's presence at these events. I remember the parade in San Francisco, before the AIDS epidemic, as very colorful and uninhibited, and this one is colorful too, but I noticed how much more mainstream it is, with the Mayor taking part, with a corporate presence (including Delta personnel pushing an airline drinks tray down the street), with many private schools marching, and with vehicles trundling along bearing rainbow-flag-waving seniors from assisted living residences. They—we—have come a long way.

Sunday, June 11, 2017

This morning the Friends Meeting, with perhaps eighty people present, continued for a full hour in unbroken silence. It was a rare and vibrant opportunity for concentrated, deep contemplation. My focus was on the inner process—in myself and in each of us—that takes various kinds of information from the world, assimilates and reassociates it, and results in the signals that we, often half-consciously, send out. I was focused on the work that goes into this process, and the tone of it.

Wednesday, June 14, 2017

I've returned to Crete. On my first day back I went to see Fotis. He gave me a happy smile of recognition and clearly understood some things I said to him, but his vitality is even lower than before. He still has an appetite and can swallow, but is a slow eater; it took him an hour to consume the ripe peach and small banana I had brought. They now give him water to drink from a syringe, rather than a spoon. He's lost weight, and his skin is losing its ability to withstand abrasion. My greatest wish at this point is that he should remain comfortable and not distressed.

The very sad news in our village is that Vangelis Alatsatianos has died at the age of forty-seven. He'd struggled for two years with lymphoma that was diagnosed only six months ago. He continued working almost to the end, stoic and always optimistic. Helpful, keenly intelligent, excellent company, he will be missed by everyone here.

Friday, June 16, 2017

Emmanuel Macron and his new party, La République en Marche, have triumphed in the presidential and legislative elections in France. With its pro-European, non-status-quo centrist agenda, its cadre drawn from various walks of civilian life, and even in its name, En Marche resembles The River, its Greek counterpart. But while En Marche has succeeded spectacularly, The River has failed to make much of an impression and is little heard from these days.

Why is this? Some of the explanation may lie in the difference in leadership; Macron, an extremely dynamic individual previously active in the Socialist party, is highly qualified to step into the position he now holds, whereas the leader of The River, a former journalist, is less forceful and less prepared. In Greece the party that sprung up from nowhere to take over space formerly occupied by our version of a Socialist party—Andreas and Giorgos Papandreou's PASOK—was Syriza, led by the charismatic Alexis Tsipras.

Tsipras came from the far left but is now governing within the constraints set by our creditors, and the country for the time being is quiet. There was suspense about a new tranche of debt service, eight billion euros due in July, which we cannot pay without support. The IMF had been refusing to participate in this latest phase of debt management unless the terms were softened in our favor, but the European Central Bank had been unwilling to agree to that until now. Today it seems that those actors have reached a compromise, so there will be no further political upheaval in Greece for the present.

Tuesday, July 4, 2017

I spent the weekend at a wedding where some sixty of the three hundred or so people present were members of our extended family who had flown from the US to Crete for the occasion. Fotis' father had a sister, Athiná, who emigrated from their ancestral village to America and married a man also from Crete. Their children, and children's children, and children's children's children, all stayed in the US, flourished, and have remained closely connected to each other and to Crete. On this occasion the bride was Athiná's great-granddaughter Smaragdhi, Greek for "Emerald," whom everyone calls "Emmy" for short, and the groom a second-generation American whose family also came from Crete.

I was very touched by the quality of these people and their relationships. All have prospered (many are doctors, and Emmy is a nurse), and now, as the fourth generation become adult, many still speak adequate Greek. The young men could, and did, dance the very vigorous Cretan men's dances extremely well, in fact better than I have ever seen this done before, which is saying something. I've known all of the older people for a long time, but the younger generation of this family were new to me and a very pleasant, and memorable, surprise.

Thursday, July 6, 2017

I've just watched the funeral oration given by Emmanuel Macron at the bier of Simone Veil, who will be interred with her husband in the Pantheon, the fifth woman to be accorded that honor (the first was Marie Curie). Her moral discernment and leadership are what made her exemplary: as an individual, a survivor of Auschwitz, an advocate of European reconciliation, and an activist on behalf of women's rights. As Macron said, she did not, as Minister of Health, fight to secure a French woman's right to abortion because she was a woman, but because she saw a need to defend any person victimized by others, including women victimized by a hypocritical society and by men. He said that she had by her life enlarged the idea—that is, the ideal—of France.

The particular word he chose to express that thought was not la gloire (which would not have been appropriate, particularly given the way that French authorities collaborated with and even exacerbated the Holocaust), but rather (a theme of de Gaulle's, and Macron's) la grandeur. Macron was profiling his own values, and ambition, by way of defining hers. Some apprehension has been felt regarding the extraordinary power that has now been placed in his hands; we must hope that he will continue to use it well.

Saturday, July 8, 2017

Natalie gave a poetry reading together with her sister, also a poet, who is visiting from Ottawa. I was particularly struck by the wisdom of something she said when introducing her work: "Lately I've made a decision to try to live more from the heart."

Sunday, July 9, 2017

Zoe and her family, plus another family with whom they are close friends, arrived in Crete today. Helen and her family will arrive shortly. I will no longer have the house to myself, and my sentiment is, "Let the wild rumpus begin!"

Tuesday, July 11, 2017

Fotis has cognitive and emotional resources that are available even now. He nodded in recognition of friends' names we mentioned, and even smiled at an old joke (his mother liked to sweeten her yogurt so much that it was said, "She puts yogurt on her sugar," and he clearly remembered and was amused by this saying when Zoe mentioned it). But, spending his days in his wheelchair and unable to do anything for himself, he continues to deteriorate overall. His body began cramping up this year, and although he is being medicated for that and is doing physical therapy, his left hand has gotten frozen in a cramped position that we can't adjust without causing pain.

I understand that he has now entered what is termed "Late Stage Alzheimer's Disease"; that is, the terminal stage. His experience of life seems to me to be not bad, in that he seems half asleep most of the time but has occasional moments of heightened feeling and understanding. We would not at this point make any invasive intervention to prolong his life; we would give him antibiotics, though, if needed. I believe he wants to live.

Sunday, July 16, 2017

We are all having a week's holiday in our favorite village of Sougia on the south coast, where the days are hot, the mountains are splendid, the sea is marvelous, and the tranquil cafés are good for sitting in all day long. Our beloved hosts, Vangelis and Georgia, whose rooms we have returned to every year for forty-five years, are still well, although Vangelis, now eighty-nine, is increasingly frail.

Wednesday, July 19, 2017

With only a few letters yet to go, I'm approaching completion of my translation of Ovid's *Heroides*. All of his fictional heroines write letters of complaint to an absent counterpart, but how differently! Each has a temperament and specific grievance of her own. There is Penelope, loyal, steadfast, the put-upon wife of a fighter missing in action; Phaedra, the older woman and would-be seductress, an unhappy victim of unrequited love; Briseis, an enslaved woman, dependent for her welfare on her former lover Achilles' (not forthcoming) support; Canace, made pregnant by her brother and condemned to death by their father; Medea, a savagely passionate, desperate woman capable of great harm; Laodamia, partner in a loving marriage, whose husband will perish in war. Dido . . . Ariadne . . .

Friday, July 21, 2017

An earthquake has struck Kos and Bodrum, where I was on holiday in April. Hundreds of people have been injured, and the eighteenth-century Defterdar Mosque that I drew has been badly damaged, its minaret destroyed.

Wednesday, July 26, 2017

Greece will remain on financial life support for another year but has returned to the debt markets this week, successfully marketing an issue of government bonds. This is a step toward restoration of confidence in the economy, a sine qua non for further recovery.

In the meantime we just came very close to running out of water at home. In our neighborhood in Heraklion the mains run only once or twice a week, and besides that, a team from the municipal water department unhooked our water supply while we were on holiday and forgot to reconnect it. Every house in the city has its own water storage tank and ours is large, but was almost not large enough. Now this has been fixed and we can take showers and flush our toilets again, but the garden remains parched. We had a lot of rain last winter, but there's no rain in summer and it seems consumption has gone up so much, for agriculture especially, that we've hit a limit.

Monday, July 31, 2017

This was the month in which the Republicans in the Senate failed to dismantle the Affordable Care Act. Donald Trump, though ever more isolated, I think, continues with his sinister antics while still enjoying the fervent support of his "base."

Monday, August 7, 2017

We will miss the upcoming solar eclipse, but the full harvest moon went into partial eclipse tonight and I watched it for a while from our roof. The event lasted for several hours, much longer than its solar sister. The moon didn't turn reddish, since less than a quarter of it was obscured while the rest remained as bright as ever, and there were no weird terrestrial effects, such as the peculiar wind that springs up or the cold, alien feeling that arises when a solar eclipse results in darkness at noon. The bite taken out of the disk by the earth's shadow was not so crisp, but otherwise similar to the bite taken out of the apple in the Apple logo.

Wednesday, August 9, 2017

The subject of birthdays came up during a visit to Fotis, and we asked him whether he'd like to live to be a hundred. His grasp of numbers is minimal, but the concept was clear to him and he nodded yes. I think of Joyce's Molly Bloom at the very end of her soliloquy saying "yes I said yes I will Yes."

Friday, August 11, 2017

My brother's son Daniel, who lives in Kyoto with his Japanese wife Mayumi and their two sons, is here for a week. We drove into the mountains to see the excavated stone village of Tylissos, 3,500 years old, and the modern village of Anogia. We discussed the differences between life in rural Mexico, where Daniel lived for several years and where people are given to casual socializing, and in Japan, which is a nation of introverts. I find Daniel to be more relaxed, calm, and open-minded than many people I know, partly because he's always been so and partly because of the kind of life he's lived.

Saturday, August 12, 2017

We had dinner at a beach taverna which—by 9:00 p.m., which is the dinner hour—was filled with people. Some tables were taken by couples, but most were occupied by family groups—such as our own—which were not nuclear families. We thought that this type of constellation is most likely to be seen in localities, such as Heraklion, where most people stay put their life long.

Wednesday, August 16, 2017

Helen's family, and also Daniel, left this morning. I'm glad that I have some work to tide me over the transition, laundering sheets and hanging them up to dry in the sun and the very strong wind off the sea.

Thursday, August 17, 2017

There's a touch of fall in the air and, not quite able to take a nap, I sit at home in the afternoon reading Colette, *La naissance du jour*, a meditation on aging, leisure, and Provence. How well those things go together! As they do here today, in my Provence, my Toscana.

Sunday, August 20, 2017

Some reflections on the news.
The general level of trust in a society is a strong indicator of

how functional that society is and how safe the people in it can feel. Unfortunately, trust is a capital good that is hard won and can be quickly lost, through one bad incident or bad actor. We need to keep building and rebuilding well-founded trust, appropriately and incrementally, in order for society to flourish.

That this is a leading issue in the United States has become blindingly obvious. We've become sharply divided over a host of issues, and so are both less able to resolve any of them and less capable of focusing our attention on the most important ones. (Our current president, need I say, is a champion divider, as well as a world-champion distracter of our attention, exacerbating our predicament.)

In that context I've just had some thoughts about displacement. In psychological terms, "displacement" is a defense mechanism which may help to alleviate stress, but may also be dysfunctional and usually stops short of solving the problem: for example, a man feels intense anger toward his wife, so he kicks the dog. In political life, we might use the term "displacement" to cover all kinds of scapegoating, along with many other, similar sorts of reconfiguration of stress or distraction from it: for example, a man feels disempowered as a member of society, so he commits himself to a struggle against some supposed global conspiracy (thereby going down the well-travelled route from garden-variety displacement to mild, or more than mild, paranoia).

Displacement is a resource to be deployed as needed, but very much in moderation; otherwise, as an unsatisfactory substitute for self-respect, it can become a great contributor to the mixups of life. In America now, it seems to me, many of our public arguments—about guns, about flags and monuments and much else—are about real things that we want or don't want in our society, but are also a means of displacing our collective focus onto things that are symbolic to us of deep feelings having to do especially with fear.

People want lots of other things, but just about everybody wants to feel safe. The escalation of so many of our disagreements is making us less functional and less safe. We need to strive to uphold our best understandings and values in the most calm and convincing ways. My humble advice: stick to firm principles, listen and engage reasonably with all others, emphasize the positive, and do your part to get us collectively back on track.

Maybe these thoughts of mine are tedious and not to the point. Or maybe such thoughts about process are helpful after all.

Monday, August 21, 2017

I watched a documentary about Joan Baez, who has followed her principles and her heart through life. She's now about seventy-five and more beautiful than ever.

Tuesday, August 22, 2017

The Greek National Theater came to Heraklion and put on Eurip-ides' play *Alcestis* last night. It's a tragicomedy, with much keening and wringing of hands, some buffoonery, and a happy end. Apollo has undertaken to save the protagonist, Admetus, from death, on condition that someone else volunteer to die in his place. Admetus asks his neighbors, his friends, and his aging parents, who all refuse: life is sweet and death is forever. At last his wife Alcestis agrees to die, out of love and wifely duty, leaving him and their small children behind. He accepts without hesitation, but they are a loving couple and he's wracked by grief even before the fact. He has a weak character, evidently, but is behaving within the norms, whereas his wife who steps beyond them is a strong and generous person. In the end all is well, as Hercules wrestles Alcestis back up out of Hades and returns her, alive again, to her unheroic but devoted spouse.

Euripides was a pathbreaker as a dramatist. A realist, a questioner of pieties and social norms, an explorer of our inner contradictions. In this play, the husband is torn between wanting to live and wanting to be with his wife: two good things, but he can't have both. Euripides' other plays explore other kinds of inner conflict. Phaedra doesn't want to be in love with her stepson Hippolytus and fights her feelings with all her strength but can't help herself, with tragic consequences for the whole family. Medea loves her two children, but when her husband Jason leaves her for another woman she murders them in order to hurt him. Pentheus disapproves of the orgiastic Bacchic rites and tries to outlaw them, but is also attracted and goes to observe them from a hiding place, with catastrophic results. These are amazing plays, composed 2,500 years ago and still relevant to us.

Friday, August 25, 2017

The hiking season has come around again. I open it with lines composed by Violeta Parra in honor of gratitude, walking, tiredness, and love:

Gracias a la vida
Que me ha dado tanto:
Me dió la marcha
De mis piés cansados . . .

I'm off with the hiking club on a five-day excursion to Gavdos, "the southernmost point in Europe," a small island thirty miles south of Crete. The coast path, today's segment of which is on sand dunes forested with juniper and thyme, clings to the sea at times and rises precipitously above it at others.

Monday, August 28, 2017

We've been walking for five hours a day, finding time for a swim here and there, returning to camp or rented rooms (I have a very pleasant room) in the evening.

I've read Bill Bryson's book about walking the Appalachian Trail, which combines the misadventures of a novice hiker with well-chosen information about the terrain he's going through. Now I'm reading *Wild*, Cheryl Strayed's survival memoir of hiking the much rougher Pacific Coast Trail. She did it to turn her life around, after it had run into the sand.

For myself, I walk because I feel happy doing it: happy when it's easy, and happy when I'm tired and it's hard. It's also beautiful, being outdoors, and interesting, and good for me.

Friday, September 1, 2017

The pomegranates in the garden are ripe. So it must be the end of summer, and Persephone will be eating her handful of seeds. I sprinkle mine on my breakfast cereal.

Saturday, September 2, 2017

Looking toward fall with an empty datebook, I can focus on projects such as resuming my painting. But what if I have no ideas for that, and also don't feel like doing it, particularly? The answer to this question is to just go to work, like going to a job.

Sunday, September 3, 2017

Today is our wedding anniversary: Fotis and I were married fifty years ago today. I told him that, and he understood it and gave me a kiss.

Monday, September 10, 2017

One of the benefits of the hiking club is the people I meet through it. Our president, who is extremely responsible, enthusiastic, dedicated, hardworking, and tireless, as well as gentle and thoughtful, is an elementary school teacher. He's married to another teacher, also an indefatigable hiker. Greece has a military draft (and a costly military budget, because of our problems with Turkey), and their son is presently doing his year of compulsory service.

My seatmate on the bus yesterday was a quiet, self-contained man who usually comes with his wife, who's also fit, cheerful, and self-contained. They don't talk much, but since we were seated together I was able to discover that he's a retired goldsmith. That used to be a major trade in Heraklion, and I learned from him that just a few decades ago there were seventy workshops like his in the city.

Wednesday, September 13, 2017

"They said that I would rue it,
They doubted I'd do it . . ."

But indeed I did today finish the last segment of my translation of Ovid's *Heroides*. (That is, of the fifteen letters known to be by him. There are six more that may or may not be.) I've also written a short character sketch of each letter writer. So now I'm done, unless there should ever be a demand for the rest.

Wednesday, September 20, 2017

I've been stimulating my thinking about personal and public questions—How should a person live? How can we live well together?—by reading some relevant books by three people whose thoughts intersect: Jonathan Haidt (*The Righteous Mind*), Joshua Greene (*Moral Tribes*), and Susan Wolf (*Meaning in Life and Why It Matters*). One very simple take-home from their interesting and complex work: Different cultures, and individual lives, have evolved to emphasize different values—perhaps more sorts of value than we may be aware of—most of which deserve respect, and when these collide in public life, a pragmatic solution is normally to be preferred.

Friday, September 29, 2017

The first rainfall since last spring is giving our garden a good soak. The manure that has been placed around our olive trees will now begin to be integrated into the soil. I can remember going into a field with Fotis' father to collect donkey droppings for his garden. Sadly, there are no donkeys around here anymore.

Donkey Droppings, Greece 1941

for my father-in-law

He'd ride his donkey uphill to a field,
use the manure to increase the yield
of olives, rye, barley, oats and wheat,
herbs, greens that were good to eat.

He'd gently lift a dry, frail biscuit,
carry it into his field in a basket,

crumble it carefully into the soil
to feed the garden he had tilled.

"There's no better fertilizer!" he said,
rubbing his hands, and laughed aloud.
He'd studied plants, what they needed
to grow in thin soil. Knew what abided.

That's how the family survived the war
when others who lived in the city starved.
He was stubborn, had a quick temper,
fathered three children, was a good dancer.

Friday, October 6, 2017

Fotis has been in bed for the past week. His oxygen count has dropped and he's very weak. He sleeps most of the time. When he wakes up his mind is as clear as before; he's lost the ability to engage with much but he's never had delusions or said anything that didn't make sense. He's still himself, with his temperament intact. He's calm and seems at peace.

We think it likely that he is close to death. The practical arrangements for that event have been made, and we are watching and waiting.

I thought this morning of the British psychologist John Bowlby and his pathbreaking work on attachment and loss (and remembered sitting on the John Bowlby bench upon discovering it in a churchyard in London). Fotis has been, for all the years I've known him, good at attachment. He admired scientific excellence and pursued it himself in a very unselfish way, being very supportive of his colleagues and students and always steady in his commitments. He disliked interpersonal conflict very much, and almost never engaged in it. He loved Greece, Crete, and his family and friends. I think he was very free of resentment, about anything. I think he lived with a high level of basic trust, and that although he experienced some losses he didn't dwell on them and they were not thematic for him.

I've arranged to have more fruit trees planted in our garden. Fotis loved to work in it, training the grapevines, and wanted the trees to bear fruit.

Saturday, October 7, 2017

I'm completing my translation of *Oedipus at Colonus*, in which Oedipus is an old, blind man very near death. Sophocles was close to ninety years old when he wrote it, and many of the characters in the play—not only Oedipus but his antagonist Kreon and the chorus—are old men. While Sophocles was writing it, his own son tried to get him declared incompetent so as to take control of his property, an ignoble effort which failed in court. In the play, Oedipus' next-to-last act is to curse his son Polynikes, who is going to die in battle. His very last is to bless the city of Athens.

Despite the conflicts in his life, Oedipus' last moments, with his death and transfiguration, are magnificent, calm, transcendental. In the very last scene life goes on toward its tragic climax in the already-written sequel, *Antigone*, which turns on a further conflict between political and transcendental values and power.

Sunday, October 8, 2017

Today's was an eight-hour hike in very steep, rocky, mostly pathless terrain. Midway, some of us, including me, sat out the optional one-hour climb to the very summit of Mt. Kryoneríti, but Nikos, the eighty-five-year-old man who often walks with us, did it easily. On the other hand, I did swim in the Libyan Sea at the end, whereas Nikos sat out the swim.

Monday, October 9, 2017

The cicadas are still. In summer they were extremely loud, in September they grew steadily fainter, and I hadn't noticed their complete departure until today. When did the last one go?

Wednesday, October 11, 2017

It's often been observed that people with Alzheimer's retain an appreciation for music into very late stages of their trajectory. This is in fact not surprising, since they also retain an ability to understand what is said to them. Today when I played music Fotis listened attentively, and as we came to the end of "Du bist die Ruh" and were about to hear "Es ist genug," I said, "That was Schubert, and the next is Mendelssohn," and he nodded with full understanding.

Thursday, October 19, 2017

Fotis' condition is thought to be improving. He's still in bed and very weak, but not thought to be in imminent danger.

Tuesday, October 24, 2017

In Willa Cather's novel *Death Comes for the Archbishop*, which I have just read and which is not about death but about living a spiritual life with commitment and dedication, the Archbishop Father Latour catches a cold. After many hard decades of service on the American frontier, and after cultivating fruit trees in retirement in the New Mexico desert, he takes to his bed. When a companion seeks to comfort him by saying, "You should not be discouraged; one does not die of a cold," he smiles and answers, "I shall not die of a cold, my son. I shall die of having lived."

Friday, October 27, 2017

I've never in the past been able to use photographs as documents to help me paint. However, I have sometimes taken a photo of a scene I've sketched, or even of a scene that I have no other record of since I couldn't conveniently sketch it. The problem is that the camera flattens things out, putting them into a kind of mechanical perspective that doesn't correspond to how I feel about color and space. Now, though, I may have made a breakthrough in learning to use this potentially helpful tool. Rather than attempt to note accurately what I'm looking at, as I do when sketching, I just loosely copy my photographic image onto a canvas and then change it freely according to what my developing picture wants to be.

Every handmade picture arises out of a combination of observation, memory, and imagination, as is true of the two paintings based on photographs that I've just made.

Saturday, October 28, 2017

Once again I'm reading through the Beethoven sonatas and have just come to the sublime Opus 53 in C, the "Waldstein," known in France as the "Sunrise." András Schiff calls it "perhaps the most brilliant" of the sonatas, and it is rich in the revelation of joy.

After seeing Fotis, I went to the beach. While swimming I watched a man playing with his dog—or rather, watched the relationship between the two of them, which was active and vital for most of the duration of my swim. Eventually the man went to lie down on the sand, their rapport was interrupted, and the dog wandered off to explore a heap of kelp. It occurred to me that when I am with other people I am not usually watching the relationship between them. I notice other individuals, mostly. It would be interesting to become more aware of people in relationship.

Monday, October 30, 2017

Our friends in Catalonia are bicultural, switching from Spanish to Catalan and back several times in a single conversation (their English is also excellent). But they feel most deeply Catalan, and have long been supporters of independence for their region. All the same, I hope they have not been supporters of the improper referendum that's taking place this fall. I'm all for local autonomy and cultural expression, but since I would not be in favor of separation, even if it were the result of a legitimate process, I haven't contacted them but have thought it best to keep still.

Conflict can be healthy and sometimes necessary, but it seems to me that too many conflicts have been escalating too fast, at the expense of civility and social comity. As the political analyst Michael Tomasky has said,

> the problem is not simply one of Mr. Trump's coarseness and divisiveness and extremism. The problem, from Brexit to Mr. Trump's election to the rise of the far-right Alternative for Germany party, is how the liberal order responds to a crisis that threatens its erasure in favor of a reactionary, authoritarian alternative.

It seems to me that to respond well we need to appreciate that, no matter how strong our particular convictions may be, moderation and open-mindedness toward others, far from being a wimpy habit of splitting the difference between alternatives, is a heroic virtue and foundation of civic life.

Monday, November 13, 2017

The English poet Ruth Padel was here this weekend, and on Saturday evening we were invited to a "kazáni," a traditional meal shared with friends in some rural location where rakí is being distilled. This takes place roughly two months after the grape harvest, when the leavings from the wine have had time to ferment. Many small stills operate, some under license and some not, during this period. Even better than the rakí made from grapes, I'm told, is that made from mulberries—but I've never tasted it.

Ruth has many ties to Crete, speaks Greek, is a direct descendant of Charles Darwin, and was here to lecture, in mixed Greek and English, about Darwin. Her talk was focused on his family life, which more or less followed the norm for Victorian households. He got into conflict with his father over his choice of life path (his father wanted him to be a clergyman). When, after sailing the world for five years on the *Beagle,* he began to think of marriage, he weighed the pros—a dedicated volunteer housekeeper, children who would be seen not heard, a caregiver for him in his old age—against the cons—primarily, the presence of an inferior being who might interfere with his intellectual pursuits. The pros outweighed the cons, and he married his cousin. She came from the very distinguished Wedgwood family and was probably an exceptionally attractive and interesting person, though we didn't learn much about that. We did learn that she was a devout Christian who accepted her station in life, and that Darwin was to become very emotionally dependent on her in the course of their long and happy marriage.

Tuesday, November 14, 2017

Fotis is very weak and frail, but he gave me a joyful smile when I greeted him today. I shared with him the news that our daughter Helen ran a full marathon—her first, and very well prepared for—in Virginia last weekend with great family support. When I asked if I should convey congratulations to her from him he said Yes.

Friday, November 17, 2017

Today we brought in the olive harvest. It took three men working all day to bring down twelve sacks of fruit from our trees. The oil was pressed and brought back here just before midnight, and there are now ninety liters of virgin olive oil in a stainless steel canister in my basement.

Saturday, November 18, 2017

Fotis died at an hour and a half past midnight this morning. The call from his residence woke me ten minutes after that. I've reached both our daughters and they are searching for flights on which to come. I've contacted the funeral home and have sent the news to his brothers, and in the morning I'll begin making more calls.

Tuesday, November 21, 2017

Fotis' funeral took place today. The days since my last entry have been completely filled with incoming visits, emails, and phone calls, more than I could keep up with. Gratefully, I have been able to spend several quiet personal hours with a few of our closest friends.

His funeral was wonderful and I don't want to forget anything about it. It took place in the patron saint's church of the city and five hundred people came from nearby, from other cities in Crete, from Athens, from Cyprus and Brussels. The memorial service was sung beautifully in the true Byzantine way. We had invited only one person—Fotis' closest friend Stefanos—to speak, but others appeared and we couldn't say no, so that the sung service was followed by tributes from, in addition to Stefanos, the Mayor of Heraklion, the President of the University of Crete, the Chair of the Biology Department of Athens University, the Chair of the Biology Department of the University of Crete, the Director of the Research Center of Crete of which Fotis is a cofounder, the Director of the Orthodox Academy of Crete, and the Archbishop of Crete. Each of their speeches was short, meaningful, and very well composed. It was announced that a street in the city, and the biology building at the University of Crete, will be named after Fotis. After that, and after our family had been greeted and hugged by every person in the church, the Heraklion Philharmonic Society appeared in uniform, invited by the City Council, and walked ahead of the coffin through the city center playing Beethoven's funeral march "sulla morte d'un eroe."

Fotis was buried in the grave in Fortetsa where his parents also lie.

Wednesday, November 22, 2017

The public tributes to Fotis have dwelt on his scientific achievements and leadership, but practically every one of the personal messages I've received, including the very many from his colleagues and students, has spoken first of all of how kind and gentle he was.

This evening when everyone else was out or asleep I spent some time with the old hymn tune "In the Sweet By and By," which I imagine my American Protestant ancestors might have sung sometime. The best rendition of it I found was the one by Willie Nelson. In the sweet by and by . . . we shall meet in the sweet by and by. I almost believe it.

ACKNOWLEDGMENTS

My thanks to Sarah LeVine, who suggested that I keep a journal and share it. To Barry and Gretchen Mazur, who thought it might deserve publication, to Paul Dry, who believed that it did, and to Mara Brandsdorfer and Julia Sippel at Paul Dry Books. To the friends who read and responded, and those who appear in its pages: Vangelis Alatsatianos, Stelios Alexiou, John Alvarez, Dimitris and Suzana Antonakakis, Sara Bloom, Will and Annie Boutelle, Ben Zoe Sophia and Arthur Bunnell, Barbara Cumbers, Catherine Dalimier, Michalis Danelis, Petros and Sonia Ditsas, Linda Dittmar, Stelios Economakis, Anne Ephrussi, Rea Galanaki, Dotty Gonson, Eva Grammatikaki, Vassilis Gratsias, Antonis Kafatos, Menas Kafatos, Stelios and Lenya Kastrinakis, Sara Katz, Vida Kazemi, Dimitris Kiousis, Vassilis Kokkas, Mary and Chrysi Konsolaki, Ioanna Kourtsidaki, Elias Kouvelas, Mimoza Kuka, Anna Louis, Frinde Maher, Irini Mamalaki, Elengo Manousaki, Annabel Markova, Judith May, Julie Mayberry, Zeke Mazur, Peter and Hilary McGhee, Susan Milmoe, Klairi Mitsotaki, Stelios Helen George and Anna Moschapidakis, Vangelis Myrizakis, Carole Newlands, Alan Niles, Daniel Niles, Jack Niles, Suzanne Ogden, Ruth Padel, Giannis Papamastorakis, Suzanne Pearce, Jack Power, Ursula Rasidaki, Kelly Rich, Karl Schonborn, Louisa Schuschnigg, Babis Savakis, Electra Sidiropoulou, Ioanna Soufleri, Fondas Ruth Marilena and Sophia Spinthakis, Alicia Stallings, Gabriele Stavroulaki, Christine Tolias, Peter Tolias, Stefanos Trachanas, Kiki Tzortzakaki, Jorinde Ulmer, Joseph and Natalie Ventura, Manolis Vergis, and Hara Vlastou.